W9-DGI-031

# PERCEPTION IN EVERYDAY LIFE

# perception in everyday life

**S. HOWARD BARTLEY**
Michigan State University

Library
S.W. ...
Weatherford, Oklahoma

HARPER & ROW,
PUBLISHERS   New York / Evanston / San Francisco / London

**TO MY WIFE**

Cover art was adapted from a woodcut by M. C. Escher, with the permission of the Escher Foundation, Haags Gemeentemuseum, The Hague.

Unless otherwise indicated, photographs and drawings are by the author.

PERCEPTION IN EVERYDAY LIFE
Copyright © 1972 by S. Howard Bartley

Printed in the United States of America. All rights reserved. No part of this book may be used or reproduced in any manner whatsoever without written permission except in the case of brief quotations embodied in critical articles and reviews. For information address Harper & Row, Publishers, Inc., 49 East 33rd Street, New York, N.Y. 10016.

Standard Book Number: 06-040512-0
Library of Congress Catalog Card Number: 71-187053

# contents

204036

# preface

The present book is a response to a need. Perhaps the need is not widely recognized but it nevertheless seems to be tangible. Textbooks are either quite superficial so as not to go beyond the beginner, or very technical. In either case, they do not contain the kind of material intentionally chosen both for its human interest value and its usefulness as a teaching aid. Because a text could hardly combine laboratory reports and findings with the material contained here, a separate channel is necessary. This book is meant to be an example. It contains discussions, anecdotes, ventures in interpretation—the kind of material that helps bring the student into the discipline of psychobiology.

The approach is informal, not too rigorous, and perhaps sketchy in many places, but enough comment is interjected to make the essays instructive as well as entertaining. I have found that individuals and groups beyond university age, as well as students, are enthusiastic about the material. It would seem that the material presented will serve two purposes: the in-school purposes just described and the purpose of entertaining and instructing people in general, whoever they may be.

I have received the gratifying cooperation of several individuals who have contributed essays: Peter L. Borchelt, Susan C. Brainerd, Richard L. Doty, and Robert W. Grossman. They all are or have been graduate students at Michigan State University, East Lansing, Michigan.

In the present endeavor, no less than in the production of previous books and reports, I have received indispensible help from Mrs. Le Ann Slicer, who has put the material into typed form and given helpful advice.

From my wife I have received moral support, an ingredient very much needed.

S. H. B.

*East Lansing, Michigan*

# part
# ONE
# the need
# to know
# oneself

Several radical and pervasive changes are coming about in society. Outwardly they seem to have little relation to each other, but they can all be broadly envisaged as kinds of awakening. The awakening that is most widely discussed at present concerns the number of things man has done to make *the earth unfit for habitation*. The second awakening has to do with the fact that his *numbers are becoming too great for survival* at the present quality level. The third awakening pertains to the kind of awareness that is given the name of *existentialism*, which, though it may be difficult to define and may have several manifestations, is nonetheless real. Supernaturalism has loosed its hold on Western man and consequently man asks a new set of questions about his place in Nature.

The fourth awakening pertains to the natural means by which we concretely relate to the environment. Seldom has it been said, let alone taught, that man is a part of Nature and and not apart from it. Little or nothing has been achieved in dispelling his alienation from the rest of the universe. The fourth development, therefore, has to do with a change in the study of psychology. On the one hand there is a growing interest in physiological psychology, a deeper realization that we are biological organisms and that awareness and behavior are body based. Texts in physiological psychology and in sensation and perception are having to handle expanded areas of information.

Relatively speaking, they are becoming miniature encyclopedias. On the other hand, texts in elementary psychology are spreading themselves to include an array of material which one would be hard pressed to call psychology. They are in curious ways giving vent to the search for human interest. It may be difficult to tell what these two developments mean, but one may hazard a suggestion.

The advanced texts are reflecting a deeper penetration into problems which may be studied by precise and intricate laboratory methods. Writers of beginning texts are attempting to deal with man as a person, probably on the assumption that few students wanting to understand man are able to derive much from laboratory reports. But a few psychologists are becoming aware that we have the kind of information on hand which will begin to describe man neither as awkwardly as precise bits of observation nor as superficially as popular writers do. They are coming to see that it is not more descriptions in the usual social science jargon that are needed but rather a new picture of the role of the environment of which man is basically a part is an energistic one. It is the sense mechanisms that make contact with this environment. The new task now for psychologists is to understand and describe sensation and perception in a new way. We refer here to the sense mechanisms that permeate the body and the natural responses they provide, many in forms of awareness and others as thermal, chemical, and mechanical adjustments to ever-changing environmental energies. These mechanisms provide for seeing, hearing, tasting, smelling, and touching. They determine both quantitative and endless qualitative characteristics of experience. They form the basis for feelings, judgments, emotions, moods, attitudes, and satisfaction of needs.

The old task was seen simply as a cataloging of sensitivities in terms of thresholds and a few primary experiential qualities, thereby giving a static, rather than an active, functional picture of the human person. It was one of the procedures in psychology that abstracted "behavior" out of the person and dealt with it as a thing apart. The study of learning was a similar endeavor.

Sensation and perception have been formally studied and taught in our colleges and universities for a long time. But those who have been taught have not been given the thrill and satisfaction of understanding themselves, for knowledge has been accumulated in disconnected items. The very textbooks which should have depicted perception as the true connector between man and Nature have provided only myopic glimpses, and few, if any, vistas of human composition, need, and potentiality. Recently, in many places, perception is becoming a magic word, still comprehended as something to explain a great deal, but still not described as the way we behave on account of how we are made and what we need.

If we fail to comprehend man as a biological creature that has emerged from the long interaction of forces in nature, and as fashioned to interact with the energies of Nature around him, we shall fall far short of making the rest of our present awakening achieve what it ought. If we fail here, we shall fail in the end. To see our rightful place in Nature is entirely indispensible, and to understand sensation and perception is the core.

The new task is to see sensation and perception in action, that is, to see the person sensing and perceiving. This carries the description beyond such things as thresholds and so forth to the roles that the senses play, hence to emotional effects, and to gratifications and fulfillment of needs. An attempt to do this only a few years ago would have been seen as outlandish and unthinkable. We can begin now.

The new task means that the conventional textbook material in sensation and perception is only half the story. A companion document is needed. It will deal with the roles of sensory mechanisms and perceptual systems; it will be a living story of human capacity, need and means of gaining satisfaction. It will relate man to man, and man to Nature.

The present document is meant to do this very thing. This task then is being undertaken to participate in man's new awakening regarding himself. We've mentioned the other three components of this awakening. These will never fully succeed if psychologists fail to describe man as a part of Nature and to explain how his mechanisms of contact and response to natural forces operate. Man's sensory mechanisms are not appendages or tools to use or not; they are man himself in contact with the energistic world. They are the machinery for transforming heat, photic energy, and chemical and mechanical contacts into experiences and gratifications. We must understand ourselves and each other in terms of them.

The book is in five parts: one, the present introduction; two, some situations which illustrate perception; three, a statement of what perception is; four, the operation of perceptual systems in everyday life; and five, some general considerations regarding awareness.

Part two is a series of illustrative situations from

everyday life that are familiar and that hold some interest for people in general. The list is followed by several more extended examples. These are not commonly seen especially as examples of perception at work, but I hope that you will be led to see them as that. The descriptions are some of those given in my original edition of *Principles of Perception* (1958) where I digressed enough from the usual scientific reporting to describe briefly perception in everyday life. The situations I have used are: looking from a high place, driving on an icy pavement, attending a symphony concert, attending a movie, and the looks of a room. In these, human *impressions* — not perceptual *mechanisms* — are the foci.

Part three explains what is meant by perception and sensation and should prepare the reader for Part four, which forms the bulk of the book.

Part four is an array of essays depicting the role of sensation and perception in various kinds of understandable situations. The examples show what perception is like, and how it is an expression of the individual involved in handling human needs. Each of the five perceptual systems is dealt with in a separate subsection containing several essays.

Part five tells about the processes that produce a response whether it be awareness or just body movements. One essay deals with the suppression of awareness and describes the action of analgesics, such as aspirin, and sedatives. Other topics are isolation and sensory deprivation. Illusions, truth and reality, and some general matters are also covered in Part five.

# part
# TWO
# situational
# examples of
# sensation
# and
# perception

Despite its common usage, *perception* is still a fairly empty word, probably because our culture is not biologically oriented. Although we have some concern for genetics, we do not think in terms of the human individual's inherent and transmitted characteristics and body mechanisms. Psychology, for example, tends to deal largely with end products rather than underlying processes. Perception is identified with *knowledge* rather than with the individual's relation to the forces of the natural environment.

We can start out in no better way than to describe a number of examples in which sensory processes and perception are involved. Therefore, I shall list a number of these cases and describe several situations in more detail before we reach Part three.

## EXAMPLES OF SENSING AND PERCEIVING

These examples will each include more than what can strictly be called perception. They will encompass memories, fantasies and mood, but only the actual processes of becoming aware and gaining information are perceptual. What and how you perceive varies from time to time and somewhat from the way certain others perceive. This variation runs indistinguishably into feeling and mood, as for example:

1/ The exuberance you feel on looking at the blue sky on a cloudless day.

2/ Your feeling when you open a gift package.

3/ Your sensations when you speed along in an open convertible or on a motorcycle.

4/ Your experience when you look at some of the first flowers in spring.

5/ Your recoil from a limp handshake.

6/ The looks of the room at home when you come in and find nobody there.

7/ Hearing a tire blow out as you drive along.

8/ The way another looks as you peer into his eyes.

9/ What you see (and feel) when someone reminds you of someone you know very well.

10/ The effect of a searching reach of a tiny hand.

11/ The effect on the bereaved of an embrace of a friend.

12/ The aroma of mimosa or wild crabapple trees.

13/ The feel of a fire in the woods when you are cold.

14/ The taste of candy your mother, wife, or girlfriend has just made.

15/ The feel of a new pair of gloves.

16/ Your jolt when you taste something quite opposite to what you expected.

17/ The taste of lumpy whipped potatoes.

18/ The sight of a long-lost article.

19/ The voice of a friend on the phone.

20/ The feel and looks of velvet.

21/ The looks of a cell to a prisoner.

22/ The sound of a child crying in the night.

Most, if not all, of the situations listed involve several components, two of which are *extended action* and *emotion*;

often, these components are given the most attention. Strictly speaking, they may be isolated and separated from perception itself. Generally, this is what has been done in the formal study of "behavior," while perception has been largely bypassed and neglected. What we are to consider in this book are the mechanisms whereby we literally get and use information from what is around us. The obtaining and the effect of this information are so bound together that continuing the traditional practice of arbitrarily trying to separate them is fruitless. The individual brings himself (a total complex) to every situation, thereby making "information" out of raw data.

The following pages contain several detailed examples in which perception is critical.

## LOOKING FROM A HIGH PLACE

For some people, going up into tall buildings is routine. For others, it is uncommon. To find oneself out on a balcony looking directly down to the street used to be a rare experience, although it is becoming much less so. For many, such an occasion provokes uneasiness. Ten to thirty or more stories up, the distance down to the street looks great; uneasiness and the idea of falling become prominent. Here we have a specific nonlaboratory example of space perception. The very same distances involved on the horizontal and in the downward vertical do not seem the same in many respects. The downward look involves definite muscular tension which is absent in the horizontal. The viewer, tensing himself as if to keep from falling, may experience strange feelings in his muscles and the pit of his stomach (see Figure 1).

It is important to note that the apparent distance to the street becomes modified with extended experience. At first it looks great and evokes the reactions just mentioned, but this effect wears off and the distance seems less after routine daily encounters. I had my laboratories on the eighth floor of a building, and after working there for awhile the distance to the street seemed much less than it did originally. The downward view to the street became very similar to that from my second-story window at home. All of the feelings associated with height disappeared entirely.

It would seem that a reduction in the apparent distance, when looking down, is one of the things that distinguishes a steeplejack or a trapeze aerialist from the average person. It

Figure 1/ Looking down from a tall building.

certainly must not seem to them nearly so far to the floor or ground as it would for another person, if taken to the same height. Probably one of the features of this reduced visual distance is the lessening in muscular tension represented in counteracting the imaginary falling experience. The steeplejack's downward view becomes dynamically more like the view of the average person in the horizontal direction.

People differ widely in this fear of falling and perceived distance downward. Some of it is possibly related to various other traceable components of personality.

The crucial aspects and variables are perceptual. This is to say, they come about through the use of sense organs — through seeing. The total reaction is to be regarded as a perceptual response. Its characteristics stem from an integration of a number of sensory inputs besides the visual.

## DRIVING ON AN ICY PAVEMENT

Another situation which illustrates perceptual response is driving a car on an icy road or street. Among other things, driving a car involves kinesthesis (sensory feedback from muscles). When first learning to drive, it is not uncommon for the driver to feel as though the car is taking him "where it wants to go." Later, however, he feels that the car is a part of him. He steers it, leans, sways, and, kinesthetically and posturally, anticipates every move of the car, even cringing as it approaches a bump in the road. This same dynamic unity between car and experienced driver is exemplified by a bicycle or a horse and their riders. The same lack of unity initially exists in all three when the person is learning how to drive or ride.

Various events can disconcert the driver of a car. A sudden gust, or a strong but variable wind may deceive him. At first he is often unable to tell what is putting the car partially out of control. Initially it may appear that the steering mechanism is suddenly faulty.

The worst condition of all for driving, obviously, is on icy pavements, for then nothing the driver does is sure to turn out right. That the usual end results do not accrue from a given muscle movement in steering, or that the same kinesthetic feedback does not eventuate from a move intended to change the car's direction, becomes very distressing and provokes a feeling of helplessness. The driver develops considerable postural rigidity, which does not add to his success. His tension is likely to be experienced as some pressure or push imposed upon him, rather than as a muscular condition of his own.

While all of the feelings that result from driving on icy pavement are well known and quite obvious from the sheer physical characteristics of the situation, certain of the same feelings may arise in much less extreme form even on dry pavement. The sensation that the car is sliding, when actually it is not, arises in some cases on a wet pavement. The only way to reassure oneself is to slow down and try sudden applications of the brakes to test the pavement. This "illusion" of slipperiness tends to arise more often when the person is tired from long hours of driving and when nightfall obscures his vision. In semi-darkness, one cannot be visually reassured from instant to instant that the pavement is not wet and slippery.

A complex of perceptual factors is at stake in driving a car under all conditions, and in those mentioned the necessary stimuli are not always present to facilitate skillful performance. Sensory feedback of one sort or another is lacking. On ice, it is literally loss of control, due to slipperiness. At other times, the lack is in visual and allied factors. At such times, the performer is subject to what is ordinarily called *suggestion*; that is, he is in such a condition that a slight and otherwise ineffective physical factor may be crucial in deciding the perceptual outcome.

## ATTENDING A SYMPHONY CONCERT

Not all young people are fond of symphonic music, whether classical or contemporary. The environment of many young people is filled with radio blare to which they pay little or no focal attention. It is used only to form some sort of an activating context or background. We refer in this section to what happens when a person gives his whole attention to more sophisticated extended musical renditions.

People, especially those of different generations, expect different things from music. The young expect one thing, and the old another. We do not know whether to assign this to age or to training and chance. We are accustomed to calling these differences of taste, but *taste* functions through the vehicle of perception.

Listening to a symphony may evoke in those who do respond an extreme amount and variety of symbolism. The listener may become engulfed by elaborate imagery, for orchestral sounds tend to mean a great many things, which are not only concrete but are related to mood and visual imagery. The reader may recall what the music has meant to him on other occasions. All of this flavors one's perceptions at the moment.

## ATTENDING A MOVIE

Attending movies is a fairly common experience for many people. Generally the stars and the story receive our attention, but here we wish to discuss the moviegoer himself.

People differ on their choice of seats for the best view of the picutre. Some people go way down front close to the screen, which makes the actors and other items in the visual target very large. The retinal images of these items are much exaggerated over what they ever are off the screen; people would have to be giants to provide the viewers with such large retinal images. Images of this blown-up size function in the same way as those produced by field glasses or binoculars. Their exaggerated size makes the actors and objects seem even closer than the metric distance to the screen would suggest, and also makes them appear *larger*. We suspect that what usually occurs is that the actors seem exceedingly close. The question is: "Why do some people want the actors so close?"

Other people sit midway toward the front, and still others choose rear seats. These three sorts of people must differ considerably in their space perception and in what a visual situation is to them.

Some modes of showing movies present new problems of viewing distance. One of these is the enhanced azimuth (horizontal width) of the screens. For anyone, at any distance, the Cinemascope screen enhances the retinal image sizes considerably. People who could sit one-third of the way down toward the front now find that they have to sit in the last row. Even there, some people are not comfortable until they can lose themselves in the story. The conditions for persons who voluntarily select the first few rows are enhanced even more with the wide-angle screens. The fact that they still choose the front rows raises a fundamental problem that needs to be experimentally investigated.

As well as magnifying the retinal image and bringing the actors perceptually closer to the viewer, the wide-angle screens tend to "encompass" the viewer — a sensation which reached its maximum effect with such arrangements as Cinerama, in which the screen itself is not flat but extends around the viewer, thereby giving him something to see out of the corner of his eye. Additionally, the loud-speaker placements provide acoustic stimulation from both sides of the viewer rather than merely from out front.

The preliminary arrangements that preceded Cinerama used a number of projectors (as many as 11), each of which cast its own picture onto a segment of the screen, encompassing the viewer and giving the scene a perfectly convincing three-dimensional effect. To look around and above him, the viewer had to move his head extensively. This required the same motor components of behavior as the three-dimensional environment in which the viewer lives every day.

Thus far, we have been merely classifying people according to where in the theater they must sit to feel most comfortable visually. Certain factors of physiological optics further explain this variance. Some people are nearsighted; some, normal-sighted; and others, farsighted. Nearsighted people must be close to visual targets in order to see them satisfactorily, while farsighted people must be at a distance. What do eyeglasses do for these people? Nearsighted people need lenses that refract photic ("light") radiation so that it would arrive at the eye in the direction it would arrive from nearby objects, even though actually coming from distant objects.

Farsighted people need glasses that make visual targets at given distances function as though they were farther away than they are metrically. By removing his glasses, a person may change the apparent distances of the actors and pictorial scenes. A myope (nearsighted) can make the scene recede, while a hyperope (farsighted) will bring the scene closer. Changing the apparent distance of objects is an important, though generally overlooked, factor in the function of glasses; the blurring or the clearing up of vision is what is most often spoken of.

Understanding that the refractive characteristic of people's eyes differs greatly provides us with one explanation of why people choose to sit at various distances from the movie screen. But there are undoubtedly other factors.

Watching the movies is an activity involving the individual's sensory (perceptual) mechanism in many ways. The individual frames of the film must be timed within certain limits. Anyone comparing the projection of films of the early twenties with more recent ones will discover this. Communication at that time was by pantomime, for hearing was not involved. Encompassment, the factor we have been describing, was absent in the early presentations when the motion-picture theaters were often simply renovated long and narrow stores, possibly 100 by 125 feet deep and only 15 to 20 feet wide. Sound effects were produced by talking machines (phonographs), pianos or organs; the last was able to develop considerable momentum of feeling and mood.

Everything done by a scenario writer, director, and exhibitor, as well as by those who design and install the technical equipment, must be calculated to take the most advantage of the laws of human perception. This is the case whether or not those involved realize that they are dealing with perceptual mechanisms. Failure to comprehend that their product must be appropriate for psychobiological characteristics of their spectators or audiences diminishes the "appeal" of their motion pictures.


## THE LOOKS OF A ROOM

If rooms do not contain enough illumination ("light"), they are not only dark but inadequate for certain kinds of human activity. Since the proper levels of illumination are not obtained merely by chance, the consideration of threshold and suprathreshold levels for various tasks has occupied the attention of certain investigators for a number of years.

Beyond the consideration of appropriate illumination levels, aesthetics, creation of moods, and overall personal comfort enter the picture. The distribution of visual stimuli or the use of certain spectral ("color") combinations can be either irritating or soothing. Some study of the relation between the spectral composition of illumination and mood has been made, but little can be definitely said as yet. Personal taste, for example, is a highly variable factor that enters into any generalization about color use, since perception is a very changeable affair.

"Beauty is in the eye of the beholder" is a more significant truth than the original writer ever guessed. Some see beauty, and some do not. In one respect, the saying points to quite a sophisticated understanding, namely, that the things we see and what we see them as being are human *experiences*. Physicists who describe the universe with man left out do not find rooms, houses, trees, buildings and so forth in at all, simply units such as atoms and subatomic particles. In vision it is photic radiation.

But we, as psychologists, are concerned with experiences, and experiences about experiences. So, let us describe some rooms. In so doing, we find that there are several orders of experience. One concerns space. We see that one room looks large; another, small. We see that the size of the room varies according to the color of its walls, or the size, number and arrangement of the pictures on its walls. The nearness of a wall to the viewer is changed by repainting it another color. Some colors make the room look cold while others do the opposite. The distance of a wall can be changed by the type of illumination. In general, tungsten lamps impart a slightly yellowish color, although the lampshade plays possibly a larger role in what color a space appears to be.

Large bare spaces along the walls not only have certain spatial properties, but they influence mood.

Uniform illumination of a room produces a very different effect from a room that is spotlighted, for instance, by table lamps. Whereas uniform lighting encourages mobility, a tendency to move about in a room, spotlighting is conducive to quiescence. The individual is drawn to one of the lighted areas and tends to remain there.

Everything just stated is surely pretty well known by most people but is mentioned here to indicate a form of relation between persons and their environments, which you will see later fits the definition of perception or perceptual response. In studying the lighting and decoration of a room, one is dealing with the operation of human perception, whether he calls it that or not.

Let us take an example of a specific interior space — a cafeteria, in which the dining portion is a large T-shaped space, so that in a large portion of the overall area one can see great distances. Within the T-shaped space one sees only solid, stark hues. The walls are large unbroken areas of deep green and orange-reds. The surfaces are slightly glossy. They look cold and excite restlessness. Some of the diners are conscious of the effects just implied, including the feeling of hurry, although other diners may be entirely unaware of them.

One evening I was sitting in this cafeteria with a companion. All other diners had gone, and the place was empty except for several waitresses who were sitting around a distant table sipping coffee and chatting. This group, seen out of the cafeteria context, that is, in isolation, would have been perceived as a picture of ease and relaxation. But the uneasiness associated with the garish walls and the cold metal furnishings of the large room was most obvious. Thus, visually, I was face to face with two conflicting sets of stimulus conditions. The scene struck me rather forcefully as I stared back and forth, at the "picture of leisure" embodied in the group of coffee drinkers, and at the colors which induced restlessness. It was actually a startling perceptual contrast. The two factors did not go together at all, and if the scene were to be the subject of a painting, it would be judged internally most incongruent because of the clashing perceptual components elicited.

This is not meant to be a discussion about interior design and decoration but an approach to the perceptual effects that light and color include.

No doubt you can recall special and unique instances of how rooms affected you as you entered them or as you gazed about. If so, you are recalling examples of visual perception at work and this perception carried with it moods of delight, comfort, and ease, or else other very different experiences.

Now that you have read some examples of situations in which perception was at work, you may want to know more definitely what is meant by perception. Merely to say that perception was involved in these situations, and even to point out the characteristics of the experiences produced, did not tell you all you may want to know. You most likely will want to be given a better statement or definition of perception and be told about the mechanisms underlying the kinds of responses exemplified here. Accordingly, the next part tells you what perception is.

# part
# THREE
# what is
# perception?

It is hoped that the foregoing *situational* examples have suggested the idea that perception is involved in virtually every moment of one's active existence. Presumably this elicits your curiosity.

It has been long taken for granted that there are five senses. Now we know that there are more than twice that many. However, a more penetrating study provided the conclusion that they may be grouped into at least five major functional clusters called perceptual systems. Hence, it is not that we have just five senses, but five modes of perceiving.

## PERCEPTUAL SYSTEMS

Gibson (1966) describes these perceptual systems very ably. They are as follows (see the table on p. 19):

### THE BASIC ORIENTING SYSTEM

The vestibular mechanism in the inner ear reacts to forces of acceleration which indicate the direction of gravity and also the forces involved when one moves in diverse directions and various rates. This includes information about the beginnings and endings of body movements. The gravitational input to the vestibular mechanism is accompanied by haptic inputs from touch and kinesthesis (muscle, tendon, and joint information). The basic orienting system participates with the four other perceptual systems since it is a ground or frame of reference for them.


## THE HAPTIC SYSTEM

This system utilizes the receptors in the skin and in the muscles and joints for touching and handling things. Thus, it is the prime system dealing with mechanical contact and its consequences such as the appreciation of temperature and of injurious forces via pain. Haptic inputs (stimuli) specify an astonishing variety of facts about the environment and the perceiver himself. Much of this information is not fully appreciated because vision usually receives the most attention in descriptions of sensation and perception.


## THE SAVOR (TASTE-SMELL) SYSTEM

This is the perceptual system whereby the individual detects, discriminates, and appreciates materials that reach the interior of the nose and mouth. In general, the receptors in the nose, when stimulated, provide experiences we call smells, odors, or fragrances. Likewise, putting something into the mouth results in what we call taste. There is such an intimate functional connection between what affects smell and taste receptors that it is logical to speak of them together as being components of a *savor* system. In addition to these two sets of receptors, the system also contains the receptors for touch, temperature, and pain that line the nasal and oral cavities. Certain foods taste very different depending upon whether the nose is clamped so as to exclude the volatile component of the food from entering the nostrils. It is also known that cold whipped potatoes taste different from warm or hot ones. The mechanical features of food (hardness, softness, lumpiness, etc.) also affect its taste. The savor system is both a defensive and appreciative system, as will be seen later when we give examples.


## THE AUDITORY SYSTEM

This system deals with minute vibrations reaching the ear. Vibratory events are propagated over long distances; hence, auditory perception deals with events apart from the body. It identifies the nature and direction of acoustic sources. Since organisms themselves can act as acoustic sources, the vibrations manufactured can be used for communication by means of the distinct patterns that are produced. Communication is more than a transmission of literal effects; it is an exchange of symbolic effects. Hence, hearing and language go hand in hand.

## PERCEPTION, SENSATION, AND ENVIRONMENTAL STIMULI

| Perceptual System | Senses | Stimuli |
|---|---|---|
| Basic Orienting System | vestibular | forces of gravity and acceleration |
| | visual | |
| | kinesthetic | mechanical contacts with supports |
| Haptic System | tactual | feedback from: passive |
| | kinesthetic | and active mechanical |
| | deep pressure | contact and mechanical |
| | pain | manipulation of objects, |
| | thermal | including people |
| Savor System | smell | gases |
| | taste | liquids, foods |
| | tactual | — |
| | thermal | — |
| | pain | — |
| Auditory System | auditory | vibrations in air and in cranial bone |
| Visual System | sight | photic radiation ("light") (plus other senses) |

THE VISUAL SYSTEM

So much is made out of vision that the viewer hardly realizes all that is involved. This mechanism combines with all others in registering environmental conditions and events. The available information gained by vision is enormous.

## MUSCLE SYSTEMS IN PERCEPTION

Muscle systems function in connection with the receptors and by their states provide a form of information as to body position, and tensional states. Muscle movement is of two sorts, *exploratory* (thus, informational) and *performatory*.

One may speak of *systems* in ways other than those used in classifying perceptual systems. Muscles are involved in the organized activity that can be given system labels. For example, there is the *postural system* whereby the organism relates itself to the acting mechanical forces, primarily those of gravity. There is the *orienting-exploratory system* — which moves the head, mouth, eyes, hands for gaining information about the mechanical and other features of the surroundings. Another system is the *locomotor system,* by which approach, avoidance, and transportation in general are accomplished. The *appetitive system* involves give-and-take between the organism and the environment such as eating, breathing, eliminating, and sexual interaction. The *expressive system* produces gestures, facial expressions and vocalization, as well as other movements which manifest personalistic attitudes and emotion. And, lastly, there is the *language* or *semantic system* which signals by movements of all sorts.

In all of these systems, it is evident that not separate mechanisms but, instead, separate kinds of activity are being manifested; some of it *performatory*, some *exploratory*.

## SENSATION AND PERCEPTION

For a long time there have been two words that have been used in various ways to label the subject areas in which we are interested. These are *sensation* and *perception*. It is imperative that some clarification be made at this point.

The early sense physiologists and experimental psychologists busied themselves with discovering, describing, and classifying man's sensitivities to his environment, used here to mean energistic or physical surroundings. Thus, men sought to determine what forms of energy the human being can respond to. This pursuit involved three other considerations, namely: (1) specific forms of tissues and kinds of organs that manifest man's sensitivity and thus act as mediators between the organism and the environment; (2) the kinds of response that the energistic impingements ("stimuli") evoked; and (3) the identification of neural pathways which carry the sensory "message" from sense organ to brain. This search has led for many years to extensive analysis wherein attention was focused on highly restricted processes and end results. The end results mostly were forms of awareness or consciousness. The whole procedure, though relatively precise, failed to produce an overall picture of the functioning organ, the human being. These restricted forms of experience ("direct experience") were called *sensations.*

Starting with Aristotle more than two thousand years ago, it has been thought that there are five classes of sensations: seeing, hearing, tasting, smelling, and touching. Along with the mediating body mechanisms, these were called senses or sense modalities. Continued use of the analytic method applied skillfully and persistently, with the help of instruments, has disclosed ten sense mechanisms. Some workers call the results ten senses. Additional classes of receptors (sensitive tissue) have even been discovered but for some reason they have not yet led to an expansion in the number of senses definitely labelled and described.

All this time, despite the discovery of additional sense mechanisms, the idea of five senses has persisted among nontechnical people, which seems strange, indeed. Within the last four or five years a resolution of this apparent contradiction has been achieved. Gibson (1966) has made it clear that whereas there may be ten or more senses as judged by specific classes of body mechanisms, there still are probably only five *perceptual* systems. This involves a new distinction between perception and sensation. It is much more appropriate than the earlier distinctions made in defining the two terms.

Whereas sensation is defined in relation to sensory mechanisms, perception is regarded in terms of the tasks imposed upon the organism by the nature of the environment ("the nature of Nature").

Each of the perceptual systems is composed of the cooperative action of several sense mechanisms and extracts information from the environment.

Since we are not taking the usual extreme analytical approach, we are focusing on how the human being interacts with his environment to cope with its forces, to gain satisfactions and to express his feelings. The subsequent description in no way ignores the nature of sense mechanisms. In fact, it attempts to show that the organism's very life depends upon their use. In what follows, however, we want to describe the aspect of daily living that constitutes the interplay between the individual and his surroundings, and the consequences of the interplay of purpose and opportunity.

# part
# FOUR
# the
# operation
# of the
# perceptual
# systems in
# daily life

## THE BASIC ORIENTATION SYSTEM

As Gibson (1966) puts it, the terrestrial animal maintains a permanent orientation to the earth. Animals that fly or swim are also necessarily related throughout life to the earth since they too operate within the gravitational system.

      Certain body mechanisms have evolved that enable the individual to operate (move about) in the gravitational system. These mechanisms are of several sorts, primarily kinesthetic, vestibular and visual. As you know, the kinesthetic mechanism includes the feedback sense organs in joints, tendons and muscles. The vestibular mechanism is the nonauditory part of the inner ear and is traditionally labelled the *"sense of balance."* The kinesthetic mechanism relays information about body position and movement and the movements of head and limbs. The vestibular system is affected by the head and indirectly by body position and movements in the gravitational field; it is connected with the nervous system in a number of ways, many of which are reflexive. The reflexes are manifested as patterns of muscle movement and/or patterns of tension or posture. The visual system, which one ordinarily thinks of as free, is dependent upon the influence of the gravitational system. Head and body position reflexively influence the behavior of the eyes.

The vestibule is sensitive to two classes of conditions. It responds to various forms of acceleration and to static postures in the gravitational field. The forces acting upon the vestibule are of two sorts: (1) those produced by the person's own movement and postures such as walking, running, jumping, leaning over, turning the head, etc., and (2) the movements imparted to the head and body by forces outside the body, when transported or supported by carriages, cars, and so forth. These may make irregular, as well as regular, motions. Ordinarily, the body's own activities do not result in motion sickness, whereas certain imparted motions are well able to produce it.

A consideration that is of interest to us is the role played by basic orientation perception in early infancy. One of the chief forms of contact the early infant has with the energistic world about it is mechanical contact with bodily supports such as bassinet, cradle or a parent's arms and body. This contact is sensory as well as motor, for it affects sense organs and these in turn provide data which the infant seems prepared to use in some manner. Either satisfaction or distress can eventuate.

Since the gravitational system is a field of force, a falling body moves faster and faster the farther it falls. This is known as the "acceleration of gravity" and it affects all movements of objects. Forces either combine with gravity to increase an object's downward velocity toward the earth, or to oppose upward movements. We are interested in the factors involved both when the human moves or is carried about. The first is called active motion; the second, passive.

The unit of accelerative force has been called G. The centrifuge (experimental merry-go-round) and other devices have come to be able to produce forces of many G's. One of the problems that investigators have studied is the number of G's people can tolerate in planes, rockets, and so forth. It should be obvious from the previous discussion that the person's orientation to G application would be crucial for high G's. For example, if a number of G's were applied, the subject used as a guinea pig should be placed so as to move feet first or to be at right angles to the direction of motion to prevent the blood being drained out of the brain. Such drainage would produce blackout.

This subsection will contain several separate essays. The first, by Robert Grossman, includes an interesting observation of basic orientation in the infant. The second essay discusses the effects on perception of motion direction, both horizontal and vertical, of flying in a plane. The third essay contains a discussion of motion sickness and dizziness with a description of the effects produced by swings and human centrifuges. Three other essays will describe basic orientation in riding bicycles and swimming, the listing of a yacht, and motion sickness in a helicopter simulator, respectively.

# A ROLE THE BASIC ORIENTATION SYSTEM MAY PLAY IN INFANCY

robert w. grossman

While I was growing up, there was no experience quite as boring as attending Sunday morning church service. One event that frequently relieved this boredom was the curious behavior of babies who were brought to church for baptism.

The religion whose services I attended taught that babies should be baptized in front of the assembled congregation as soon after birth as possible. The mothers would bring their babies for baptism within two or three weeks of birth. During the service, the baptismal ceremony would begin with the congregation's singing of a traditional hymn.

This hymn was the signal to the mother of the child that she should bring the infant to the front of the church. By the time they met the minister at the baptismal fount, the child would be crying at full capacity. About halfway through the ten-minute ceremony the mother would hand the crying infant to the minister. Shortly thereafter, for no apparent reason, the child would stop crying. In fact, the baby usually remained quiet till the baptismal water was sprinkled on his forehead.

This quieting effect of the minister seemed to be just opposite to what I would expect. I had often seen a mother give her child to someone else to hold, only to have the child cry till he was back in his mother's lap. What special force was operating in these situations that would cause a baby to act this way? My first explanation ascribed magical power to the minister. This was soon corrected by the more religious members of my age group to the conclusion that it was the power of God working through the minister that gave him this strange ability.

One Sunday I came up with a less mystical explanation based on a new observation. Our family happened to be sitting at the rear of the church near the mother and family of the child who was to be baptized that morning. As the congregation began singing the baptismal hymn, I noticed that the mother was trembling. When I thought the situation over I decided that I, too, might be trembling with fear if I had to walk in front of six hundred people. At the same time I noticed how relaxed and calm the minister appeared to be.

Could this difference be the key variable in the situation? To answer this question, two areas must be explored. The first has to do with the relationship between trembling and fear. Is there a type of muscle movement associated with fear which would be characterized as trembling if it were great enough to be noticed? The second concerns the perceptual capacity of the infant. What sensory modalities would be involved in the infant's perceiving this trembling? Are these modalities sensitive enough at this time for the infant to make the necessary discriminations? Is it even remotely reasonable to suggest that the baby would be annoyed enough by the mother's trembling to be relieved by the minister's calm?

The perceptual questions are, of course, the main concern of this essay, but we should give the first area at least a brief discussion. In checking the psychophysiological literature, I found, as always, no complete answers to this question, but by making reasonable inferences from the available studies, some statements can be made about this situation. Studies of stress, anxiety and fear do show a significant muscle component associated with these variables (Goldstein, 1964; Williams, 1964; Malmo, 1966). No one had measured the exact amount of movement involved but the type of movement was found. It is not smooth. There is a small but measurable tremor or vibration-like action associated with all muscle activity and this stop-and-go action occurs with frequencies between 6 and 40 cycles per second. Thus there is imposed on muscle movement of the type associated with anxiety and fear small but measurable periods of rapid acceleration and deceleration. The amplitude of this vibration is very small so that if the infant discriminates it, his perceptual mechanisms must be very sensitive.

The second area for investigation, then, is the baby's sensitivity to vibration. Since the baby is totally supported by the mother's arms, any movement of those arms will be perceived as movement of the child's whole body. Our concern is therefore with the sensitivity of the infant to vibratory movements of his whole body.

The perceptual system available to the human for perceiving whole-body movements is the *basic orientation system.*

Of all the perceptual systems, it is the most difficult to describe because adults have little clear experience of this system.

The basic orientation system is sensitive to body position and changes in body motion. Physicists call an instrument which is sensitive to changes in motion an accelerometer and the study of these changes in motion is the study of acceleration. Before we go any further, let's take a look at an example of acceleration in operation. Think of driving a car, on a driving range, with a glass of water fastened to the dashboard. You should imagine the glass to be full and the car to be going forward at 35 miles per hour. If the car stays at that speed and the road is perfectly smooth, the water will stay in the glass. If the driver jams on the brakes, the water will splash all over the windshield. On the other hand, if the driver steps on the accelerator, the water will splash out over the passengers. Thus, the water in the glass will splash out only with changes in motion.

Other changes besides slowing down or speeding up will have an effect on the water. If the driver tries to make a left-hand turn at 35 miles per hour, the water will splash over the right edge of the glass onto the passenger. If he makes a right-hand turn, the water will splash all over himself. Thus the water is sensitive to changes in the direction of motion as well as speed. If the road is bumpy instead of smooth, the water will splash in all directions. This occurs because the glass goes down with the car when it drops into a pothole while the water stays where it was, only to have the glass come up and hit it when the car bounces out of the pothole, sending the water in all directions.

## THE VESTIBULAR ORGANS

The water in the glass registers any change in the motion of the car, either of direction or of speed. Although the vestibular mechanisms are much more complicated than the glass of water, they operate on the same principle. There are two vestibular organs, one a part of each ear. They are filled with a fluid which acts much like the water in the example. One part of each organ is sensitive to any movement of the fluid and so responds to all changes in head motion, whereas another part is sensitive to the static position. Because the head moves with the body, these organs are sensitive to body-motion changes.

## THE KINESTHETIC RECEPTORS

If we change the glass in our example to a flexible plastic glass, we can use the analogy to discuss the role of our muscle and joint sense receptors. When the car slows down, the flexible glass will bend toward the windshield. If the car speeds up, it will bend toward the seat. In a left turn it would bend toward the passenger and on a right turn it would bend toward the driver.

In our body, the things that usually bend in this way are muscles, tendons and joints. (If the bones themselves bend too much, of course, they break.) We have sense receptors in our muscles, tendons and joints that are very sensitive to any movement. Close your eyes and bend your fingers. You can feel the movement because of the muscle and especially because of the tendon and joint sense receptors. The muscle sense receptors are much less noticeable but they can be experienced if you pay attention to the sensation in the latter portions of your forearms. Now if you will swing your arm letting your hand and fingers swing freely, you can still be aware of the movement in your fingers and hand. That is, even when the hand is being moved passively, these sense receptors allow you to be aware of it.

## THE HAPTIC RECEPTORS

When you swing your arm, you may have noticed that you could perceive your fingers moving "through the air." This comes from your touch, or haptic, receptors in the surface of your skin. You experience these receptors bumping into the air molecules and perhaps into pockets of temperature change in the air.

If you were in the car mentioned above and didn't have your seatbelt fastened when the driver stepped on the brakes, you would receive two kinds of haptic information that there was a change in motion. First, you would receive information from the part of you that is in contact with the seat that you were moving from the seat. Second, you would receive information from other parts of your body as it bumped into the windshield. Information about the latter case would not be pleasant but it would make it very clear that the car's motion had changed.

# THE VISUAL RECEPTORS

That the eyes are a major source of information about changes in motion is too obvious to do more than mention it and move on.

Because the basic orientation system is made up of a combination of receptors, there is no one distinct experience which can be labelled basic orientation perception. But with all these receptors in action one can see that the basic orientation system has the potential of being very sensitive. Indeed, it has a perceptual threshold to vibration whose amplitude is only a tiny fraction of an inch.

A prime reason we are not aware of the experiential aspect of the basic orientation system is because it is so basic to our perception of reality that we take it for granted. It is one of the first perceptual systems in operation. Studies have shown that it is sensitive to changes in motion immediately after birth and there is some reason to hypothesize that it operates even before birth. Since it has been with us from the beginning, we've just become accustomed to its presence.

It is also basic to all our perceptions because it's always with us. If you have had a physics course or ever closely examined an object falling toward the earth, you know that the object goes faster and faster the closer it gets to the earth. That is, the speed of the object is constantly changing so that we say gravity is an accelerative force. Since the basic orientation system is sensitive to all accelerative forces, it is always sensitive to gravity. Thus we can always tell whether we are upside-down or right side up with respect to gravity. It seems quite foolish to ask if you know whether you are upside-down or not because "everybody knows;" it is less foolish to ask how you know.

There is some reason to believe that an infant's basic orientation system is sensitive to the same tremor range as an adult's. Since it is also reasonable to infer that movement in this range accompanies fear or anxiety in an adult standing in front of a crowd, we can reasonably hypothesize that the basic orientation system plays a role in the curious behavior of the babies during the church service.

Once it became clear that the basic orientation system might play a large role in this vital social relationship, I began to look for its operation in other situations. I began to want to find out how we as adults experience this system's operation. I began to get a clearer view of the role this system played in my life when the experience was not taken as much for granted. The experiences I recalled could be divided into two groups: those which were exciting, and those which were nauseating. As I thought of these experiences, parallels in my adult life became immediately clear. To help you in this process I thought I might give you some examples of each.

## EXCITEMENT

For children the basic orientation system can be experienced as fun. Have you ever watched four-year-olds spin around and around until they were so dizzy or disoriented they couldn't stand up? After they fall, laughing and giggling, they get up again and do it some more. If you think of the water-glass analogy, you can see that this spinning would send the water in every direction at one time. This means that the vestibular mechanism is sending the brain contradictory reports. Though we can process these reports for a while, eventually it becomes too much; we lose our sense of what's happening and we fall down.

There was a game I played as a child which took advantage of this lack of control after spinning. It was called *Statues*. The person who was "It" had to think of a statue like "a bird in flight" or "a galloping horse" or a "swimmer." After he thought of the statue, he would spin each of the other participants in turn around and around till they were quite unable to orient themselves. When he let go of them, the player was to "freeze" in whatever position he was in when he stopped moving. Most would fall down with one leg in the air and find it impossible to remain frozen till all the others had been spun. The spinner then would tell the group what he had thought of as a statue and pick the person who most closely resembled it. That individual then got to be "It." The fun was spinning 'round and 'round and then being thrown free, unable to control yourself.

Another example of the basic orientation system providing excitement for children is to be found in youngsters' sheer delight at being thrown up in the air and falling back into their parent's arms. I can remember my youngest sister being very tense and stiff the first few times my father swung her just a few inches up in the air. Not long after that she would push him to exhaustion yelling, "More, Daddy, more!" Her total joy in the experience is still very clear in my mind.

I think some of this same thrill must be available to adults in skydiving. The closest I've come to experiencing this was on the parachute ride at Coney Island. The total free-fall on that ride was only about two-tenths of a second, but I can still feel the eerie exhilaration which was produced by it.

Other rides at carnivals, fairs and amusement parks also take advantage of the basic orientation system's ability to produce excitement. Even as mild a ride as the merry-go-round constantly changes your motion in two directions. While you are going 'round and 'round, you are also going up and down. The ferris wheel depends mostly on heights to produce excitement. It also gives you a little extra thrill each time it jerks to a stop and your free-swinging chair rocks back and forth.

## NAUSEA

Discussing the excitement generated by stimulation of the basic orientation system on rides brings us to another feeling which overstimulation can produce—nausea or motion sickness. I suppose I was 10 or 11 years of age when I first went to the fair without my parents. The combination of the foods I ate and the various rides I took was too much for a small boy's stomach.

Overstimulation of the basic orientation system seems to be what's involved in seasickness. The ship rolling from side to side, and at the same time from front to back, very clearly involves large changes in motion.

The purpose of this article has been to describe the operation of the system in such a manner that you will be able to understand how it plays a role in the interaction between infants and the adults who are holding them. I have tried to describe a situation where this system may be operating as well as to relate the infant's experience to our own. One of the proofs of correct understanding of a process is to apply the knowledge you have gained.

## APPLICATION OF KNOWLEDGE
## APPLIED TO A STICKY SOCIAL SITUATION

Not long ago my wife and I were at a party with several new friends. We were all graduate students, too poor to afford babysitters, so one of the couples brought their baby. As conversation drifted along, I noticed that the only two people who weren't deeply involved in conversation with someone were the baby and myself. I thought I would get out of this mildly awkward situation by entertaining the baby. He was quietly sitting in his little travel seat on the floor near his mother. I politely asked her if she would mind if I picked him up. She told me to feel free but she had that "do you really know what you're getting into" look in her eyes. I confidently gave her a smile, trying to give her that cool "I do this all the time" look, said thank you and proceeded to pick the baby up. The conversations slowly ground to a halt, and I began to get the feeling of "everyone watching me." I reached for the child and began to lift him from his seat. When I had lifted him free from his chair, his face began to pucker as if to cry. I noticed immediately that my hands were quite tense and that things were getting worse every second. Realizing this, I let my hands relax and continued to lift the child. As the tension left my forearms, the puckered face relaxed.

To ensure that he wouldn't cry, I began to quietly rock him back and forth in my arms. As the conversations began again, I reflected on the whole situation. Was it really the stimulation of the basic orientation system that was at the root of this situation? I thought I would try to find out, so I stopped rocking him. He didn't seem to mind but appeared to be fine. Then I tensed my hands trying to be sure that I didn't squeeze him any harder. Sure enough, he became a little fussy and squinted up his face as if to cry. I relaxed my hands again and his face relaxed. I tried it several more times and the same thing occurred each time.

This fast-moving stimulation of the basic orientation system seemed to be quite annoying. On the other hand, the gentle stimulation of rocking seemed to be quite soothing. Would middle-range stimulation be exciting for the child as it is for adults?

I decided to give him a short bit of free fall without letting my hands leave the surface of his body. He stopped all of his movement and looked vaguely at a spot far in the distance as if he were "checking out" this new experience. The baby was too young to laugh or show overt signs of enjoyment, but he didn't show any signs of being bothered so I tried again. He appeared to find the experience interesting, if not exciting.

If the child does perceive this type of stimulation as exciting, then small amounts of gentle free fall should be more effective in stopping a child from crying than rocking. Indeed, I have found this to be the case. If the child is somewhat older, he usually enjoys it so much that he begins to laugh.

At the same time that this method is useful in stopping a child from crying, it is definitely not effective in aiding a child to go to sleep. Here the standard old-fashioned rocking chair seems to be a much better device to use.


## CONCLUSION

Our experience of the basic orientation system is indeed vague when compared to that of the visual or auditory perceptual systems. For this reason, the role it plays or may play in our relationship to the environment around us is relatively unexamined. I have suggested that the system may play a very large role in the early social experience of an infant. And there is a great deal of evidence to indicate that early social experience is vital to the development of a fully functioning adult.

I have also suggested that one of the reasons we, as adults, pay very little attention to the basic orientation system is that we take it for granted as the basis and background for all our relationships with the energistic environment which impinges on us. If this is so, it would seem to have a vast role to play in early experience when we are developing and organizing our perceptual worlds. If we pay more attention to the operation of this system, we will more thoroughly understand our relationship to our environment and will be able to relate to it more effectively.

# SENSORY MECHANISM IN RIGHTING REFLEXES AND STARTLE PATTERNS

A funny thing happened as I was walking down a large hallway in a building on campus. To briefly describe my surroundings, about thirty feet from the end of the hallway the floor dropped down two steps to a lower level. The walls contained a number of bulletin boards which were filled with notices and announcements of various sorts. As I walked along the hall at my usual pace, a curious incident took place.

All of a sudden I became surprisingly aware that some performance of mine had partly happened without my knowledge, and that I was in the midst of experiencing the terminal part of the performance—I was gracefully landing on my feet on the floor two steps down. The telling takes far longer than the event itself. Nevertheless words are the only means of informing you. One of the impressions was that I was in mid-air with nothing under my feet to support me. About this time I experienced an erect graceful landing without a thud or a lurch. One of the chief aspects of this affair was that I was not directing it. It was something happening to me. I had not been looking where I was going, and as I came to the steps I did not see them, for I was looking off to the side at the bulletin board. I did not become visually aware of falling and begin to tense up or do something consciously to brace myself. It was all over before any consciousness was involved except, as mentioned, of being in mid-air and of landing smoothly on my feet.

I am telling this story to illustrate some features of *basic* orientation — sensorially apprehended and guided performance in the mechanicogravitational world.

Obviously, I performed the correct movements to land unawkwardly on the floor below. One way of looking at the matter is that it was pure chance, since it was not directed consciously and with the aid of vision. Another alternative is to suppose that I must have had mechanisms whereby I was reflexively prepared to meet the situation. The best answer I can think of is some form of a *righting reflex*. It could well have been a combination of both.

You are familiar with righting reflexes in animals such as, for example, the cat, which can be thrown or made to fall from any sort of gravitational position and land on its feet. This is an example of what is called a righting reflex. Even here it would seem that vision is an aid in the actual landing. The righting reflex only helps the animal to get oriented right side up.

I am not aware that adult humans are thought to have clearly demonstrable righting reflexes such as the cat has. If we have such reflexes, they may be vestigial, i.e., hidden leftovers in the long process of evolution. They would be covered over by more dominant modes of conscious and intended behavior and would not have a chance to operate. For example, when beginning to fall, a person often is aware of what is beginning to take place and tries to prevent or modify it to advantage. In some cases, a fall happens so fast that it is largely over before he is aware of much of anything. Nothing then seems to be effective in lessening or guiding the fall. Also, falls occur in places where there is not enough room for a complete or successful righting reflex to operate. When falling down stairs, one is on uneven terrain with no good place for the feet to land. Furthermore, the conscious corrective measures that are introduced might interfere with the built-in reflexes which when acting alone could do a fair job in certain circumstances.

My best tentative conclusion is that man has some vestigial righting reflexes and that under favorable conditions they are brought into play. Most of what I did (unconsciously) to keep erect (right myself) was done under the direction of the orienting system (minus vision). In other words, kinesthesis and the vestibular system succeeded in providing for an appropriate maneuver without the direct guidance of vision and without the consequent interference of skeletal muscle action which would have so dominated a possible righting reflex that it couldn't function.

Of course, it was lucky that there were only two steps down, thereby providing me with a suitable place to land, rather than having my heel or heels land on the edge of a step. This would have been an unsuitable place and an injurious fall would have ensued.

Righting reflexes are usually discussed and dealt with as examples of motor behavior which, of course, they are. But the mediators of these motor responses are sense organs and thus the performances are pertinent material for our consideration in describing the relation of humans to their environment.

Another basic reflex pattern, known as the *startle pattern,* is pertinent in considering basic orientation in emergency situations. The pattern which includes overt behavior and a number of sudden shifts in internal processes such as heart rate and blood pressure, is elicited in two major ways. One is a sudden, unexpected "loud noise;" the other is sudden withdrawal of body support. In fact, the acoustic stimulus hardly needs to be fully unexpected. When the acoustic source is behind you, you simply manifest a pattern of overt self-protective movement. Several decades ago, considerable attention was given to the study and significance of the startle pattern, but by now little seems to be said about it. Nevertheless, it is a significant form of behavior, and one that helps to supplement our knowledge of the relation between you and your environment in which sensory mechanisms obviously are involved.

When the startle pattern is evoked by an acoustic stimulus, the reaction is haptic. Nothing was done to the person by gravitational changes. When the startle pattern is a response to sudden loss of body support, the pattern is an example of regaining basic orientation.

The actual pattern of startle to an acoustic stimulus includes blinking the eyes, making a unique facial expression, lifting the shoulders and drawing them forward, flexing the elbows, pronating the forearms, flexing the fingers, making a forward motion of the body, contracting the abdomen, and bending the knees (Landis and Hunt, 1968).

The startle pattern is found in the various races that have been studied, in infants as well as adults, and even in certain lower animal forms. It has been tested in people who are psychotic, feebleminded, hysterical and epileptic. It was found to be absent only in certain epileptics.

## ORIENTATION IN THE AIR

Since man has produced airborne vehicles he has a whole new cluster of forces to contend with. Our sensory mechanisms of basic orientation are pushed to their limit and beyond. We are not only involved in simple ways with the force of gravity, as when we are on foot or in ground vehicles, but also with forces which are even greater, and they are applied in various ways.

In the introduction to this subsection, the nature of gravity and its force (the G) used as a unit have been described.

Our nonauditory labyrinth is affected by acceleration and also by the position of the head with reference to gravity, or as we more often think of it, with reference to the earth. There are three general forms of acceleration. *Linear* acceleration, the best known, is the increase in velocity when moving in a straight line. If you were to move faster and faster in a straight line, at the same rate as the body falls faster and faster toward the earth, you would be subjecting your semicircular canals (and whole body, for that matter) to the force of 1 G. Another form of acceleration, and thus the production of force, occurs when you are on a merry-go-round. It is the force outward from its periphery and is called *radial* acceleration or centrifugal force. Mud flying from a rapidly revolving wheel is a good example of its action. A third form of acceleration is brought about by the change in rate of the revolution of the merry-go-round. Whereas radial acceleration is produced by an ever-changing *direction* of motion, the third kind of acceleration is simply the change *in rate* of changing direction. This is called *angular* acceleration.

All of these forces are produced by our behavior on the ground, but they are greatly enhanced in air transportation, owing simply to the rate at which planes must fly and to the fact that planes operate in a markedly three-dimensional space. An additional factor is involved, namely, the motions involved in the air are passive motions, i.e., not produced by your muscles as if you were a bird flying. The motions of the plane, your vehicle, are not those that you can do anything about in a direct sensory way. You may be the pilot at the controls but, even so, some of the actual muscle movements you make to pilot the plane, especially if you are piloting a huge jet, are not rigidly connected to specific behavior of the plane. Part of your actions are intellectual performances rather than purely sensory controlled ones. Most of us are passengers rather than pilots; consequently we do nothing to control flight. It is fortunate that all we are generally subjected to is more or less linear flight except at take-off and landing.

To bring to vivid recollection the effects of acceleration we can recall the experience we've had in swings.

As a swing is released at one end of its arc of excursion, it positively accelerates till it reaches the halfway point. As it passes this point, it negatively accelerates (decelerates) till it reaches the end of its arc. Since actually the path of motion is an arc, you are subjected to radial acceleration (both positive and negative) and since you speed up and slow down you are subjected to angular acceleration. This example is of use here because you can in memory relate acceleration to the sensory effects you have experienced.

In planes, part of the time the unexpected effects result from the relation of vision to labyrinthine action, as when viewing the earth when the plane is banked for a turn. On land you use the earth as the most fixed frame of reference. In the air in a steeply banked turn you are likely, when first flying, to see the earth tilted rather than experiencing your plane tilted in a bank (see Figure 2). In other words, the labyrinthine or vestibular input to the brain has not been used to make you feel tilted. You use what you see. The visual pattern shows your bodily axis as not perpendicular to the earth. Since you are being subjected to the forces created by the plane's motion and since the the plane is making no quick acceleration *changes,* your vestibular mechanism is adjusted so that you feel upright. Since you don't feel tilted, what you see must be tilted. What you see out the window of the plane is the earth's surface which is tilted and in a frightening manner. However, after a bit of experience in flying, you will be able to utilize the input from the vestibule (however slight) to feel as though you are tilted. When this occurs, you have made an achievement. I have no statistics to show whether every person goes through this evolution, or whether some are able to use the vestibular input to feel tilted the very first time they bank in a plane.

Before we examine the curious "errors" produced by flight, a brief description of some land-based experiments will be helpful. The major ones we have reference to are those of Witkin (1959) in which his subjects were placed in a room that could be tilted or revolved. The subject was in a chair which could also be tilted. Both the room and the chair were on the same axis and the tilts were to the right or left rather than forward or backward.

Let's say we start with both the room and the chair placed in the gravitational perpendicular. The subject, of course, senses both of them to be in the normal upright position, just as we would in any regular room. The experimenter can leave the room in its original position and rotate the chair. With lights on in the room, the observer will see that he has been tilted to the right or to the left. Let's say that instead of having tilted the chair, it is left in the original position and the room is tilted (revolved around the axis holding the chair). Now there are two al-

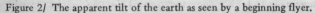

Figure 2/ The apparent tilt of the earth as seen by a beginning flyer.

ternatives. He may feel that he has been tilted and that the room is practically upright, or he may feel he has stayed in his original position and that the room has actually revolved.

The room is the entire visual world to the subject, and it can be tilted out of the normal relation to the gravitational field, while the subject retains his usual upright postural relation to the field. The major fact, for our purposes here, is that the visual and gravitational fields can be brought into conflict. In certain ways these conflicts are like those that can occur in flight, even though the gravitational factor here is not one of acceleration but rather any one of a number of fixed positions with respect to the earth. The Witkin setup is thus a very suitable arrangement whereby the interrelations between vision and vestibular-kinesthetic perception can be studied.

Perhaps in no other type of sensory situation is the human as much a captive of his sense mechanisms as when the factors involved in this experimentation are brought into play. He is not only captive but he often possesses a panicky awareness of it.

The following paragraphs illustrate some effects that may ensue in flight. Much of this is not actually experienced by passengers in today's planes, for most of the time in the air is spent in more or less straight flight and, furthermore, they are not called upon to operate the plane and make decisions. The pilots and navigators of planes have learned to rely on instruments, a very subtle achievement.

The effects listed below are found in McFarlund (1953) who quoted them from Vinacke (1947). The results fall into two classes: (1) those in which there is insufficient stimulation of the proper sort to enable effective response, or in which there are conflicting stimulus factors at work; and (2) those in which an erroneous interpretation is given the sensory effects the pilot receives.

Some of the errors of the first sort are the following. In a level turn, the pilot may experience continued straight flight, for the rate of change in direction is not enough to activate the *semicircular canal*. Also, in a level turn, the resultant forces acting on the *otoliths* are the same as in ascent; hence the experience is often one of ascent. In the plane's recovery from a level turn, descent may sometimes be experienced. If a turn is continued for some time, the result may be the experience of straight and level flight since the semicircular canals are sensitive only to rate of change and not to sustained change.

If in a left-hand turn the pilot's head is suddenly tilted forward, he may experience falling to the right. The actual stimulus is the *combination* of the plane's motion and the pilot's head motion with reference to gravity.

If the plane skids in a flat turn, the experience tends to be one of banking in the opposite direction since the resultant forces on the otoliths are the same in each case.

Level flight following a slow recovery from sudden roll tends to result in a feeling of tilt and the pilot leans in the opposite direction to compensate for it. The rate of the plane's change in orientation was not enough to activate perception of the recovery movement.

Gradual ascent, descent or a slow bank produce insufficient forces on the otoliths to activate them; hence level flight is the experience obtained.

In the darkness, a fixed distant light often appears to move when it is being approached. One often appears to be following it. This is an example of what is called the *autokinetic phenomenon*, which is predictable in a fixed land situation.

In the darkness also, when approaching an external object, it may seem as though the object is approaching the pilot. Here we come to several of the ambiguous situations which may be misinterpreted.

In a straight and level flight, when nearing a row of ground lights at an angle to flight direction, it may seem as though one is banking or tilting.

There are still other effects, but these should suffice to indicate the kinds of predicaments a pilot can get into if he relies only on his sensory equipment.

# DIZZINESS AND MOTION SICKNESS

One of the ways to understand basic orientation mechanisms is by learning what happens when such mechanisms are not functioning properly. One way to produce ineffective function is to apply extreme or unusual stimulus conditions. Another is to produce dysfunction by chemical means, such as drugs. A third method is through disease, such as cases of middle-ear infection.

Some malfunctions are brought to attention by discomfort symptoms such as dizziness, and some by overt failure to cope with the features of the gravitational field manifested, for example, by mispiloting a plane or simply by falling down stairs.

Dizziness is a symptom that many people have experienced; hence, its nature and basis are of interest. It is generally said that the basis of dizziness is in the disturbance of the nonauditory labyrinth in the ear, the best known parts of which are the semicircular canals. While it is true that one of the major sensory mechanisms for basic orientation is the labyrinth or vestibule, other factors have been shown to contribute to dizziness.

It is well known that posture (basic orientation) is achieved mainly by three major sense modalities: the vestibular mechanism, the kinesthetic sense mechanism, and the visual system. Any two of these three will serve quite well for static posture. One alone will not suffice. Neurologists utilize this fact in what is known as the *Romberg sign*. When a normally functioning person is asked to stand erect with his eyes closed, he can do so without swaying, collapsing or falling down. But when some segment of the vestibular mechanism, which includes part of the brain, is not properly functioning, the patient cannot stand with his eyes closed and his feet close together. He is left with only one of the three mechanisms functioning and this is not enough. If left alone, the patient sways or even falls.

Dizziness and motion sickness are dependent on the mechanisms mentioned above. The three terms — dizziness, motion sickness, and vertigo — are not clearly distinguished from each other in most of what you read. Downright *dizziness* occurs when the person experiences the visual field whirling around. Another term sometimes used is *giddiness*. *Motion sickness* is the syndrome or group of symptoms sometimes caused by motion of vehicles in which one travels. An age-old example is sea-sickness. Another term used here is *vertigo*. Motion sickness, or vertigo, involves dizziness and nausea, a kind of headache and certain other features of general uneasiness, some of which are difficult to describe. It must be realized, however, that this syndrome can be conditioned so that the same sickness is induced under certain conditions without actual motion. Thus, some persons who have traveled by sea become slightly sick later merely upon boarding a vessel.

Dizziness seems to be a very subtle matter and the individual's suggestibility can easily become causally incorporated into it. On the other hand, many concrete factors operate to produce it. Sometimes it is difficult to distinguish between cause and effect. Does nausea lead to dizziness or motion sickness, or does the disturbance of the vestibular mechanism come first?

It is difficult to study such complex matters as dizziness and motion sickness, and a clear and complete picture has not as yet been produced.

The major point I wish to make here is that while posture and the experience of a stable world are said to depend upon vision and kinesthesis (the muscle, tendon, and joint sense), as well as upon the vestibular mechanism, too little attention is paid to the first two factors — especially the role played by kinesthesis. Griffith (1920) as early as 1920 made a systematic effort to determine whether factors other than the vestibular mechanism (ordinarily and erroneously called the "sense of balance") are involved in dizziness. He did this by subjecting his observers to rotation in a revolving (Barany) chair and having them carefully introspect regarding all of their bodily sensations before, during, and after rotation, and during acceleration from immobility and deceleration to a complete stop. These subjects were able to isolate and describe many features of bodily sensation involving both skeletal and visceral muscles which led Griffith to conclude that motion effects on muscle and visceral organs formed an important part of the overall set of conditions producing dizziness.

A specific form of moving vehicle that is often avoided by people on account of the unpleasant effects produced is the *common swing*. Swings vary greatly in their effects depending upon their pendular radius. Swings of short radius, of course, repeat their excursions rapidly and their possible arcs are shorter. Swings at the other extreme repeat their excursions more slowly.

Children generally like swings while adults generally don't or at least they tend to enjoy swings much less than children do. Adults are often made ill by swinging, whereas this is not nearly so common with children. There are various reasons why a person of any age might be made ill some of which lie in the ears themselves. Ear infections and other systemic conditions produce anomalous tissue conditions in the ear. Often overloads of sodium produce edema in the inner ear. Various forms of visual malfunction sometimes underlie dizziness.

The sort of facts disclosed by Griffith leads to the plausible conclusion that dizziness or motion sickness produced in adults by swinging are partly of visceral origin. The abdominal walls sag, fat accumulates, and internal organs are not held as snugly in place as they are in children. I know of no experimentation that would clearly bear on this problem, although it seems to be a relevant matter for testing. Some differences might be found between those adults who are left free and those whose abdomens are experimentally bound so as to more snugly contain the visceral organs. It ought to be possible experimentally to preclude the operation of some of the visceromechanical factors found by Griffith and thus to discover more about the role of visceral sensations in the production of motion sickness. With all that can be said regarding the importance of the muscle mechanisms as the body is spun or otherwise moved or tossed about, the effects attributable to the vestibular mechanism are not to be minimized.

One of the effects produced by rotation is nystagmus, an ocular effect in which the eyes reflexively move slowly in one direction and quickly jump back in the opposite direction. This is horizontal movement and the person is not aware of its occurrence. The most likely effect if at all pronounced is some such untoward effect as dizziness.

In subhumans, patterns of repeated movement of the head (mystagmus) are produced by rotation. Humans show little of this whereas long-necked reptiles and birds definitely manifest it.

Tonic neck reflexes are also set up by disturbances

in the vestibule brought about by shifts in relation to gravity. These reflexes are such that the head regains or maintains its normal position to gravity. This is part of a larger complex of reflexes whereby the animal such as a rabbit or cat is enabled to land on its feet even when beginning to fall in a very awkward position. The righting reflexes are known as the reflexes of Magnus and de Kleyn (see Magnus, 1924).

Landau (1923) reported righting reflexes in human infants.

Wendt (1951) lists a number of the more usual factors producing motion sickness. The vestibule is principally involved in most, if not all, cases as is shown by the fact that deaf persons who show no vestibular sensitivity do not become sick (McNally & Stuart, 1942).

# SPECIAL SITUATIONS FOR BASIC ORIENTATION: RIDING BICYCLES AND SWIMMING

In addition to the more commonly discussed abilities of the human to move about and otherwise orient himself in the gravitational field, there is: (1) the ability to operate (ride) vehicles such as the bicycle which has no permanent equilibrium of its own, and (2) the ability to orient and propel oneself in water. Thus, in addition to sitting, standing, walking, running, and riding in such vehicles as wagons, automobiles and airplanes, there is the question of what is involved in riding a bicycle or in swimming. These two skills are among the more unusual and not all people develop what is required. Moreover there is much that nobody knows about them as yet.

Bicycle riding is a skill that has to be learned. It involves the operation of the basic orienting system, but obviously in a way that is not "natural." By "not natural" is meant that the adjustments to remain upright while riding a bicycle are different from those involved in remaining upright while standing or walking. For example, let's say one is standing and leaning a bit. So long as he does not tilt enough to shift the center of gravity out beyond his feet he can remain there. If he tilts too far, the action his body takes to correct this is to try to lean in the opposite direction which is the very thing not to do when riding a bicycle. Hence the individual must be able to act one way on foot and the opposite way when riding a bicycle. There is far more to it than that, of course. For example, instead of trunk movement in leaning, the major operations are to be performed by the hands and arms which turn the front wheel. In relatively straight courses, the bicycle can be kept upright by appropriate body action without the use of the hands on the handle bar, but this accomplishment generally comes long after success with the handle bars, if at all.

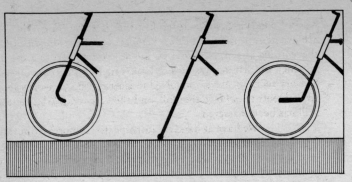

Figure 3/ Some of the modifications of the fork for the front wheel of a bicycle.

Jones (1970) has reported a study on the dynamics of the bicycle. First he determined what was in the literature to account for the means by which bicycles would remain upright. None of the theories seemed to account for all of the features of bicycles. Consequently, he adopted an experimental procedure which consisted of making modifications in normal modern bicycles and testing them for their ability to maintain equilibrium when given a shove straight ahead. This was measured by determining how far they would go before falling over. Some fell quite readily and others went for considerable distances. The latter sort could be divided into two classes: (1) those which described a large arc before falling over, and (2) those which righted themselves by alternately going from side to side, before finally falling.

It was his supposition that some bicycles would be unrideable, for they could be so constructed that no adjustments through manipulating the handle bars would keep them upright.

Because it is the turn of the handle bar changing the direction of the path taken by the front wheel that is primarily involved in keeping the bicycle upright, Jones modified the front fork. Figure 3 shows some of the modifications and Figure 4 shows an actual bicycle that the author found a young boy riding in a small town he visited. The boy and Jones had no connection with each other. It was an interesting coincidence to find a modified bicycle in action.

Our concern is not with Jones' mathematical equations on the manner in which equilibrium is maintained, but rather with bicycle riding as an example of basic orientation in

# MOTION SICKNESS
# IN A HELICOPTER SIMULATOR

Miller and Goodson (1960) describe motion sickness in a helicopter simulator. Such a simulator was used to determine to what extent the device might be useful for the initial stages of helicopter pilot training. The simulator consisted of four components: a cockpit, a visual projection system, a computer, and two loudspeakers to produce acoustic stimuli simulating engine noise. The cockpit contained the controls that the trainee had to learn to use. The visual projection system consisted of two screens on which the "environment" (sky and land) was projected. There were two projectors, each displaying its own portion of the environment. One projected the near and distant terrain and a portion of the sky while the other continued the sky. The two projections overlapped. The position and attitude of the simulated helicopter were produced by motion of the transparencies. The computer took inputs from the cockpit flight controls to manipulate the transparencies and thus produce the visual effects.

The only actual motion of the cockpit was sound vibration and rough land jolts simulated by rotating imbalanced weights in the cockpit frame.

From the beginning it was found that a large number of persons using the simulator, particularly veteran helicopter pilots, developed some degree of motion sickness. The vertigo or motion sickness was enhanced if and when the "pilot" lost control of the simulator. Critics of the device apparently thought the motion sickness stemmed not from the simulator's incorrect visual representation, but from the lack of associated effects on the body.

The sickness that developed usually occured during the first ten minutes in the simulator and often lasted for several hours after leaving it. Sometimes the sickness did not come on until some time later that day.

Miller and Goodson undertook to find out why the simulator produced the ill effects. One major feature of the simulator was that no actual motion of the cockpit was involved. Some people who had suggested earlier that such an absence was in conflict with the visual impression that the cockpit did move assigned this as the cause of the sickness. The authors thought this factor was hardly enough to produce the ill effects. For example, they said that in actual flight in the HTL-5 (a real helicopter), there was a lack of perceptible cues in many situations and these, apparently, did not occasion any ill effects.

Some individuals did not get sick while in the simulator, but did several hours later. Some persons became so averse to the simulator that the very sight of it made them sick. Those who did not actually get sick typically complained of becoming very tired by a session in it. In fact, the greatest effect was felt by experienced instructors and not by the students.

The authors believed that possibly the ill effects accrued from conflicting *visual* factors rather than from conflicts between visual and proprioceptive factors. It is possible that some of the later conflicts existed and had an effect.

In the operation of actual helicopters, one of the most unnatural features is the time lag between executing a control and having anything appreciable happen. It requires one to two seconds, during which time it seems as though nothing is happening and that no response will occur. The pilot's natural reaction is to add to the adjustments he has already made.

It is in the *action* of the helicopter and the simulator that there is a difference. The helicopter begins to move in the *direction* it is to go as it begins its *attitudinal* adjustment. The simulator makes its full attitudinal adjustment *before* it begins its directional movement. This *increases* the lag between a control setting and the device's execution of the response to from two to three times as long in that in the HTL-5 helicopter.

Here is an interesting point. The only way for the simulator to take a nose-down attitude is to shift the scenic view upward, thereby presenting a visual appearance to the pilot of flying backwards instead of nosing down. Of course, this induces the pilot to make a further control adjustment and thus to "over-control." Actually, the so-called illusion appeared so vivid and extreme to one experienced pilot in the simulator that he reversed his control.

When over-controlling occurs, it is as though the pilot is "chasing" his craft. That is, the simulator is doing a number of things in sequence as a result of the controls given it, but it turns out that the pilot's action at any instant is one or more steps behind the simulator sequence. The maneuvers become violent because of the pilot's actions and this adds to his sickness.

# THE HAPTIC SYSTEM

The haptic system is first of all the body machinery which enables animals and humans to appreciate mechanical contact and manipulation. It is a detector system with sense organs in the skin for touch, temperature and pain, and in the muscles, joints and tendons for the appreciation of motion and position as well as muscle tension. It is a system that *explores* and *appreciates* what the individual comes into contact with. The system is involved when objects are manipulated to discover or utilize their mechanical qualities. It is the device by which both humans and subhumans become intimately acquainted with each other.

You will find descriptions of the complex sensory structures in skin, muscle, tendon and joints in textbooks. What we are interested in here is the fact that we as humans are equipped with body mechanisms whereby we can come to know our environment, can satisfy our needs and avoid what may be harmful. A major and pervasive aspect of the environment is that it is mechanical. This calls for both negative and positive behavior and forms one of the foundations of our existence. We must make adjustments to concrete objects every moment of life. Moreover, mechanical things — what we can touch — provide us with innumerable satisfactions.

It is not strange that the skin is the seat of so much that is important to the individual for the skin is the *juncture* between the body and the physical environment. As such, the skin performs several classes of function. First, it is the protective barrier between the organism and various kinds of impacts or intrusions from outside. It also contains devices for regulating body temperature; it is an organ of excretion and of identification, attraction and repulsion in terms of color, hair growth and the production of substances which other organisms smell. Additionally, it contains numerous kinds of sense receptors for detecting qualities of external objects experienced by the human being as varieties of hardness, softness, roughness, smoothness, coldness, warmness, wetness, and dryness. We wish to discuss this category of skin function. In so doing, our concerns transcend the simple qualities just mentioned, particularly as the individual deals with other members of his own species and even other creatures which can actively respond to him.

The haptic system while being a *detection* and a *receptive* system is also an active agent, a *doing* system. It takes part in mediating information whereby not only the mechanical properties of objects are appreciated and evaluated but also other active organisms, particularly humans. Thus the skin deals not only with exploration, appreciation, and manipulation of the mechanical features of the environment but with communication between persons.

When it is realized that these sensory mechanisms have to do with the essence and core of existence, their relevance becomes quite apparent. We speak of contact, closeness, remoteness and detachment to describe spatial properties of the environment. But these same spatial terms aptly describe the evaluative and qualitative aspects of existence. The same sensory mechanisms that deal with physical space supply meaning to something which is not actually spatial at all, but which we nevertheless talk about in spatial terms.

In attempting to understand haptic perception, we must distinguish between *touching* and *being touched* because the sensory experiences are different. That is to say the way objects feel is different. Moreover, the broad effects upon the person himself are different. We shall call touching *active touch,* and being touched, *passive touch.* In general, sensory physiologists have confined their attention to passive touch. This is not surprising for it eliminates the subject's active behavior and restricts him to reporting upon the effects of experimentally controlled impingements on the skin. However, we are interested here in what touch means to the individual and how he uses it in his daily life, which is quite a different story.

Révész in Europe and Gibson in this country seem to be the only two psychologists who have made much out of active touch. Révész (1950) termed it *haptics* and later Gibson (1966) identified the haptic system as one of the five perceptual systems. To deal with haptics as a perceptual system is to consider more than the tactile and kinesthetic sense mechanisms. It is to include the individual in the act of searching or exploring. He is doing something to obtain information and/or certain satisfactions. Sometimes the information itself may be a kind of satisfaction for it can be the basis of decisions, while at other times certain sensory experiences are qualitatively satisfying in and of themselves. The haptic sense is a vehicle for associating with other persons, and in this connection haptic perception becomes extremely significant.

When an object is placed in your hand or when you place your hand on it, you tend to bring your other hand to the object. You are likely to curve your fingers around the object if it is small. At least you do not usually extend your hand to make it a flat surface unless you wish to make it more visible to someone else. If the object is very small, you finger it; if larger, you move your fingers over it in a variety of ways.

Once you gain a certain amount of information, you verbalize regarding surface qualities and name the object. After that, your explorations cease or become minimal, unless the very tactile qualities bring unique satisfaction.

Whether one, two, or more fingers, or both hands, are used to contact an object, the experience is a unitary one, transcending the multiplicity of separate contacts. This is true even when vision is not involved in the act.

As in vision, what is apprehended tends to remain stable, despite the exploratory movements that provide a succession of bits of information. This impression of stability goes beyond the specific object being touched, encompassing the remainder of the room or other surroundings and providing a still more extensive stable world.

When you press on a surface or when you squeeze an object, the impression is not of an increase in the intensity of the cutaneous experience of your own hand or other body surface, as it may be, but of something about the object. It is hard or soft, rough or smooth. Even the softness possesses different qualities. It may be soft like putty, soft like butter or something else. Hence through experience you are able to identify putty, rubber, and other *classes* of material — if not specific substances. Differences between textures are also perceivable as, for example, the dissimilarities of wrapping paper, blotters, good bond and cheap typing paper.

The haptic perceptual system and the basic orientation system overlap if we judge them by the sensory mechanisms involved. However, if we judge them strictly by the function served, i.e., the kinds of information obtained and the satisfactions derived, they do not overlap. For example, by tactile and kinesthetic mechanisms, that is by touching and handling objects (even with eyes closed), you can determine positions, orientations, and even tilts. Tilt, however, is basic orientation when it has to do with the relation of the perceiver himself to the gravitational field. The touching, grasping, identification of object, quality, size, texture, and many other things are actions in haptic perception.

Touching and being touched involve two different sorts of relation to the environment, particularly in relating to other people. Touching conveys something to the other person and being touched conveys something from the other person.

Tactile communication gains its efficacy by being one of the first modes available to the developing infant and child. To the adult, tactile communication may seem crude, primitive and inadequate when viewed in a newborn baby. But the mechanism is there ready to be used, and used it is. Haptic communication is never completely superseded; it is elaborated through the development of symbolism.

The meaning and significance of many symbols in adulthood depend upon previous tactile experience. This experience gives the symbol its cognitive meaning and its affective quality. Huxley (1939) has pointed out that "direct animal intuitions are not rendered by words; the words merely remind you of your memories of similar experiences." Thus it is that life is made up of concrete experiences and the memories of them. Many of the experiences themselves are tactile. In all symbolic communication such as language, verbal or written, the recipient can receive the message only insofar as previous experiences provide the necessary meaning and affective coloring.

That meaning which is not tactile in intent can be aptly conveyed by the use of tactile figures of speech is a significant demonstration of the role played by touch. We use the statements "I was touched" or "I felt" by which we can mean as readily an emotional experience as a mechanical contact. Many tactile adjectives such as *rough, hard, tender* and *smooth* likewise convey affective and evaluative states as adequately as mechanical contact.

Being touched conveys something different depending upon what part of the body is touched. To commend a person, one pats him on the dorsal rather than the ventral surface of the body. Some may argue that this is simply custom. While an added factor of meaning does accrue from custom, certain experiential (sensory) differences between ventral and dorsal contact have a more fundamental basis. These dorsoventral differences show up in infancy and are quite apparent in adult life. They are manifested in the different effects of various prone positions both while awake and asleep. Relaxations achieved from lying on the back differ from that obtained on the "stomach" and on the side. Some of these differences have to do with muscles, tendons, and joints, but some of them are definitely tactual. *Amount* of surface contacted is another variable which underlies meanings derived from contact.

While we often turn our backs to the wind on a cold day, this may be more for protecting the uncovered face than the ventral surface of the body. Actually, coldness is less objectionable when striking the front of the body than the back. When we warm ourselves at a hearth, we of course face the fire part of the time. Even here, part of it may have to do with warming the hands, but the greatest pleasure comes from warming the *back*.

We can better tolerate something of low temperature suddenly touching the ventral than the dorsal surface of the trunk. Other regional specializations result in tickling in some places contacted and not in others. Here again the amount of area makes a difference. Certain forms of mechanical impingement produce itch. Contact with some body surfaces in certain ways produces reflex effects. The point of the nose is one such surface. Water ready to drip from the nose can be very annoying. Certain contacts with the nose elicit a sneezing reflex.

Contacts (touching, stroking and biting and the like) with some body surfaces produce results which are called erotic but these must be associated with other conditions, most of which we call cognitive.

## HAPTIC MECHANISMS,
## REALITY, AND WELL-BEING

What we wish to depict here are the consequences of sense organ activation that go beyond the simple analytical qualities just outlined. We wish to show what senses have to do with the active behavior of the organism as a person as stimulation of sense organs may fulfill certain needs in addition to mediating specific information. If there is considerable restriction in sensory activation, certain developments in the young may fail to occur as shown in studies made of the consequences of rearing animals in complete darkness.

Since the haptic system deals with the mechanical features of the environment, no perceptual system is quite as concrete and as final in the information it provides. The haptic system deals with and/or produces the things that language can only *talk* about. It is no wonder that action seems more genuine than the language describing it.

The activation of mechanisms of haptic perception makes all the difference between being in harmony with one's surroundings (particularly when the object is another person) and being remote from it in every respect. While vision informs of the presence or absence of objects, including persons, vision alone does not suffice. What is seen can refer to something at great distances, even in another world. The recent live moonshot scenes totally changed our feelings about the moon. It is no longer so remote, but haptic contact would bring it experientially all the way to us.

While many social contacts are made through language, many others are made directly through the senses at a nonverbal level, particularly through the haptic senses. Whereas language, at its best, is supposed to be a superior means of communication, words are not sufficient for some things. Direct contact and experience are necessary.

Tactile sensitivity is one of the very most primitive sensory processes. It appears in subhuman animal forms as tropisms and thigmotaxis. Many forms are guided by their antennae, Even the sense of smell may be looked upon as a form of tactile response as when airborne particles land upon olfactory organs. The tactile sense appears early in the fetal life of the human and is likely the first sense to become functional (Carmichael, 1951; Hooker, 1952).

## THE ROLE OF THE SKIN AND HAPTIC MECHANISMS IN WELL-BEING

Several years ago Ashley Montagu (1953), the noted anthropologist, pointed out the role that stimulation of the skin and underlying tissues played in various species including the human. He mentioned that the skin and nervous system are derived from the same embryonic layer and that there is a wide tactile-cutaneous representation of the skin in the brain. He assumed that this implied considerable significance for the skin and that what is so basic phylogentically must have physiological significance. We might add that what is important physiologically must also be important psychologically. In considering the various forms of behavior which fulfill the requirements of basic need, it seems that cutaneous stimulation must play a large part.

Montagu pointed out how stimulation of the skin plays a role in the development and well-being of the young animal. That animal mothers spend a great deal of time licking their young, has usually been thought of as simply a cleaning process. But this hardly covers the possibilities. During this licking process, the young receive a great deal of cutaneous stimulation involving considerable impact and manipulation of deeper tissues. This licking has a total consequence aiding the young all the way from social development to the functioning of the gastrointestinal and genitourinary sustaining systems.

The question of whether licking the skin has functions other than merely cleansing it has been experimentally answered in studies comparing young not licked with those that were. Previously, experienced animal breeders had noted that the young not licked died of failure of the gastrointestinal system or malfunction of the genitourinary system. Montagu suggested that stimulation of the peripheral sensory nerves is part of the process of activating these two systems.

Study of rats and dogs has indicated that the genito-urinary system will simply not function when there is no cutaneous stimulation in the region of the perineum. Professor Reyniers (1946, 1949), in raising germ-free animals, found during the early days of his work that his animals died from an apparent failure of the genitourinary and the gastrointestinal systems. In later batches, the young animals got along all right when their perineum was stroked after each feeding until they urinated and defecated. Apparently, the first animals died of occlusion of the ureter and a distended bladder. It has been found that mother rats raised from birth with a cardboard ruff around their necks were less able than unruffed mothers to care for their young by licking them. The ruffs had been a means of preventing the licking of their own bodies (Frank, 1957). Young kittens, also, cannot urinate or defecate unless the mother licks the urethra and anus.

Windle (1940) says that the human fetus is capable of defecation in utero, and apparently the young require no cutaneous stimulation as in the case of the animals just cited, but it is not certain whether this is true throughout the Order of Primates nor does this call for the conclusion that handling the child is not helpful.

Many years ago, Hammett (1922) found that in certain surgical operations, "gentled" (stroked) rats were far better risks than those not so handled. The unstroked rats presented a picture of high irritability and tension. In the ungentled series, 79 per cent died in parathyroid tetany within 48 hours, while only 13 per cent of the gentled died of this difficulty during the same period. While these figures applied to the animals that were thyroidectomized, it held in the same way for those parathyroidectomized.

For many centuries, it has been known that if a newborn child fails to breathe, a vigorous slap or two on the buttocks often induces breathing. The significance of this remarkable fact has seldom aroused much curiosity. Another procedure for inducing breathing was the immersion of the child in hot and cold baths. These baths act on the autonomic and, in turn, on the respiratory centers.

Montagu asks whether or not it may be that the contraction of the uterus during labor provides a sort of massive stimulation of the vital systems including the respiratory. An affirmative answer would presuppose that Caesarean and some prematurely born children would have difficulty in beginning to breathe. We have no evidence on this but the respiratory behavior of prematurely born children later on has been studied in respect to their respiratory behavior. Such children have been shown by Drillien (1948) to have a significantly higher incidence of naso-pharyngeal and respiratory troubles than the normally born. This difference was marked during the first year of life. Shirley (1939) found that prematurely born children have greater difficulty in developing bowel and bladder sphincter control than children born at term.

While the foregoing examples may be seen simply as a group of physiological facts, the connection between them and higher order behavior emerges as one continues to look for relations between skin stimulation and behavior.

Haptic contact between infant and mother is obviously of some systemic and organismic value to the infant. This contact generally constitutes the first act of communication between them, and it seems to be a language that provides satisfaction for the infant. Specifically, the contact of the infant's lips to the mother's nipple seems to be one of the most satisfying forms of behavior. The representation of the lips in the somesthetic cerebral cortex is enormous as compared with other body parts. The comparative rarity of gastrointestinal disorders manifested by the breast-fed baby, in contrast to the bottle-fed one, is possible testimony to the benefits it derives from sucking and perioral stimulation. Montagu thinks that further investigation will disclose that the breast-fed baby is a more efficient organism in respiration than the bottle-fed one. He suggests that cultural differences in clothing or nudity in the nursing situation will also have some effects on the later development of the child. This problem has, of course, received no adequate attention and study.

In all cultures physical contact between persons exercises an important role in interpersonal relations. Handshaking, kissing, nose-rubbing, holding hands, hugging, walking arm-in-arm and the like are manifestations of friendliness. In western countries, however, it is the common practice of well-bred persons to apologize to others upon accidental touch. All bodily contact is significant in one way or another. To establish tactile contact with another person is an act of communication and recognition. Such contact in some circumstances is entirely out of place and unwanted. Taboos against various forms of contact have arisen to preclude the unwanted and unfavorable occasions.

The connection between some illnesses in the human and lack of cutaneous (haptic) stimulation in infancy is suggested in the following case cited by Montagu. A 30-year-old woman, an identical twin, had suffered from very frequent attacks of asthma as far back as she could remember. The same was true of her twin. She was in and out of sanatoriums over a six-year period for treatment and was told that perhaps another major attack would be fatal. A certain visitor to her home, noting some of her mannerisms, asked whether her mother had died when she was young. The woman said that her mother died when she was born. The visitor suggested that perhaps she had not received enough cutaneous stimulation as an infant. In the discussion it was suggested that she go to a physiotherapy clinic where she would be massaged by an expert masseuse. She agreed and a few days after her first massage she was bubbling with enthusiasm. She was told it might be possible that if she continued massage for a while she would never have another asthmatic attack, unless she was involved in some emotional upset. She took the advice and for more than five years up to the time the case was reported she remained in the best of health with attacks reduced to a minimum.

## MONKEYS REARED WITH SURROGATE MOTHERS

One of the most enlightening programs of study in recent years has been that by Harlow (1958) of monkeys raised with surrogate mothers, which are mechanical devices resembling mother monkeys in a faint way. Some are simply wire-mesh bodies which, of course, are rough and tactually unlike the natural mother. In some cases, this wire mesh was covered with terrycloth, which made the body softer and a little more like a natural body surface. Some monkeys were even reared in isolation. Obviously, Harlow's technique was not originally designed to separate the haptic features from all others such as, for example, those that could be called social. But in the various situations, the haptic features were a kind of variable.

In the first two weeks of the infant monkeys' lives the floor of the cages were warmed by electric heating pads, but most of the monkeys climbed onto the unheated cloth mothers. Clinging and cuddling up to the terrycloth mother occupied more and more of their time as they grew older. The monkeys who were given only the wire frame as a mother spent no more time on her than was required for feeding from the nipple, thereby contradicting the common assumption that the source of relief from hunger and thirst would be preferred to other things. It showed that the immediate effects of bodily contact were of overpowering importance. Because the surrogate mother could take no responsive part in the haptic situation by fondling the infant monkey, this important factor was lacking.

The experimenters subjected the infant monkeys to stress by confronting them, for example, with a mechanical teddy-bear that walked forward beating a drum. This, unquestionably, was a disturbing event. The experimenters wanted to see whether the monkeys would go to their surrogate mothers for protection. Regardless of whether they had nursed from a wire mother or a cloth one, they sought refuge from the cloth one. As they grew older, this difference in behavior toward the two types of surrogate adult monkeys became increasingly marked. In early infancy, the monkey might dash to the wire mother, but if it did so, it soon backed away and sought the cloth one. Later, it went directly to the cloth mother. After cuddling onto the cloth mother, it would turn and look at the originally menacing teddy-bear with seeming calm. After a time with the cloth mother, it might even become so reassured as to leave her and walk up to the bear. This all seems to be emphatic evidence that the tactile or haptic factor was the overwhelmingly important one.

The monkeys were also placed in less stressful but, nevertheless, strange circumstances. For example, when they were put into a room much larger than their usual habitat which contained strange objects (but including the cloth mother) they would immediately rush up to the cloth mother and climb upon her, rub against her and hold tightly to her. If the cloth mother was absent, the monkeys rushed across the room and threw themselves upon the floor face downward, clutching themselves and screaming in distress. The wire mother, however, provided no more help in this situation than a completely absent mother.

A more recent report (Harlow and Suomi, 1970) indicates that nursing is a factor in monkey development which original papers treated as of no importance. Recent experiments show that it does have an effect but one which is of far less importance than the tactile and which probably decreases with time.

The surrogate mothers were static, thermally cold, and not as tactually pliable and responsive as natural mothers. Hence, although they formed objects to which the infant monkeys could retreat and seek refuge, they failed in many ways to provide the haptic interaction with the infants that the natural mothers would. This resulted in certain developmental failures in the growing infants.

All sorts of aberrant behavior were produced in the animals reared under these conditions. When reaching adulthood, these infants were generally unable to mate and those that did become mothers rejected their offspring and were unable to participate in raising them.

It is easy to speak of the basis for the trouble as being social. But what we are trying to make clear here is that a large part of what is social is the pattern of haptic stimulation the mother provides as she nurses, preens, and fondles her children. Various forms of sensory input constitute the ingredients of what is called social.

## ROLE OF HAPTIC MECHANISMS IN INTERPERSONAL INTERACTIONS

Some of the most subtle but forceful examples of the role played by the haptic mechanisms can be found in the work of certain social psychologists showing how certain deficits in human behavior can be relieved by group activities. These activities involve the substitution of nonverbal, but haptic, interactions between two or more persons.

These techniques are described by William C. Schutz in his book, *Joy* (1967). While the usual interpretations of the activities and their effects are not the same as we are suggesting here, the effects do constitute the very kinds of examples that we are portraying for the haptic senses.

The subtitle of Schutz's book, *Joy*, is "Expanding Human Awareness" and the techniques used actually do this.

There seem to be two features of this procedure: first, the things done to get the participants to discard inhibitions; and second, the involvement of the haptic senses. The participants are asked to interact with each other in reckless and absurd ways, all of which at times must be nonverbal. In fact, the interaction was not even to be primarily mediated by sight and hearing, but by the haptic senses of the skin, muscles, and joints. In our culture, the free exercise of this form of interaction may seem strange, crude, and ridiculous and, in fact, our mores and manners prohibit it, but it has potency that is undeniable.

Schutz's underlying suppositions are as follows: While young infants reach out and poke and grab each other and seem to derive certain kinds of satisfactions from so doing, adults have stopped doing this and thereby have stopped responding to each other on the basis of their impulses. He supposes that if people do respond to each other on this basis they will derive joy and satisfaction. In fact, this is the only way they will obtain full joy. We would say that adults have largely disjoined feeling and action. This has minimized the exercise of the sense mechanisms which are the bodily media of connection between the individual and what is around him. Feeling leads to action; action produces feeling.

The therapy Schutz described uses what are called *encounter groups* which involve from six to twelve people who are instructed to be deliberately absurd at one time or to act exactly as they feel at another. The group members touch each other; they hug; they slap. When they have their session outdoors, they touch and feel not only each other but also touch and feel the grass. They pantomime and act out their life situations as in a play. Schutz asserts that in being forced to confront others, they are forced to confront themselves. We would say that the whole procedure is a matter of achieving maximal directness of action. Much of this directness unavoidably has to occur in terms of haptic rather than verbal activity. Schutz says that the techniques used imply that in *doing* one's feelings become more available than in talking. This is to be granted. But what we are stressing here is that much of what Schutz describes comes about by the exercise of the haptic mechanisms. Everything becomes more real than when action is withheld and the mediating mechanisms are not brought into play.

The results of Schutz's techniques have been quite dramatic. Those activities entered into by people in pairs (dyads) or in groups which involve simply the exercise of haptic mechanisms (nonverbal behavior) give the participants new insights into themselves by producing feelings of relationship to other people and to the rest of their surroundings that they had not previously achieved.

Much of Schutz's encounter technique is not new in psychology, for other therapists have had individuals act out their feelings—i.e., play roles. Little if any of this role-playing involved the haptic encounters that seem to be a part of Schutz's procedures. Sheer role-playing in which pairs of individuals *say* to each other what they feel or what they believe their acted role to require is not what we are referring to here.

Get me out of here! I want sensitivity training! I wanna join an encounter group!

## RECOGNITION OF THE HAPTIC IN THE ART WORLD

It is significant that those outside of science and its fringes are coming to realize that a great deal of reality is couched in the consequences of stimulating the haptic senses. The major example is what is happening in today's world of art and literature. Of particular interest is a tactile (haptic) environment that was set up at California State College at Long Beach. It consisted of an unilluminated room or rooms in which the experiencer pushed through a "many layered curtain of black vinyl and entered a pitch-black world." As described in the July 25, 1969, issue of *Time*, the experiencer's only guide was his sense of touch. There were tubes and rubbery barricades, up-and-down slopes; passages between that felt like oscillating fur muffs. As the experiencer reached the end of the maze, he sank into a water-filled plastic mattress at about body temperature. Many of these affects, including the engulfment by the mattress, were possibly never experienced before. It was not only a kind of bewilderment but a demonstration of the overpowering potency of the haptic senses.

This maze was the major feature of The First International Tactile Sculpture Symposium. Some experiencers of the maze called it "fearful;" others, "sexy." One young woman—dragging her garments—came out saying, "It's too much of an experience in there."

One of the professors responsible for this demonstration said that its purpose was to demonstrate his conviction that we are in a touch-starved world. He had reached this conclusion after spending ten days blindfolded busily touching everything he could reach.

The producer of the water-filled mattress called it the Pleasure Pit, and advertised it as "a friend in love with you, beckoning you to grovel in rapturous sensual splendor." The punch line of the written copy was, "The Pleasure Pit is like taking your bed to bed with you."

Gunther, the associate at Esalen where Schutz's encounter techniques are used, asserts that the increasing promiscuity and use of drugs are manifestations of touch hunger. Gunther denies, however, that touch has any necessary connection with sexuality.

Curiously enough, after several days the maze had to be shut down for repairs. The gallery director said that the experience has taught him what a bull the human being really is. I would simply say that the haptic stimulation was so potent that violent reaction (mechanical response) was unavoidable.

Much of this is likely to seem like a publicity stunt in which crudity and flaunting the usual societal taboos of good taste are used for sensational purposes. The affair contains much of that, but awakening people to the role of the haptic sense mechanisms in their own composition is a legitimate intent. The haptic modality possesses considerable potency, and many of its features either are not understood or are glossed over by society. In some ways, its potency has long been indirectly recognized in the form of taboos on certain kinds of touching, many of which have been pretty well observed.

What is needed from this point on is to examine the meaning of haptic experiences to the individual and to re-examine taboos. Perhaps, there are ways of exercising haptic potentialities which will enrich life without intruding on privacy and offending certain other features of human tastes and sensibilities. Generations have been living in accord with fixed taboos; perhaps there has been insufficient evaluation of what is to be countenanced and what is not.

## THE ROLE OF HAPTIC PERCEPTION
## IN YOUTH AND LATER

With all that we have said about haptic perception, some very important aspects have not been discussed. One of these is the role of haptic perception as it varies with age.

Gaps between young and old are among the most frequent topics of casual conversation these days. Most generally the gaps are described as differences in viewpoint, values, and motivation between young and old.

We can add something by pointing out differences in the operation of sensory mechanisms. Here we shall discuss certain features of haptic perception only in a broad and general way by comparing youth with persons in the age range in which contrasts to youth become quite noticeable. In dealing with haptic perception here, we shall be concerned with how people feel bodily, how this affects their initiative, and what they find pleasure in doing. One of the major topics will naturally be how they react to thermal conditions. Body temperature regulation and its ensuing comfort or lack thereof is a function of the haptic system.

Recently, a rather unusual article appeared in the newspapers under the caption, "Wanted: Girl Who'll Live in a Cold Tent." This article described a University of Michigan student who had been living in a tent during the winter of 1969-70 and, who, the article said, was looking for a girl companion to live with him. One need not be reminded that Michigan has sub-zero temperatures and plenty of snow. Because of such weather, many persons reading the article recoiled in aversion and/or puzzlement. It is easiest for many people to regard the article as simply a description of a publicity stunt and a demonstration that some people would do anything to gain attention.

This side of the matter is irrelevant for us. The young man has been living in an unheated tent. That is, he sleeps there at night after going about his business as a student majoring in fisheries and wildlife during the day. The problem is, how can he do it? The first retort is that he is young—a fairly sensible remark. If he were not young, he would not likely find the situation possible, let alone attractive in any way. We shall describe what is meant to be young partly in terms of the role played by haptic mechanisms and perception. Haptic mechanisms, as you will remember, include the senses of the skin (touch, temperature and pain) and of muscles and joints, called kinesthesis. However, the object of this article is not only to discuss the conditions that make living in a cold tent possible but also to show why it would be desirable or pleasurable. The newspaper item brings to attention a situation which by its very nature is a good example for our purposes. We take it as an occasion to discuss the way haptic mechanisms operate as a function of age.

## TEMPERATURE REGULATION

One aspect of the haptic system is its involvement in temperature regulation. The receptors in the skin are sensitive to thermal conditions and provide the signals which result in our feeling warm or cold or comfortable. These receptors send signals to the internal body mechanisms that regulate body temperature. Determination of body temperature involves some combination of three processes: production, dissipation, and conservation of heat. Although all of these processes are reflexive, they are somewhat controlled by the cerebral cortex. They do not function independently of processes that we attribute to the cortex such as thinking, perceiving and feeling. On account of this cortical participation these basic processes can be modified in level and in pattern by conditioning.

You choose, to some extent, what you are going to consider comfortable. And you choose whether you are going to achieve comfort by raising room temperature, by putting on more clothes, or by being more active muscularly.

In middle life, and particularly in later years, body-temperature regulation runs the chance of becoming rather inflexible, and thus discomfort is easily produced by environmental temperature extremes. In fact, in sedentary situations such as working at a desk or simply reading or writing, room temperatures may easily become too low for comfort. A degree or two

Fahrenheit makes considerable difference to some people. Mild ambulatory activity indoors, however, provides comfort when temperatures are a number of degrees lower. Even so, the ranges are very narrow in comparison to those which are easily tolerated or even provide definite comfort in the young.

The temperature range within which one may feel comfortable as he goes through life typically becomes changed in one way or another, and a person can develop an abhorrence for high temperatures or for low, despite the fact that he did not start out that way as a child. Since much of this change may be brought about through a conditioning process, it is not something intentional and purposive on the part of the individual, who hardly realizes he has had a hand in it. The mere fact that the regulatory mechanisms for temperature start out as quite adaptive to shifts and extremes in ambient temperature and later become less so is one factor that helps to make behavior in youth and old age quite different. What the young will enjoy doing may well be something totally abhorrent to older persons due to the operation of the haptic mechanism.

Those who have continued to possess quite flexible temperature regulation, and have maintained bodily comfort under environmental temperature extremes are not likely to cringe at the mention of cold weather. But those who have not maintained this regulatory flexibility are apt to recall various uncomfortable experiences of the past and will have no yen for encountering cold weather, let alone sleeping in a "cold tent." Thus, the tent example may appear one way to one person and another way to someone else. Obviously, imagining being in the tent must not evoke feelings of coldness in any case, else it will be shunned. For many young persons, the tent suggestion would not evoke images of coldness, but rather images of snuggling up to a partner and keeping adequately warm.

No such anticipations of comfort will be possessed by most individuals in their fifties and sixties. This may partly be because the matter seems like a "foolish stunt" in the first place, but it is certainly based upon the imagined sensory consequences.

The young's greater adequacy for producing, conserving or dissipating heat as needed for survival and comfort in various environments enables them to enjoy a wider variety of everyday circumstances. Were they as little adaptable thermally as many older persons, they would not show the enthusiasm for many activities that now entice them.

No stuffy old dorm!

Thus far we have singled out temperature regulation to contrast young and old. It is far from being the only haptic factor; various others are important as well. Actually, the several factors that constitute haptic perception are so intimately intertwined that, for some purposes, they had best be treated together rather than in attempted isolation.

The other considerations besides temperature are metabolic conditions induced by exertion, and disease conditions such as rheumatism and arthritis.

In the young exertion must be more severe in order to produce untoward haptic effects (aches and paints, feelings of stiffness) than in persons several decades older. In fact, a gymnasium workout produces very favorable results in the young even when they have had little exercise for long periods. Instead of feeling worse from exertion when out of training, the young tend to feel better. This differs from the consequences to older individuals from the same workout. In the 20s, unpleasant effects are likely to be practically nil. Somewhat older persons are bound to have sore and aching muscles and considerably older individuals can be made quite ill. Some people prove totally inadequate. Recovery from overexertion and its attendant unpleasant symptoms when they do occur is much slower than in the young.

This is one of the reasons why the relative amount of time spent feeling muscle aches and pains is far less in the young than the old. In youth it may be so little that it doesn't count. Later it begins to be enough to count by diminishing the person's enthusiasm for doing a great many things he used to do or otherwise would be doing. The young spend so little time in muscular discomfort that it scarcely figures in negating action and initiative.

Conditions such as *rheumatism* and *arthritis* are examples of chronic bodily discomfort in muscles and joints which act to preclude the desire to do those things which might be "fun," since they might involve discomfort. Very often what most adds to this discomfort either would be subjection to cold environments or would involve extra exertion.

In general, it may be said that many persons in middle life begin to avoid overt activities for the very reasons stated. Not all who do so are actually incapable of exertion; they simply either are made more uncomfortable by overt activity or suppose they will be made so. They are not enticed by cold tents whereas the young may be.

Textbooks tell us of *paradoxical cold* and *paradoxical warmth*. The former is supposed to be fairly easy to produce in the laboratory and is brought about by touching something which is slightly *higher* in temperature than the skin. While the object should feel warm, it feels cold instead. When the thermal conditions are just the opposite, paradoxical warmth is sometimes produced. In the skin there are supposedly two kinds of receptors represented by "warm spots" and "cold spots." These are simply tiny areas which, when appropriately stimulated, produce one or the other of the two experiences—warmth or coldness. Apparently, in paradoxical coldness, "cold spots" are activated by stimuli which would normally be expected to activate "warm spots."

Be this as it may, textbooks do not generally cite any examples in everyday life where the paradoxical effects apply to the way the total person feels. Perhaps the following example will illustrate this. When a person has a curious uneasy feeling which he is prone to interpret as chilliness it generally occurs when he is somewhat achy in the limb muscles, possibly from previous overexertion. This feeling of coolness is somewhat paradoxical for the room temperature is not necessarily low enough to produce chilliness at other times. It is possible that the temperature sense receptors function somewhat differently from normal as a result of the overexertion. The feeling of chilliness under these conditions is not a clear one but only resembles chilliness more than anything else the person has ever experienced. It is true that raising the room temperature tends to eliminate this paradoxical chilliness. However, one of the things that helps to connect the chilliness to muscle state rather than simply temperature level is the fact that aspirin, if and when it is noticeably effective, relieves this feeling of coolness, as well as the other features of sensory discomfort.

This illustration is meant to show how very small drops in temperature can make certain people very uncomfortable. Such people would certainly not be candidates for the "cold tent," nor would they likely be able to understand how anyone else would care for it.


## EROTICISM

Some regional specializations in haptic mechanisms assume dominant proportions at times. We are referring to the erogenous zones and eroticism. Eroticism is loosely called sex, when people fail to distinguish between *sex*, *love*, and *eroticism*. Sex, more specifically, refers to the differences in two genders and includes eroticism. While the word *sex* is admittedly a broader term than the other two, much of what is customarily discussed would be more appropriately labelled eroticism. Eroticism includes the kinds of sensory experiences that are brought about by the various contacts (primarily bodily) of the two sexes with each other or, in some cases, by interaction of two individuals of the same gender. Eroticism is the relevant issue at this point, for it is evoked by sensory stimulation.

While visual perception is one erotic vehicle, and auditory perception may also play its role, the dominant mechanism in eroticism is haptic.

Since considerable sensory pleasure (or aversion) is evoked by bodily contact of various sorts, it often makes an existence that otherwise might be monotonous or empty, quite attractive. This sort of thing would be involved even more significantly in a thermally and spatially restricted environment such as a "cold tent." The erotic factor along with the young's thermal regulation adequacy would more than offset what might appear to older persons as abhorrent.

One would expect the erotic factor to vary with age, which it does for many reasons, among them the muscular factors already mentioned. Thus, in older individuals the aches and pains, or their mere anticipation, along with lack of the erotic component make their haptic existence quite different from the young.

# SWADDLING AND ITS EFFECTS

Pertinent to our consideration of haptic perception is the ancient custom of infant swaddling in which the baby is wrapped from head to toe in strips of cloth. While not a common practice in the Western world, it is practiced in some other parts of the world today and has been studied by people interested in child development. In some respects swaddling is a rather unique form of haptic stimulation. In our society, because it is likely to be viewed as restricting a child's movement, it would be looked upon adversely. Of course, its good or bad consequences might depend upon whether the child was bound constantly or only under certain circumstances. One of the most noticeable results of restricting a child's movements is his resistance to it. Holding his arms to prevent them from flailing around is fairly sure to produce evidences of resistance, both haptic (motor) and vocal. The child typically tries to jerk loose and in some cases may scream or express displeasure.

One of the effects expected from swaddling, then, might be resistance, struggle, and general arousal. It is more easily seen by adults as a form of thwarting. Strangely enough, swaddling quite readily pacifies and induces sleep in young infants.

Since the infant's response to swaddling is very different from his reaction to restraint of movement, one is first inclined to see a contradiction. Let us instead attempt to find consistency.

Although both of the things done to the infant are forms of sensory stimulation, we need not expect the responses to be similar. It is necessary, however, to find an explanation for the difference in the two cases.

Before we get into further discussion of swaddling, the observations of Mead (1954) on the kinds of haptic stimulation that seem to be favorably effective in young children are quite pertinent.

She says that the very young infant with undeveloped means of maintaining its homeostasis requires tactile aid from outside for maintaining its internal equilibrium when upset by fear or pain, such as results from digestive upsets with their consequent stomach ache and gas. Close contacts with the mother including rhythmic tactile stimulation such as stroking and patting are effective remedies. Too great an emphasis cannot be placed on the fact that the infant usually responds with increasing composure even to vigorous rhythmic slapping on the back.

This is reminiscent of the effects of treatments given adults consisting, in part, of a kind of back-and-forth rolling of the patient's body while he is lying face down. This, along with other mechanical manipulations, produces in a very few minutes a feeling of great relaxation, comfort, and freedom in use of lower limbs and body. It would seem that this rhythmic manipulation is analogous to the pacification of infants described by Mead.

The several kinds of mechanical (haptic) treatment that can be favorably applied to humans emphasize the important role of haptics in living.

## SWADDLING AND LEVEL OF AROUSAL

Discussions of swaddling often involve consideration of the concept of arousal. A broader term for this topic than arousal is *state of excitation*.

Authors differ in the number of excitatory-state levels they distinguish. In some scales there are six stages of *sleep*, while the simplest scale recognizes only two—active and passive sleep. The next state above sleep is *drowsiness*. Often three stages or states of *awakeness* are distinguished, namely, quiet awake, active awake, and crying awake. Even novices agree without difficulty in the identification of these last-mentioned states.

One problem consists in determining the sensory input conditions that will cause the child to go from one state to another. A prominent question is what will produce sleep or pacify the child.

Swaddling has been found to be one answer. This has caused some authors to distinguish between the basic conditions in adults and infants for sleep production or for pacification. While it is said that adults and infants require different conditions for falling asleep, actually the differences may not be what they seem once we examine matters carefully. Simple generalizations often bypass variations that lurk within.

When it is said that adults seek low illumination and quiet surroundings to fall asleep and that infants require definite sensory input to do so, the contrast seems undeniable. The requirement described by Brackbill and Fitzgerald (1969) for infants is a monotonous (unvarying) sensory input. They say that a "noisy" environment arouses an infant less than a "quiet" one; illumination arouses it less than darkness; swaddling arouses it less than nudity; jouncing arouses it less than letting it lie quiet in its crib. All of this may be true, but it is nevertheless easy to make false interpretations—first, that these facts differentiate the infant from adults, and second, that sleep is an active state requiring more stimulation than the waking state.

It would seem that we must look to the pattern of sensory input as well as to its intensity. We shall take our first example not from the haptic modality but from audition, even though it is haptic perception that we are primarily interested in here.

We know some insomniacs who often use music or whatever is on the radio to enable them to go to sleep which, in a way, tallies with the conditions described for infants.

In general, one must recognize that all sensory inputs do not evoke the same kinds of response and or the same level of arousal. Thus it is probably too simple merely to divide environmental conditions into those with and without stimulation. Some attempt at classification of positive sensory input should be made that goes beyond a simple scale of intensity.

Adults do not respond to all they hear simply on the basis of intensity. The intensity range or ceiling that lies within tolerance or pleasance may be quite wide among people.

In considering haptic stimulation, it would also seem that the *pattern* of sensory input is a salient factor in producing the behavioral end result. Swaddling is an *overall*, somewhat uniform kind of bodily contact, while restraint of arm movement is a localized form of contact. That distinction in itself may be significant. To illustrate, one need only recall the effect on himself of point contact, as by a sharp stick, and broad contact as provided by a flat surface. One can further recall distinctions between contacts made by soft and hard material. Roughness and smoothness is another effective dimension. So it is not surprising that the young infant reacts differently to various haptic contacts.

How am I going to swaddle *her*?

The comforting or pacification effect of swaddling is not greatly different from the effect produced on adults by heavy bed covers. While some persons may not like them, in general adults do like covers. When room temperatures preclude the use of at least a moderate amount of covers, many persons neither get to sleep as easily nor sleep as well. While I know of no direct experimental evidence here, I do have the testimony of people in everyday life. Both covers and bed partners are bases for snuggling and "pacification."

From the pacification effects of swaddling just reviewed, it is somewhat surprising that it has not been used in our society, especially since it is not one of man's recent discoveries.

The contrasting effects obtained by local haptic restraints and swaddling should suggest appropriateness of a whole program of haptic investigation in which variables of amount of body surface and loci of contact would be studied.

## TO WEAR OR NOT TO WEAR:
## THAT IS THE QUESTION

Further insight into temperature regulation (in part a sensory process) and personal comfort may be gained by examining the effect of clothing.

Comfort depends upon the heat exchange between body and environment. At times more heat is produced than is needed to hold body temperature at its optimal level. At other times the opposite occurs, more heat is lost from the body than is produced, requiring either increase in production to take care of the conditions at hand or resort to added means of heat conservation.

Clothing may help or hinder the achievement and maintenance of optimal body temperatures. Of course, the assumption is that anybody would know when he is cold and what to do about it. However, it is a bit easier to know when one is too warm than when he is cold, strange as this may seem (see "The Role of Haptic Perception in Youth and Later").

Despite the fact that much conversation touches upon humidity and the discomfort it produces, many people are not clear about the matter and very mistaken notions are often expressed. Humidity is attributed as a cause for discomfort in a climatic or weather situation when it is not in operation at all.

I would like to talk about humidity in connection with clothing. When the body is warmer than its surroundings, the humidity of the air reduces heat loss from the body because of the limit in cooling effect from evaporation in humid air. On the other hand, when the air is humid and *warmer* than the body, the exchange of heat from the air to the body is accelerated. Thus, the cooling effect of evaporation is minimal and in addition there is heat exchange from air to body. Humidity retards heat exchange when it ought to be accelerated and accelerates it when it ought to be minimized.

Some examples of how this operates are derived from experimental studies. In one case, young men acclimated to hot surroundings daily marched at the rate of three miles per hour carrying 20-pound packs. Heart rates, rectal temperatures, sweat losses and skin temperatures before and at the end of the task were recorded. In one test, the men were nude, and in another clothing made of a single layer of herringbone twill was worn. The clothing imposed a heat load equivalent to an air temperature elevation of from two to four degrees Fahrenheit. The unclothed men could walk at wet-bulb temperatures two to four degrees higher than the clothed men.

Wet-bulb temperature is a measure of relative humidity. Thermometers are of two kinds—dry bulb and wet bulb. The ordinary thermometer is of the dry-bulb type and the reading it gives you is simply the temperature existing where it is placed. The wet-bulb thermometer is one in which the bulb is covered with a gauze-like material kept moist with water. If the humidity of the air is low, evaporation takes place rapidly. Evaporation absorbs heat. The greater the rate of evaporation the greater the rate of heat removal from the thermometer bulb. Thus the wet-bulb thermometer reading is always lower than that of the dry-bulb thermometer unless the air surrounding it is fully saturated with moisture, as for instance when it is raining. There the water in the gauze that covers the wet bulb cannot evaporate to reduce the bulb temperature.

A table can be consulted to determine relative humidity existing for the difference in recorded temperatures between the wet and dry bulbs for any given dry-bulb temperature. The study indicated that unclothed men could work at a dry-bulb temperature of 120 degrees and at a wet-bulb temperature of 92 degrees (relative humidity, 34 percent). The same men clothed were able to work only if the wet-bulb temperature did not rise above 88 to 90 degrees.

Winslow (1941) found that if the temperature of the air is above optimum but below 95 degrees, the unclothed person can adjust to a higher relative humidity than the clothed. However, at environmental temperatures of about 95 degrees, clothing becomes advantageous. At such temperatures the body is absorbing heat from the air by convection. Clothing tends to limit this process and at the same time increases cooling by evaporative-heat loss by increasing the evaporative surface. That is, the surface of the clothing dampened by sweat adds to the cooling effect of the moist body surface itself. This accounts for the

Figure 6/ Three ranges of temperature regulation in the unclothed resting subject. (After Gagge, Herrington and Winslow, 1937.)

protection clothing offers in the intense dry heat of the desert.

Thus the three forms of heat exchange—evaporation, convection and radiation—at times work for and at times against regulation of body temperature and comfort.

To reduce conditions to their basic form when studying temperature regulation, the unclothed subject is used. This does away with the complications brought in by clothing impeding heat transfer from body to environment, or by acceleration of heat loss due to damp clothing.

With unclothed subjects Gagge, Herrington and Winslow (1937) found that the environment could be divided into three temperature ranges. They found a neutral zone of from 86 to 89 degrees Fahrenheit within which the heat losses by radiation from the body and by convection and evaporation equal each other. That is, the heat lost by the body just balanced the heat produced by the metabolism of the resting subject. Below this *neutral* range is a *cold* range in which no regulation of heat loss occurs. The body simply loses heat like any physical object. Drop in skin temperature as the surroundings cool is not compensated for by additional vasoconstriction.

The third zone lies above the neutral zone and is called the *zone of evaporative regulation*. In this range, blood flow to the skin and periphery increases with temperature. Evaporation rises but not strictly with temperature (see Figure 6).

Whether or not you are comfortable depends upon certain combinations of relative humidity and the amount of perspiration on the skin. Winslow, Herrington and Gagge (1937) studied the relations between these factors and the perception of *comfort* and *discomfort*. The results are a bit complex to depict here, but it may be said that humidity reduces the temperature point at which you begin to feel discomfort.

There is an indifference zone between feeling pleasant and beginning to feel uncomfortable. This zone covers the greatest temperature range when relative humidity is low, or when the amount of body area thinly covered with perspiration is high.

A general rule to remember about humidity is that it limits the free exchange of heat when the exchange is from the body to surroundings, and accelerates the exchange when it is from the surroundings to the body.

# HAPTIC PERCEPTION OF OBJECT AND FORM

Révész states some principles that characterize the haptics of form and describes how an individual apprehends form, a spatial property, by the use of haptic perception. His material relates to two of our discussions on perception—haptic and visual. It pertains to the latter inasmuch as it shows what the individual can and cannot do with vision absent. We prefer, however, to place this discussion with the rest of our material on haptic perception.

The first principle Révész calls the *stereoplastic principle*. It is exemplified by what the blind or the sighted person with blindfold does when some item is first handed him or when he touches it under other conditions.

As soon as an individual receives an item, he does not stop with the mere experience of touch, but tends to enclose the item in his hand if he can. This seems to be his most immediate and direct route to gaining some notion of three-dimensionality. Of course, we do not know what this concept really is for the blind, but at least we know that the perceiver is using a three-dimensional contact.

Enclosure of the object is the first stage in the subject's gaining as full an apprehension of the item as possible. This plastic impression includes perception of the mechanical resistance (hardness and rigidity) and some notion of volume character without, at the very first, gaining an accurate impression of the item's form. He recognizes the item as part of the external world. Indeed, touching by the hand in this fashion gives him the most vivid realization of the distinction between himself and the physical world. This realization is less vivid when touch occurs without enclosure, and even less, so Révész says, when another part of the body comes into contact with an object or surface.

Both the sighted and the blind have the urge to touch items from all sides, not merely to come into contact with a single surface.

The next principle of haptic perceiving is called *successive perception*. This simply means that by haptic perception one cannot become aware of most things as totals at the very first instant, but must proceed bit by bit. The blind person explores portion by portion successively, thus in effect requiring a series of tactile acts to achieve what the sighted can generally achieve (see) in a single instantaneous act.

This same successiveness is required when a blind person is asked to imagine an item, let's say a chair or set of stairs. Whereas the sighted can summon a single image of the complete object, the blind person imagines a staircase by remembering how it feels to walk up or down the steps.

Both the sighted and the blind use haptic learning. Learning to trace out a finger maze is one of the best examples. The sighted can either watch himself learn the shortest path to the goal, or he can do this simply by haptic perception. I am not sure which is the faster of the two forms of learning. Perhaps the tactile (haptic) form is preferable in some respects.

When the maze is learned visually, the person may not be able to trace the maze as fast as he could when learned haptically. Vision can get in the way.

A better example is typewriting in which the faster way to type is by the "touch system." No one expects to type as fast by the visual "hunt-and-peck" system as by touch.

Even with the maze learned, there is a difference in how one traces it. Visually one would tend to look ahead and generally be aware of factors beyond the immediate location of the hand and stylus. By the haptic system, although the person is not at any instant aware of the plan or "map" of the maze, once he begins to trace it by means of muscle and touch, he makes the proper next move at every instant. While this may not imply a cognitive map in the usual meaning of the term, it does suggest a means in the person's neuromuscular system whereby the right *sequence* of movements unfolds.

The next principle of haptic performance has been called the *kinematic* principle and is exemplified by the fact that tactile experiences in and of themselves do not provide for a successful act of identification. Let's say we try to achieve knowledge by merely having a series of static tactile experiences while keeping fingers, hand and arm motionless. This does not allow us either to get an adequate idea of an item or to learn to trace a maze. Movement of muscles is necessary.

A further principle is what Révész calls the *metric* principle. This pertains to measurement. The full recognition of an item implies a recognition of the *quantitative* relations and orientation of the parts to the whole. Visually this can be done in a single act of perception. Haptic perception provides a far less accurate gauge of the quantitative aspect.

In the haptic sense, the basic method of measuring is by use of thumb width, finger length, and span of the spread hand from thumb tip to little finger.

## "SEEING COLOR" BY TOUCH?

Now and then one reads in the daily papers of a person who can "see color with his hands." Some cases have been investigated by men interested in vision.

Quite different meanings are attached to the statement "seeing with the hands," or "seeing by touch." Immediately, one can reject a literal interpretation, for by definition, we only see with the visual system. Seeing is the name for what a person can do by means of this system which is sensitive to photic radiation, the energy that is generally called light. Thus, to see is inescapably to involve this energy and its action on a visual system.

By saying that the result in question is obtained with the hands would either be to say that the hands contained a system something like the eye sensitive to photic energy, or else to rule out the performance as being visual at all. There is no anatomical evidence that the skin contains this second visual system, so the performance cannot be called visual.

The next question to ask is whether the performance can occur in the dark, i.e., in the absence of photic radiation (illumination). Most laymen do not bother with these questions. The claim is simply so unusual that it evokes his curiosity and wonderment. The average person, in his thinking, does not use criteria that have to be met in order for a performance to be called visual. It is simply taken for granted that it is vision that is being discussed since the stimulus material is what he as a sighted person sees, for example, as a set of colored papers. Any device that will provide for some kind of identification of the papers is thought to be visual.

Let's "see" what comes out of an actual case. The mother of D, a girl about 15 years of age, phoned me about her. The girl seemed able to identify colors pretty well by touch, according to what I was told. D was quite reticent about her ability, for she saw it as evidence of mystical power. She did not tell her schoolmates, thinking they would either not believe it or would tease her about being a witch.

I agreed with D's mother to see and test her. The mother thought I might have some explanation for the power and could dissuade D from believing in the power's mystical nature.

After the mother agreed to bring D in, I began to prepare for her. Whereas the usual way of testing involves a blindfold to insure that the tested person is not visually aided, I chose what I thought would be a more convenient method. I placed a box on my desk with the two ends open so that D could reach in from her end, and I from mine. I draped a black cloth over the box to help exclude illumination and any chance of the girl seeing the pieces of colored paper I would use.

When I tested D, she did no better than chance. This failure seemed to dismay both her and her mother. I decided to try the more usual condition. This time I tested the girl with the box removed after asking her to close her eyes. Although by not placing a blindfold on her I left the way open for cheating, I took the chance. This time she did somewhat better, but nothing near a perfect performance.

I recognized an essential stimulus difference between this set of conditions and the original one. In the first case illumination did not fall on the colored sheets D was tactually exploring at the time. In the second case, it did. My best guess as to what might have produced the improved performance was that the illumination heated the sheets in different amounts according to their hue. That is, the paper coated with a substance seen as one color might absorb or reflect more than a paper coated with another color. However, the girl's performance when out in free illumination was far from perfect. My next step was to shift from fluorescent to tungsten illumination. This was done for two reasons: (1) to bring the luminous source closer, and (2) to use a more heat-productive source so that if the thermal factor was providing the stimulus difference, there would be more chance for it to operate. Under tungsten illumination from a desk lamp not far away, the girl did her best job of color selection.

There is still one more thing to take into account. The girl had hedged from the start on being able to name specific colors, at least with any great accuracy. Her major claim lay in being able to distinguish light from dark colors. After I had seen her performance under the three conditions, I could understand why she could best discriminate between light and dark colors, if any distinction at all were possible.

Had her performance under the three conditions been the same, I would have been left totally puzzled about why D's touching the colored papers enabled her to make her choices. There is still much to be learned, but what I did brought the understanding of her performance back into the tactile (haptic) realm.

D was able to make somewhat better than chance designations of light and dark colors but, in naming them, she still failed to do well—or as well as she wanted to. Possibly, her belief in her ability was based on sketchier demonstrations than I have just described, so that she was not as successful in my tests as in her own.

What I first did was to prevent any illumination from falling on the test color sheet by having the girl's hand inside the box. Another factor operated under this set of conditions which ought to be recognized; namely, that I allowed the girl to keep her eyes open, thus precluding her paying the same undistracted attention to how the test sheet felt than would be possible with eyes closed. Of course, in the second and third test conditions, she did have her eyes closed and this may have been a factor helping her to pay better attention. But since she did best under the condition of more intense ("warmer") illumination, I suspected it was the thermal differential felt by her fingers as she examined the test plates that enabled her to make her choices.

It certainly would be expected that if a tactile-thermal process was involved it would take some concentration of attention. In line with this, it did seem as though she was attending carefully or making a careful guess. Her choices took some effort and consumed a quarter to one-half minute or more to reply in each case.

Further research with similar subjects and then with unselected subjects may begin to tell us about a kind and degree of sensitivity that has seldom been explored.

## IS IT HEAVINESS?

When you pick up something, is it heaviness you sense? It may be, for sometimes you pick it up for that very purpose. It turns out, however, that when you judge weight the size of the object makes a difference. If for a given mass an object is large, it doesn't seem so heavy. At least that is what we have been accustomed to conclude. A small steel ball weighing four ounces seems heavier than a larger object weighing the same amount. This has long been called the *size-weight illusion*.

Illusions have been defined as mistaken perceptions, but in a later section you will find that this stems from inappropriate ways of looking at the matter (see "Illusions, Perceptual Constancy and Objectivity").

When picking up an object, a person regards its size or volume and he expects large objects to weigh more than small ones. However, he does know that this is not always the case.

One might try to answer the following questions: Is the object light or heavy, or is it simply light or heavy for its size? It seems that these two questions have long been mistaken for each other. The consideration often uppermost to the lifter in an everyday situation, and also in most laboratory experiments, is whether the object is heavy or light for its size. Nevertheless, the thinking and conclusions unwittingly switch to answering the question of whether the object simply is heavy or light. If the sensory scale used were only one of heaviness in the absolute, a 4-ounce item would seem less heavy than a 12-ounce item, for example. Size would have nothing to do with it. By custom or otherwise it doesn't seem to work that way. Size is involved. So, the judgments deviate greatly from those expected, i.e., from those that would follow the absolute scale. Hence, our behavior is called illusory.

The question I would like to ask here is whether our sensory mechanism is mistaken or whether we in our culture don't draw the right conclusions about our own behavior. I believe it is the latter. Customarily we take it for granted that we ought to be able to sense absolute weight, and that this is the easiest and most natural thing to do. So, when it is found that this does not happen, it is quickly concluded that the sensory mechanism (and, as a consequence, perception) is mistaken and that it does the job wrong!

Couldn't it be that when you pick up something, you are sensing something else than absolute weight (mass)?

Physicists have isolated other phenomena besides weight and have defined and established units for them. The one that seems relevant here is *density*. You will admit that you do come to the conclusion at times that steel is denser than balsa wood or even than most other woods. So you know what is meant by density. But still you call it heaviness. Actually, you could have become accustomed to saying steel is denser than wood, but instead you say it is heavier.

What is density? That is, how is it defined? It is mass per unit volume. Steel has more mass per unit volume than wood. If, when picking something up, we regarded the experience as *density,* there would be no "illusion." The sensory answer obtained would follow the physicist's density criterion and the notion of illusion would never have arisen in our society.

Can one sense heaviness? It may be possible, under conditions in which one can't include the factors of size, softness, etc., that judgments tallying with the absolute mass scale can be made.

If what I have just said is generally true, our conclusion would be that under the usual conditions a person cannot sense ("judge") mass (weight); he can only sense density. Except under some carefully controlled conditions, he cannot judge what the physicist calls mass (weight). So the preferable way to state the matter as we presently know it is to say that what we usually sense is density. Obviously, whatever the sensation is it does not tally with mass, the property measured on a set of scales. The property of size, which can be isolated, enters in. This ought to tell us that it is density that is being sensed since in the definition of density, size and mass are the two factors. If and when one is blindfolded or otherwise unable to perceive the size of the object lifted or held, the property could be called heaviness. It is probable that the act of perceiving is different here from when a second sense modality, such as vision or touch, is involved. One's attention is somewhat different, and it could be expected that a kind of a tally between mass (physical) and heaviness would emerge. In fact, this must be so, else Harper and Stevens (1948) would never have arrived at a psychological unit for heaviness, the *veg*. The behavior relating vegs to pounds is essentially the same kind of behavior (response) manifested in the auditory response of *loudness* or *pitch*, and in the *gust* scale for taste, three sensitivity scales developed during the last several decades.

Even if by experimental test, the subject's response does not correspond perfectly with the mass-per-unit-volume criterion, it does not nullify the idea that density is the factor in question.

For our purposes as students of sensation and perception, the present example would suggest that we had always better be sure we know to what the human sensory mechanism is responding before we conclude that perceptual behavior is illusory. Many illusions will disappear when we understand perception in this way.

## ESTHETIC EXPERIENCE

The esthetic refers on one hand to the beauty of an idea or object, and on the other to the feeling or behavior that recognizes this quality. In the following discussion, the behavior expressing recognition rather than the quality itself will be concentrated upon.

Obviously, beauty expressed in behavior is generally sensorially aroused. Here we deal with one kind of sensory response that can be distinguished from others. While borderline cases may possibly occur, we believe they will not confuse us.

The specific question at issue is not whether what we call beauty can be sensed by haptic perception, but whether blind persons can have esthetic experience, whether they derive a kind of feeling that could be classed as esthetic. Some investigators think so and others do not.

Most often when we talk about esthetic experience we refer to the experiences that arise through *seeing* and *hearing*. Less often, we make much of tactile experiences derived from manually exploring surfaces. Perhaps there is more to be recognized in such experiences than is customarily expressed. But for what is most explicitly thought of as beauty we rely on sight and hearing. Having this bias we do not expect much that is esthetic from touch. However, the blind describe tactile experiences with a definite appreciation that we might call esthetic.

If we were to rely solely on the reports of the blind, there would be no question. But we know that words do not mean the same to the blind as to the sighted.

Révész seems to say that unless one can perceive something as a total at a given instant, the experience cannot have the qualities we define as esthetic. This would seem to outlaw music or anything that is essentially sequential and temporal even for those who can hear. We know that the impact of a musical work is temporal. A symphony, for example, can begin with a small impact in the first few bars and build up minute by minute. Appreciation can wane, as well. Surely the experience is esthetic at all instants, and not simply when the piece has been completed, for there is not an instantaneous total.

Révész says that the procedure of haptic contact is confined to determining the properties and spatial arrangement of parts and schema of the object by exploration and, on this account, the procedure results in a synthetic product. What is achieved in the sequential tactile analysis is lost in the synthetic process whereby the individual tries to make a whole. So it is that Révész concludes that little is possible in an esthetic way from tactile exploration alone.

Révész is thereby assuming that the overall experience gained from whatever is sequential is never integrated. If this were true, the blind could not learn to get around even in familiar quarters and would not be able to make use of their muscular feedback.

If we now examine the kinds of experience the sighted get, we may discover people differ greatly in the degree to which they can indulge in pure sensory experience. For instance, some may get a positive thrill from a cool breeze or from touching velvet, and experience abhorrence in dipping their fingers in an unknown mushy substance in the dark. Others so link every sensory contact with the ideational that they cannot claim "pure" sensory pleasure. Perhaps this is where many sighted persons have lost something. It would not be surprising if such persons denied esthetic experience to those who could not see.

Seemingly, it is one thing to ask a person about an object not present, and a very different thing for him to determine an effect when he can use his senses at the moment. A blind person questioned about the beauty of what he is tactually exploring may answer by telling about experiences of parts of a total object rather than the whole. However, he may be "put too much to test" when asked about the beauty of the whole object, and so he "fails the test," whereas in a casual situation he would derive pleasure out of exploring the same object. If we find that a tactually explored object does not thrill someone who is blind, we must remember that there are many sighted persons who do not derive any great amount of pleasure from *viewing* certain well-recognized works of art.

Obviously, even if the blind do not have a sensory basis for the ideational scope attributed to sighted persons, it is no argument against a kind of esthetic pleasure they derive from touch and haptic perception.

Révész points out cases in which blind subjects are asked about the beauty of a Renaissance figure. They often say they do not know. They make remarks only about the parts of the figure. There are plenty of cases in which the blind subject explores a sculpture with great enthusiasm. Only if a display of appreciation is absent could we suspect lack of ability for esthetic appreciation.

We can say that the *esthetic* is the emotional or affective result evoked by direct sensory experience, or in contemplation of something that can be sensed. Thus, when a sensory experience is neutral there is nothing for us to talk about, but when it is pleasant or unpleasant an esthetic scale surely is involved.

Révész says that the blind person does not stand in a "free relationship to pictorial art." The same may be said about the sighted. Both have to be trained to like and dislike. Much of that comes incidentally to anyone. Some results from formal training or social influence. In the case of vision there is so much detail of form going into the overall perceptual result that it is easy to talk about esthetics and to build systems of esthetics (patterns of *taste*). The excitement or pleasure derived from touch is of a different sort.

Cutsforth, the famous blind psychologist, made himself a desk when he was a graduate student at the University of Kansas. He had developed considerable competence in working with his hands. One of the cardinal objectives in his craftsmanship was to make the desk as smooth as possible. He worked longer and harder than most sighted persons would have. But his delight lay in the smoothness. He pointed out to me how awful is the practice of having blind persons work with rough material such as broom-straw since he felt roughness to be extremely ugly and distasteful. From this I had no reluctance in crediting the feeling of smoothness with being an esthetic sensory experience in his case.

Sighted persons like certain objects to be smooth, and possibly other things to be rough. The roughness they feel can be articulated with the objects they see, the result being that there is no aversion in certain cases to roughness that might be felt by the blind. The rough-smooth dimension probably stands out more nearly by itself.

Helen Keller, in *The Story of My Life* (1954), beautifully described the esthetic effects she claimed:

Museums and art stores are sources of pleasure and inspiration. Doubtless it will seem strange to many that the hand unaided by sight can feel action, sentiment, and beauty in cold marble; yet it is true that I derive genuine pleasure from touching great works of art. As my fingertips trace line and curve, they discover the thought and emotion which the artist has portrayed. I can feel the faces of gods and heroes, hate, courage, and love, just as I can detect them in living faces I am permitted to touch.

Undoubtedly, Miss Keller derived results by touching which were very pleasing to her, and with all that we have said in this subsection about haptic perception providing basic satisfaction, we must conclude that her words are to be taken as evidence thereof. The question arises as to whether she might have obtained just as much pleasure from a piece of sculpture not considered by the sighted as a work of art as from one that is. If she could, it might have indicated that the inspiration of feeling "cold stone" is not as highly dependent upon its detailed form as upon what she had been told about the piece she was feeling. However, the "cold stone" *per se* might have been highly pleasurable to touch.

According to Révész, "The process of modelling by blind pupils shows that *their creative activity is largely governed by the same rules as the perceptive process operative in the haptic examination of solid object.*"

He demonstrates that the sculptural parts are modelled separately and independently of each other. Seemingly all this shows is that the scope of blind people's perceptions is not as broad as that of the sighted who, for example, can take in not only a part of the clay object but also the object's surroundings at the same instant.

Munz and Löwenfeld (1934) believed that the spontaneous plastic creations of persons born blind are essentially only the symbolic expressions of what they feel. He supposes that the blind person creates his figures out of himself, or in accord with his haptic sensations.

This is exemplified by a sculpture entitled *Deserted* which was a poorly formed figure with long arms and huge hands. The figure was seated with legs crossed and its legs were tiny compared to its arms. While these features seem to be out of proportion, he says that if we place one leg over the other while seated and stretch our arms out far from the body, we actually get the feeling of our hands growing larger and our legs smaller and less significant. This is just what the blind sculptor depicted. It is to be expected that the blind person will not only produce over-sized body parts, but will even omit others—those from which he is deriving no significant sensation.

## HAPTICS, RELAXATION, AND THINKING

Tension is a word that we often encounter, both in conversation and in reading. Sometimes it refers to a person's uncomfortable orientation to his obligations. At other times, it refers simply to the local muscle effects we experience. When the reference is general, as in the first case, we often say we are "all tense." The condition is a complex encompassing a general attitude and an intellectual awareness reflected in our muscles. Tension and ache are often closely allied.

The state called tension is often difficult to get rid of. Some of the measures taken to do so are medication (including alcohol), exercise, and/or massage and rest. All are aimed at more or less directly affecting muscle. Many persons are not too successful in the use of these measures.

Various authorities have their own specific understandings of the bodily conditions that exist in tension. Not all of these views are alike and not all are applied equally successfully in attempting to relieve tension. Our interest in tension lies in the fact that since tension involves muscles, it involves the sense mechanisms which mediate between muscle and the central nervous system. Thus, tension is in part, at least, a haptic phenomenon and the topic is relevant to this chapter. We are interested in how tension is produced, what it is, and how it is relieved, but we are not posing as therapists. All we want to do is to set forth a few insights regarding kinesthesis as it relates to relaxation and to such activities as thinking and feeling.

One of the authorities who has concentrated more on understanding and relieving tension than almost anyone in our country is Edmund Jacobson (1957), a psychologist and physician, as well as a laboratory experimentalist.

He believes that there is an effective way to relax; for many years he has taught patients to do so and more recently he has helped one of his associates, Dr. Arthur Steinhaus, to demonstrate that the technique can be transmitted from person to person. An examination of some of the essentials of Jacobson's technique may prove helpful to us in understanding muscle activity and haptic mechanisms.

Jacobson has assumed that muscle tension underlies many forms of the discomfort and emotional distress for which clinical psychologists are often consulted. Many years ago he undertook the study of relaxation and how to produce it. He assumed a very simple principle, namely, that if an individual knew how it felt to have a body part relax, he could relax it intentionally. While this may seem to be a gratuitous or unfounded assumption, it is perfectly plausible. In many other situations involving posture and body movement a prerequisite for producing them is the ability to recognize the bodily sensations associated with them. We are usually able to know when a required stance or posture is achieved simply by how it feels. To learn a new posture one must be able to feel it. Of course, a certain amount of visualization goes along with this feeling when muscle state is involved in body posture, such as in a golf stance.

Accordingly, one would suppose that *all* kinds of skeletal muscle tension would routinely be recognized when they occur. This is not the case. Some feelings of tension result only when one practices directing attention to them. Learning to relax is brought about by achieving and utilizing this awareness.

A good example occurs in one of the beginning situations used by Jacobson to teach an individual to relax. For example, he may have the person lie on his back on a treatment table with his arms alongside his body but not touching it. He would then have the person bend one of his hands backward at the wrist as shown in Figure 7. When the person does this, he is likely to feel the muscles pull on the undersurface of his forearm and wrist. This pull or stretch produces the major sensory experience at the time. Whereas the person is likely to call it tension, it is actually a sensation of *strain* and not what should be attended to. Actually the person does not at first feel tension in the muscles that pulled the hand into the required position. While this failure is strange (but typical), it is this feeling that has to be isolated and attended to.

The person will next be asked to let his hand fall limp on the table, and to pay attention to how the back of the forearm feels (Figure 8), which will likely be different from when the hand was in the bent-back position, or even before that. The identifi-

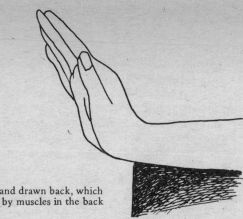

Figure 7/ The hand drawn back, which is accomplished by muscles in the back of the arm.

able feeling is the "relaxed" one. The procedure can be repeated a few times till the person becomes more and more able to isolate this special feeling and is able to identify it definitely as relaxation. When he has progressed this far, he no longer needs to go through the procedure of bending his hand back. Merely letting his hand go limp will produce the feeling in the forearm muscles.

Furthermore, the person need not be lying down to achieve and experience relaxation in the forearm, but can easily achieve it when sitting in an armchair by resting his arms on the chair arms with his hands extending beyond them. He then lets his hands fall into a drooping position and can feel his forearm muscles and wrists relax.

Relaxation can be accomplished in a variety of postural conditions, some of which are better than others. While it should be understood that relaxation is not a positive act into which energy and neural innervation are put, it occurs quite well when incipient muscle movement is involved at the beginning. Lying recumbent in a bed or reclining in an easychair might be supposed above all others to provide for the relaxation we are talking about, but this is not necessarily true. One person reports that some of the most marked effects of relaxation can be obtained in other postures and circumstances. This individual is often "keyed up" when he goes out to get in his car to run an errand or at the end of the day's office work and realizes he is tense and too impatient. To counteract this, he tries the following technique for relief. Dropping his head forward (not much if he is driving), he repeats a self-command to relax which is timed to coincide with

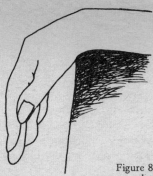

Figure 8/ The hand relaxed and dropped over the edge of an armrest. The muscles that had contracted to draw the hand back, as in Figure 7, are now relaxed and one can attend to how this feels.

a long exhalation. The head is dropped as if he were obeying the command. The point here is that the incipient *movement* of "relaxing" (dropping the head) produces greater relaxation than were he to attempt the same thing lying flat on his back. He doesn't dare repeat this self-command more than once or twice else he claims he would be too far gone to drive properly. He finds it a brief but effective way to "unhitch" himself. Some may argue that he is merely practicing a bit of self-hypnosis, but it matters little what it is called. However, the exercise does require a certain pattern of motor performance; just any action would not have sufficed in the beginning to produce the effect.

This same principle of incipient movement in the direction of relaxing can be applied in other situations. For example, when hurrying along on foot to reach a destination, a person may conclude he is too tense and not in the need of such haste. Naturally, his first move is to slow his pace but he may also let his shoulders drop and his arms dangle as he gives himself the command to relax.

This is a modification or a deviation from Jacobson's simple rule of merely discovering what relaxation feels like and then putting yourself into the state where you get the "feeling." It involves the incipient or overt "obedience" to the command in time with one's exhalation. Something seems to be accomplished by relating the two. The very act of exhalation is a let-down or relaxation performance in and of itself.

Jacobson's relaxation training involves the development of skill in relaxing all the various muscle groups of the body, large and small, including the muscles of the throat, face and eyes and also the forehead. Whereas it may seem possible to relax skeletal muscles that have to do with haptic exploration and manipulation such as fingers, hand, wrist, and arms, it seems ridiculous at first to think of relaxing the muscles of the forehead or eyes.

In all cases, a way of definitely contracting the muscles in question must be found in order to discover how tension feels. Next, you must let loose, i.e., terminate the contraction. Feeling of relaxation is easiest to discover just after definite contraction. When you find out what relaxation feels like you become able to produce it at will.

The whole learning procedure requires months and possibly even a year or two, depending—among other things—upon your success in identifying the feeling of relaxation.

When eye muscles are well relaxed, a person is unable to think. The field of imagination ("mind") becomes blank. This may be difficult to believe, but it has been testified to by those who have been able to use the technique.

As soon as you begin to examine yourself when relaxing, your attention becomes very different. Instead of thinking over and over again about the things of the moment (a process we call worrying), your attention tends to focus on your own bodily feelings. Your consciousness shifts from the details of situations that occupied you and moves toward more of a blank. Whereas this might seem to be too much of an introspective procedure, defeating its own ends, it isn't necessarily that at all. The pleasurable feeling of relaxing as it involves gross musculature is a diffuse affair, and it constitutes, as might be expected, much more of a feeling state than an analytical type of self-inspection.


TRANSCENDENTAL MEDITATION

Narrowing of attention and simplification of visual imagery is reminiscent of what was described to me by a woman who took a course in transcendental meditation while in Burma. In such a course, the person is put into a kind of cell where it is quiet. With eyes closed, he attempts to follow instructions. One of the early exercises is to imagine a spot between the upper lip and the nose. While you may wonder what this is for, I believe it is simply a procedure whereby the learner is made to concentrate his attention. The more effectively and consistently he does this, the more it narrows and focuses his field of awareness and concern.

A later exercise is to imagine a small point of light located at the navel or just above which then is imagined as becoming more and more diffuse, spreading to fill the whole visual field. Later, one begins with a diffuse field of light which contracts gradually into a point and disappears. Apparently, one of the objectives of Burmese meditation is to be able to go into trance. The narrator told me that when the light narrows down to a point and disappears, one enters the trance. I was also told that one can decide beforehand how long to remain in the trance.

My purpose in referring to Burmese meditation is to point out that the ways of narrowing attention and reducing or eliminating awareness (consciousness) which seem so mysterious, particularly as features of Yoga and oriental meditation, are not greatly different in many respects from the ways of achieving relaxation I have just described. The control, minimization or elimination of muscle activity is apparently involved in both. In the meditation procedures, it is the form of consciousness or the production of unconsciousness that is the central objective. A form of relaxation is necessary for reaching this objective, even though little or nothing may be said about it. In Jacobson's relaxation technique the kind of consciousness required is an awareness of how muscles feel when relaxed so that relaxation may be achieved. His procedures are somewhat similar to those in meditation. That is, the eyes are closed and a specific object of attention is involved.

It is at first possibly surprising to realize a close connection between some of our practices and those mysterious ones of the Orientals, but right away it is rather gratifying and enlightening to discover their resemblance. Even before hearing the details of Burmese meditation, I was very much pleased with my own experience of narrowing the attention during the relaxation procedure or, one might say, as a consequence of it. The extremes that the Orientals achieve and practice are possibly only more complete forms of the same thing.

Knowing that the Orientals do achieve extreme detachment from their surroundings, and that this enables them to transcend many kinds of worries and troubles, there is considerable comfort in supposing that we are capable of some degree of this simply by following some of our own relaxation procedures. However, we are characterized by our unwillingness to avail ourselves of this form of comfort.

We are beginning to see accounts here and there by certain physicians and therapists of transcendental meditation helping to deal with drug addiction and alcoholism. Since the "cure" is oriental, it probably has more allure and fascination, and more would be expected of it, than something we ourselves had discovered or advocated.

## EXPERIMENTAL STUDIES ON PHYSIOLOGICAL EFFECTS OF MEDITATION

A number of experimental studies have been made on Zen monks and upon students who have learned transcendental meditation to determine what physiological changes, if any, differentiate meditation and trance from the normal waking state. The findings would show the nature of some body states associated with shifts of attention and diminution or abolition of consciousness.

A few of the results are worth mentioning here (see Wallace, 1970). The findings from all of the studies, it will be noticed, may not be alike. The differences can easily accrue from the differences in what constitutes meditation in the various groups.

Meditation has brought out such changes in expert Zen monks as decrease in rate of respiration, lowered oxygen consumption, changes in galvanic skin response (GSR), and a slight increase in pulse rate and blood pH. During meditation, the brain wave records (EEGs) manifested alpha waves predominantly. These progressively increased in amplitude and diminished in frequency. Now and then another sort of wave ranging from 4-7 cycles per second (theta waves) would appear.

A group of college students who had practiced a simple type of easy meditation from six months to three years was tested. Nine subjects whose oxygen consumption was tested manifested a decrease within five minutes after beginning to meditate. The average decrease was 20 percent. Skin resistance rose markedly as meditation began, although it fluctuated some during the period. Heart records were taken on only five subjects and these showed a decrease, the mean being about five beats per minute. In all subjects, alpha waves increased in amplitude. In some, theta waves appeared. (Theta waves are sometimes referred to by physiologists as a form of arousal response.)

Alpha blocking (momentary cessation of alpha rhythm in response to a sensory stimulus) showed no habituation as it does in the waking state. Habituation means lessening or elimination on repeated occasions to produce "blocking." The brain wave pattern during meditation seemed to be distinguishable from that during sleep. It was also different from the pattern in hypnosis which, however, varies a great deal with what the subject is doing or, possibly, in accord with his "emotional" state. Thus, comparisons with other states are not too satisfactory.

There is a form of meditation in which the individual gets rid of his body, as it were. Such statements sound so absurd to people in our society that we scarcely give them a second thought. But let us examine what the person does who is attempting to achieve this goal.

First he focuses his attention on his feet and visualizes them as not being part of himself or his body. Some of what he is actually doing is relaxing his feet to the point at which he no longer feels them. But in accord with his mystical teachings and belief, when he no longer feels them they no longer exist. He believes he has gotten rid of his feet. Stage by stage, he progressively discards other parts of his body, such as legs and abdomen.

Of course, it takes a non-Western mystical view of life to make such an interpretation, but it does not take an Oriental to become as comfortable as described. A "nonmaterialistic" view of the universe makes the body disappearance interpretation a very natural one to make. With such a view, the job of ceasing to "feel" is easily accomplished and may become more certain. If we compare this "meditation" with Jacobsonian relaxation, we need have no mystical interpretation whatsoever of what happens.

While the Oriental works for self-effacement and annihilation, we do many of the things that bring about *self-agitation*. We are enthusiastic about self-fulfillment and unwittingly produce self-agitation instead.

Western man focuses on the achievements and rewards of *doing*. The Oriental pays more attention to the matter of *being*. What he has to show for it outwardly doesn't entice us at all.

We tend to focus on our feelings and, if they are uncomfortable, to focus on the discomfort, thereby maximizing the discomfort instead of working in the opposite direction. The mediator develops the means whereby he sidesteps much of the discomfort he otherwise would have.

What we can largely gain out of the various findings, all of which we have by no means mentioned, is that the forms of attention and "concentration" in connection with a passive bodily state are accompanied by changes in various vital processes, the ultimate results therefore being by no means mystical.

## DREAMING

In some respects, what I said earlier about eye muscle activity and thinking seems to apply to dreaming, or at least to some forms of it. Those who study dreaming use REM's as an indicator. (REM's are rapid eye movements.) It is not my intention to discuss dreaming here, but I would like at least to mention this connection between eye muscle activity and a form of experience in sleep. That there is this connection in dreams tends to enhance the general credibility of the relation of eye muscle tensions to thinking in waking life.

## SUMMARY

In the foregoing discussion we have then an example of the haptic mechanism in the production and relief of tension and, in the special case described, an example of haptics involved in the reduction of thinking and worrying and dreaming.

## A NEGLECTED KIND OF CONTACT
## WITH THE ENVIRONMENT

In several previous essays we dealt with the subject of *relaxation*. The examples were cases in which relaxation was brought about by certain forms of attention, concentration, or meditation. These were skills developed by the individuals themselves whereby innervation to muscles was temporarily reduced or nearly obliterated, and a form of desired well-being resulted.

In the present essay we are pursuing the same general topic — the production of comfort and ease. But, to reach this comfort, the aid of *external* agents such as cold and hot baths and massage are involved.

Countries both in the Western world and in Asia employ various forms of massage, along with baths and other things. While the techniques are somewhat diverse, they still have many features in common.

Recently, Richard Atcheson (1970-71), who claims to be a great believer in the effectiveness of massage for recuperation from stressful situations, has related some of his experiences in various parts of the world.

In discussing massage, I am here taking another occasion to illustrate a role of the sensory systems in everyday life and in human welfare. When baths and massage are mentioned, the typical person thinks of achieving comfort, but he does not attribute the experience to something in which sensory mechanisms play an essential role. It is this role that impresses me, and I feel its recognition is another way of understanding human behavior.

Atcheson travels a great deal in the routine of duty and sometimes has to endure sitting for 14 hours at a stretch in a plane seat. At the end of such a trip, bed rest does not seem to be the first thing that is of much help. Knowing this from experience, he seeks out the nearest local masseur. He says that even the worst ones enable him to face a day's appointments. At the very least, it permits him to sleep instead of enduring 24 hours in knots of tension and discomfort. He says that we need to be "rubbed the right way."

He describes some of these occasions as alternations between hot steam baths and cold dips ending up with a pummelling by a husky masseur, and then a short snooze. The baths and massages he tried out while in the Army, taken not for "physical therapy," but for sheer sensual pleasure, made him and his buddies "absolutely giddy with good health."

Saunas of one sort or another are becoming more and more common in city life in this country. People's experience in such saunas must vary quite widely, but the self-treatment does not involve massage. What can be accomplished by massage varies greatly and, at best, can be very effective.

A thorough osteopathic treatment (not as commonly resorted to as formerly) can accomplish remarkable effects in a very short time. One wonders, therefore, what the more vigorous and extended kneading and pummelling accomplishes that osteopathic treatment does not. We shall have to take Atcheson at his word that for the young and able the pummelling can have wonderful effects. Since milder forms of manipulation produce unexpectedly good results for most persons, they would seem to be more appropriate for older individuals.

The mechanical treatment given in osteopathy is not called massage, but *manipulation*, but it still comes within the broad definition of massage which applies various kinds of mechanical effects from rubbing, kneading and slapping. Osteopathic manipulation varies from physician to physician, but the form I am referring to involves rolling the body from side to side and its effects are accomplished in a very short time. This "loosening up" is a prelude to the treatment which produces mechanical adjustments of the spinal column. I am not aware of what feeling of well-being manipulation without this adjustment would produce, but the whole procedure is effective and far less violent and extended than the bouts described by Atcheson.

What I am saying here is that to be knowledgeable about haptics and related matters, one should learn about what can be accomplished by subjecting the body to certain simple thermal and mechanical conditions that aren't the usual part of our customary routine. Massage and osteopathy undo the unfavorable effects of accumulated tensions in muscles, putting them in a condition whereby the sensory signals emitted are a joy.

# PERCEPTUAL MECHANISMS INVOLVED IN THE DEVELOPMENT OF LOVE

Harlow and his associates (1970) have done a great deal to disclose the factors involved in the development of attachments between individuals among primates. When we deal with attachments in man or in other animals, a number of words are used, one of them being *love*, and others being *affection, fondness*, and *sex*. As humans, we have a vocabulary for designating what we experience (feel or sense), and other vocabularies for behavior apart from feeling and sensation. Very often, however, distinctions between the acts or states that constitute experience and those that do not are very poorly adhered to. When one talks about love, what does one mean? Does he mean simply what he *feels* toward some object or person? Or, is love spelled out simply in terms of overt reactions toward people or things?

If we recognize that we do not *know* how animals feel, or what they actually experience, how can we talk about love in their case, unless love simply refers to a form of overt behavior?

For present purposes and in keeping with frequent usage, we shall define love as the relational attitude or behavior of one animal toward another when it displays attraction and performs an act that seems to contribute to the other animal's welfare. If we mean simply something of this sort, we can talk about *love* in monkeys and we can assume that its basic features are not utterly foreign to love in man. I think this presumption underlies the work done by Harlow and his associates, who describe clearly certain behaviors in infant monkeys that indicate the perceptual components in the development of love.

One of the components is the haptic. It has generally been thought that the mother's behavior or the sensory stimuli she produces when breast feeding her young is of the greatest potency and that other factors, whatever they be, have less weight. Demonstrations have shown that this is not the case. Harlow's investigators used two sorts of surrogate mothers (crude, artificial "mothers" of cloth) one of which lactated while the other did not. The infants voluntarily spent somewhat, but not a great deal more time with the lactating mothers, whether they were made of cloth or of wire, but the difference was not great. The same degree of preference held for the two types of surrogates when the infants were exposed to a typical fear-producing stimulus.

Harlow and his associates also investigated a visual component in the development of attachment or love. In one case, an infant monkey was given a surrogate mother whose head consisted of a round wooden ball on which no facial features were painted. To the monkey the face became attractive. Harlow and Suomi said that the face became "beautiful" and the monkey frequently caressed it with hands and legs beginning around 30-40 days age. When the infant reached 90 days of age, the experiments substituted an "appropriate ornamental cloth-mother face." After one glance at it, the infant screamed and fled to the back of the cage. After a few days of terror, she solved the problem most ingeniously and effectively by simply revolving the face 180° so that the blank side of the head was in evidence. Now she could again see only a bare round ball. Every time the experimenters rotated the head to show the face, she would turn it back to expose the blank side. Finally, within a week, she lifted the head and rolled it into a corner. As the authors say, she could not be blamed. She had come to love a faceless mother and could not love a two-faced one.

The evidence seems to show that the infant reacts visually to the initial version of the mother it encounters. The infant becomes used to this mother and she is the one relied upon.

The importance of human faces to human infants can be seen in the ways they scrutinize strange faces and sometimes shy away from them.


## THE TACTILE OR SURFACE VARIABLE


At this point we wish to distinguish between the tactile aspect of breast feeding and the effect of large surface body contacts with external objects.

Infant monkeys do not react aversively even to a wire-mesh mother. They spend a great deal of time climbing upon and pressing against the wire-mesh surface of cages, exploring it both orally and tactually. However, when given an opportunity to choose between terrycloth, rayon, vinyl, and rough-grade sandpaper, they preferred the cloth surrogates.

In another experiment, the infants were given the chance to choose between a wire-mesh mother heated by coils to above room temperature and a cloth mother at room temperature. The unheated cloth mother was preferred, particularly in the early infancy. At 15 days, the preference reversed.

The investigators manipulated the temperature factor in another way. For example, an infant monkey was raised from Day 15 on a warm surrogate mother 7° above room temperature for four weeks. Then the infant, which had become strongly attached to the surrogate, was shifted to a cold surrogate (5° below room temperature). Within a couple of minutes it was evident that the infant noticed the switch. It responded with a piteous cry and a huddle in the corner of the cage. For a week, the infant resorted to the surrogate very seldom. When the cold mother was replaced by the original warm mother, the infant established its old degree of contact with it. The next step was to switch the warm and cold mothers each day for two weeks. The infant clung to the warm mother and ignored the cold one.

With another infant, the cold mother was used as the original surrogate for four weeks. Then the warm one was used for a week. After this, the cold one was subsequently returned for a week and then there was a two-week period during which a daily switch was made. The infant failed to become attached to the cold mother at the beginning, instead spending most of its time in the corner of the cage. In the succeeding periods in which the warm surrogate was used, the infant never became as intimate with the warm mother as the warm-reared one did even to the cold mother. Seemingly being raised by a cold mother had "cooled" it to the mothers even when they eventually radiated plenty of warmth.

As a further test, the two infants were exposed to a typical fear-producing object. The warm-reared infant ran to the surrogate and clung to it vigorously, and the cold-reared one ran into the corner of the cage. Thus the behavior of the infants seemed to show that temperature as a haptic component is a material factor in developing the affectional/behavior of monkeys. The investigators were willing to suppose that this would apply

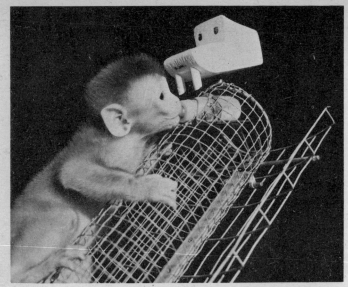

Figure 9/ A surrogate mother with a nipple. (By permission of The Regional Primate Research Center, University of Wisconsin.)

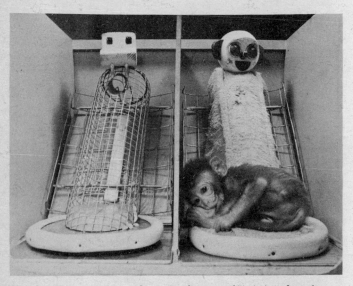

Figure 10/ Two surrogate mothers. One has a rough (wire) surface; the other, a soft terrycloth surface. (By permission of The Regional Primate Research Center, University of Wisconsin.)

not only to mother and infant, but to age-mates both homo- and heterosexual, and to maternal and even paternal behavior.

Figures 9, 10, and 11 are three illustrations of the nature of surrogate mothers and certain reactions of infant monkeys to the surrogates. In the first figure, the surrogate is a nursing mother. The infant clambers onto this mother, accurately finds a nipple to suck and receives milk. The second figure contrasts two types of surrogate mother. They exist in adjacent compartments and, in this case, an infant has chosen the terry-cloth mother. In the third figure, an infant monkey has apparently sought protection from some disturbing item in the environment. Certain reactions of monkeys can be seen in facial expression, just as in humans.

The behavior of the monkeys just described adds considerably to what was outlined in the earlier essay on surrogate mothers. What we call love seems to stem from some very basic sensory conditions.

Figure 11/ Infant monkey resorting to the comfort and "protection" of a surrogate mother when alarmed. (By permission of The Regional Primate Research Center, University of Wisconsin.)

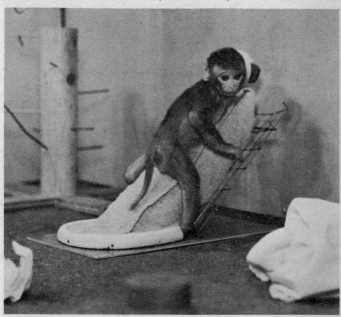

# WHAT KIND OF AFFECTION IS THIS?

The following is an account of human experience which ordinarily would be overlooked as something based upon haptic mechanisms. Most stories of human behavior are couched in language that has little or nothing to do with perceptions and sensory mechanisms. It is as though they hardly pertain to living and associating with other people. These descriptions of human affairs deal with ideational and emotional items, totally disregarding the roles played by perception and sensory processes. The very same stories can be retold bringing out the role of perception and sensation. When this is done, the stories take on a new significance.

The present story has to do with Mr. X and two persons with whom he associated for many years. Both were women, and the main point to be made is the consequence of the *outward show* or *lack of show* of affection between him and them. One of these women was his aunt; the other, his wife's mother. Mr. X was in his sixties and was thus able to look back over a long period for his examples.

Mr. X's mother died very shortly after he was born. As a result, his aunt and grandmother reared him till he was about eight years of age when his father remarried. One might expect that X would have recollections of his aunt in a mother role which would include rocking him as a very small child, feeding him, hugging and comforting him when in trouble, and doing many things which would involve various forms of bodily (haptic) contact. One would expect that he could relive the warmth of feeling arising from recollection of such contact, but he had no memories of this sort. About the closest he could come to this was sometimes sleeping with his aunt as a very small child.

When X was young, he lived in a region of the United States where he never saw outward displays of affection or heard people praising and complimenting each other. He was taught not to make remarks about how people looked or what they wore. One was supposed to "mind his own business."

It was not the custom for relatives and close friends to embrace and kiss or show any overt sign of affection when they would meet or separate. This same affectional vacuum operated in all of X's early environment. He remembers, for example, how strict and conservative his high school environment was. On one occasion, a student was quite strictly disciplined for having merely put his arm around the waist of a girl. However, X grew up not really knowing that something was lacking in his environment. Although X's recollections of his early life contained no examples of outward show of warmth, he came to revere his aunt. She constantly did things for him for years without appearing to expect any reward. She was so kind to him that she became his ideal of altruism. Nevertheless, the affection between him and his aunt was never manifested in overt ways as in the usual spontaneous embrace and kiss when expressing gratitude.

This is a picture of a boy growing up to idolize an aunt who reared him, but whose associations were entirely devoid of the usual elements which comprise much of the usual content and basis for warm feelings and love.

The second person X described was his wife's mother. She, too, was a small, quiet, completely unobtrusive person, who, like X's aunt, always "minded her own business." She was able to live amiably in the household of one of her daughters for 30 years or more without getting in the way at all. She was brought up in a part of the country where warmth of affection and outward displays of it were the rule. X first became acquainted with her when she was a frail, plain common-looking person on a small Southern farm. After her husband died, she went to live with a daughter in a city. There, of course, she was treated affectionately and fitted into the situation helpfully and harmoniously. In this context she began to wear much better clothing and to make a transformation that was nothing short of amazing. The older she got, the more she looked like a queen.

It took X some years of living in an environment in which affection was outwardly manifested by mutual compliments, kissing, and other bodily contacts for him to behave that way himself. This is not at all surprising when considering his early environment. In later years he was able to be "demonstrative" to his wife's mother but not to his aunt. In fact, it would have seemed unnatural and artificial to make an outward fuss over her.

Nevertheless, his aunt was still an ever-growing ideal.

This comparison was meant to indicate that affection and high regard can be of several very different sorts, based upon the sensory relations of two people. X had the very highest regard for both these women. Each was someone unique to him. He never saw two other women to compare with them. But, owing to the differences in the way affections were displayed in the two families, they presented entirely different images to X. One was somewhat of a neutral (genderless) ideal while the other was clothed significantly with femininity. X often wondered to himself how his aunt really "got through life" receiving as little outward warmth as she did. (She lived to be 94.) He wondered what kind of a self-image she possibly could have had. He did not wonder about his mother-in-law; she was in a warm social context, elicited no pity and did not fail to be treated as a full-fledged woman.

Life and living are truly made up of the very components that people either take for granted or are in many ways oblivious to. After I had read this essay to a class, a student suggested to me that the human story seemed like the case of the monkeys with surrogate mothers. This, of course, was in essence the message I was trying to convey.

## HAPTICS AND CONTINENCE

In picturing the role of haptic perception as it is involved at different periods of life, it is appropriate to deal with more than thermal sensations. For various reasons two people treat each other differently as they go through life. I have already mentioned that various muscular and other tissue degenerations set in to cause pain and discomfort and, consequently, to minimize various sorts of bodily contact between people that are routine when people feel physically well. This often precludes a number of kinds of close association that were common earlier. For example, eroticism plays a far smaller role as these conditions develop.

Other reasons sometimes develop as years go by that preclude haptic stimulation and its benefits. I know of a married couple whom I shall call E and G. When the third child arrived and there was hardly enough money to take care of the family, E decided they had enough children and that she would have to do something about it if they were not to have more. In this context she kept in mind the kind of family G "came from." His people all had big families and to E, with her puritanical religious training, this meant that they were a carnal low-grade lot. So she decided that she and G were never to sleep together again. This wasn't just a decision to have twin beds. It was a decision never again to get into the same bed together. She enforced it from the time they were in their middle twenties till G died at the age of about 72. They had separate bedrooms and she was as aloof from G as from any other man. This turned out to be a case of old-time puritanical "continence" taken too far. Continence is a word seldom heard today, but it means total avoidance of coitus.

I never saw E show any affection for G whatsoever. Whereas once in awhile E might have said "poor G" when describing him or his faults to others in his absence, she never spoke in complimentary terms to his face.

The explanation for most of the way that E treated G seems to lie in the complete elimination of all the haptic factors in their relations. This inescapably produced a coldness between them which could not be compensated for in any way and it brought humane interaction to a standstill. Were either to make any moves toward the other to rectify the miserable situation, E would very naturally have seen it as a step back toward an erotic relationship, which she would not have tolerated because of her vow that no more children would be born to them.

This story thus concerns two people living in the same house without kissing, embracing, holding hands, or patting each other on the back to emphasize a commendation. Even affectionate glances were totally absent year after year. Thus, besides additions to the family, E eliminated kinds of behavior that show warmth and closeness and harmony between people. She relied on her "righteousness" to handle everything. Like many in her generation, she was not taught that there are natural ways of producing closeness and promoting good feeling (love). Harmony was to be achieved simply by "doing right" and was a part of "serving God."

E obviously keenly felt the marriage was a failure as far as happiness was concerned, but she blamed this on G. Although she didn't know it, she was totally awry about how the basic role of haptics provides for the kind of intimate relations needed in married life.

It is astonishing to us now to realize that any form of religion could blind people to the roles played by mechanical (tactual) shows of affection, and to the effects produced by certain forms of bodily contact. All that bodily contact meant to people like E was sin ("carnality").

As time went on, this couple fared less and less well. Their lives were totally empty, with E becoming increasingly righteous and pious in her own eyes while G became more an object of her criticism.

While the ideational basis for the behavior was a perverted religious outlook, what brought about the emptiness and distance between E and G was the absence of tactual contact between them. Thus we have two things to blame — a belief and a daily way of life which eliminated a natural psychobiological function and permitted empty bitterness that "serving God" could not make up for.

## HAPTICS IN RELIGIOUS SERVICES

In the present essay we shall discuss some practices in church services that concern rather intimate behavior involving haptic mechanisms. The old-time Wesleyan procedure in the Methodist Church whereby the membership was divided into "classes" of about 12 people each is an early pertinent example, although it is not as full and frank an illustration of haptic behavior as some of the contemporary practices we shall cite.

The classes met separately once a week with the intent of producing behavior that constituted "serving God." The device broke down formality and demanded individual participation. The class leader asked each member very personal questions regarding his or her past week's behavior. This procedure was widely employed in certain fundamentalist congregations and probably still is being used. All this time it was not looked upon with any great approval by the larger religious body from which the fundamentalist congregations sprang.

Now that society has become permissive in many ways, some of this permissiveness has spilled over even into the liturgical conduct in churches. Informality, which was formerly tabooed, is now creeping in.

The groups we are about to discuss indulge in personal self-disclosure and similar activities. Lounsberry (1970), in a recent article, describes the activities of various church groups which have taken up "sensitivity training."

In a church in California the congregation sits in a circle, claps hands and expresses their innermost feelings. In closing the service they are asked to stand shoulder to shoulder.

Elsewhere a large group of priests and nuns gather in a hotel ballroom. Grouped in circles of six, the participants first exchange their impressions of each other and then begin a discussion of the participants' problems. Before the service is over, everyone is supposed to pat the others' shoulders, touch their faces, or squeeze their hands.

At least a third of the denominations belonging to the National Council of Churches are said to be sponsoring some form of sensitivity training for both pastors and lay members. Whatever else it is, the training consists of *physical contact* — touching, bumping shoulders, and other actions. Church leaders have come to realize that handclasping or hugging can be more effective than words. One of the procedures sometimes used has been to pass one another around. The group, which is in some kind of close formation, lifts and passes around within it a person who has allowed himself to become relaxed and inert.

One church, for example, has done away with pews, because they are said to keep people apart, and has substituted circles of folding chairs so that people can face each other. Some people have testified to a "real spiritual discovery" derived from these new conditions.

Even those who do not approve of this radical change in the nature of church services recognize its potency. Various newspapers and church papers have lashed out against it as a form of brainwashing and a means of destroying the natural defenses of society. One disapproving Episcopal diocese points out that the changes pose too many hazards and that the trainers are not sufficiently "professional."

The example of the growing indulgence of church groups in forms of confrontation and physical contact is but added testimony of the power of haptic and other forms of sensory input. The customs of society have generally been those of inhibition and control. The haptic procedures just mentioned have greatly helped many people.

We mention "encounter" in churches only to add to the examples of the potency of feedback from haptic behavior. Bodily contact and its perceptual repercussions are more potent and far-reaching and lead to far different effects than even most adults had supposed.

The whole trend of human conduct has rapidly and definitely moved toward direct *participation* in all avenues of life. Life is coming to be seen and lived as something the individual does by the exercise of his own capacities whether they be called instincts, senses, or anything else.

In this trend, as well as in the particular examples given, the discovery of the role played by haptic perception is one of the major features. Even with this discovery, its total interpretation may still be naive and erroneous. It is so new and so surprising to most people as to be given a purely mystical interpretation. What we are saying here is that the results are only an example of what the exercise of everyone's sensory machinery produces.

Our enthusiasm for the exercise of haptic perception is not to be taken as a sort of naive and unlimited endorsement of everything that is going on in the name of "encounter" and "sensitivity training." Society is simply waking up to some things that people with the most insight about sensory mechanisms have known for some time. The result can only be a great deal of "experimentation" with all its consequences, good or bad. Even those who are enlightened about social movements and sensory processes cannot predict what the overall outcome will be.

Whatever else can be seen in this new enthusiasm and adoption of "encounter" tactics, they demonstrate what bodily contact (haptics) does in human relations, be they religious services or whatever.

## PAIN SENSITIVITY — THE
## DEFENSIVE SIDE OF HAPTICS

Is everybody equally sensitive to pain-producing stimuli? Sweeney and Fine (1965) used immersion of the right hand in a thermostatically controlled water bath at 40°F for 10 minutes as a situation to try to answer this question. Duration of the intended immersion was not told the subjects to begin with, but they were instructed that if pain became intolerable they could remove their hand. Out of 76 soldiers ranging in age from 18 to 28 years of age, 48 completed the test.

The purpose of the investigation was not only to determine whether subjects differ in their sensitivity to pain-producing stimuli, but to compare the performances of the same subjects on a test of "field dependence." Some persons have a tendency to be *analytical*, to extract the focal experience from the more general background of awareness. These persons are called *field-independent*. Others tend to be more general or *global* experiencers. The item that is mainly attended to is somewhat more submerged or embedded in the background awareness than is the case with the field-independent person. These persons are said to be *field-dependent*.

Sweeney and Fine found that the peak pain was reported within two minutes of immersion and that the ratings following this were the same or lower. The subjects were asked to report their sensation according to a scale. The range of results was broad and allowed the subjects to be divided into three classes — high, medium, and low pain experiencers.

The test given to determine field dependence was a standard one having to do with detecting single geometric figures embedded in complex geometrical patterns. When the results were compared with the pain ratings, it was found that the analytical perceivers (field independent) experienced greater pain than the global perceivers.

Collins (1965) made a study of pain sensitivity as it related to social matters. He tested 62 soldiers for pain sensitivity by using a D C constant-current square-wave stimulator. The electrodes were placed on the second and fourth fingers of the right hand. Two measures were obtained — one of *threshold* pain and the other, *tolerance* of suprathreshold current intensity. The subjects were given a Childhood History Questionnaire which produced scores on (1) protection, (2) independence, and (3) stimulation. Collins' supposition was that childhood experiences had something to do with sensitivity to pain in adulthood. Of course, in dealing with the content of early life there are many factors. Some investigators pick out the specific factors they wish to study. Others study such broad considerations as socioeconomic level, which may contain the aforementioned factors hidden in them.

Schluderman and Zubek (1962) had reported that college students from upper socioeconomic levels manifested significantly less sensitivity to pain than nonstudents of the same age from lower income levels. Although not dealing specifically with the factors involved in Collins' check on childhood, their findings indicated that something in early experience later predisposed persons to react in certain ways to noxious stimuli.

Collins found that the *protection score* correlated positively with both threshold of pain and pain tolerance. The *independence* score was negatively related to both of the pain measures. "Stimulation" was not related to either of them.

While it is not clear what the meaning is of a positive relation between Collins' "protection" score and sensitivity to pain and the negative relation between it and the "independence" score mean, the finding does suggest a connection.

I derive two conclusions from the experiments. One is that those who readily isolate an experience will be more affected by the stimulus producing it than those who tend to keep such an experience embedded in their general awareness at the time. The other is that adult sensitivity to potential pain-producing stimuli is influenced by childhood experience. Thus, pain is not an end result determined solely by sense-organ sensitivity, but is determined also by the central nervous system which represents the individual as a person.

## HAPTICS UP AND DOWN
## THE ANIMAL KINGDOM
peter l. borchelt

The importance of the visual and auditory sensory systems in our daily life, and in the lives of other animals, is readily apparent. These sensory systems mediate a variety of behaviors important in our welfare and survival; for example, we, and most other animals, rely on these systems for acquiring food, for finding others of our species, and for establishing comfortable homes (or nests). Another sensory system, the olfactory, is also of vital importance for the survival and comfort of many species even though people do not usually consider it of importance for humans. Its importance is described in the subsection on "The Savor System."

The present essay describes a variety of behaviors involving the haptic system manifested by many species of animals. Many of these behaviors are seen as instinctive acts achieving ends which provide for the welfare and survival of the species involved. Those behaviors of humans and, possibly, some of those of the higher primates which are described are regarded as cognitively initiated, but sensation and perception are involved nevertheless. The purpose of this essay is to indicate the many ways that contact sensitivity and movement (haptics) are involved in mediating these behaviors.

First of all, we do not know nor can we rightly conceive of what the feedback from muscles is like in other animals; we know nothing of their awareness. But we cannot fail to conclude that feedback of some form occurs from muscle systems. Even if the feedback plays no role other than the initiation and guidance of the succession of subsequent movements, we would still be dealing with sensory systems. It is hoped that the examples given below will reveal the ubiquity of haptic activity.

The haptic system has been described in previous essays as the sensory system by which the organism is literally in touch with its environment. It includes the muscles, joints, and the skin. The sensory modalities involved are touch and kinesthesis, although temperature and pain may be involved. However, discussion here will be mostly limited to the sensory modality of touch.

Five different classes of behavior of this sort will be described: care of the young, sexual behavior, fighting, predator defenses, and care of the body surface. Certain features pertaining to the relations between mother and infant and some aspects of sexual behavior are discussed elsewhere, so descriptions here will be brief. The role of haptics in initiating and guiding behaviors related to fighting and predator defenses have not been discussed previously. Much of this essay is concerned with care of the body surface, which involves a variety of interesting behaviors. It is hoped that these will be seen as sensorially initiated and guided and of great importance to the survival and welfare of many animals, including humans.

## CARE OF THE YOUNG

When a mother cares for her young, often both the haptic and basic orientation systems are involved. The mother contacts the young in many ways; one example is licking. During other maternal behaviors, such as retrieving and cradling, the young are not only touched but also experience changes in basic orientation.

Licking the young occurs even in invertebrates. Adult ants frequently exchange regurgitated liquid food with each other. The most elementary form of exchanging food occurs when ants care for their young. The worker ants feed the larvae and lick, stroke, and handle them incessantly. In turn, the larvae secrete fluid from the salivary glands and fat from their bodies which is frequently licked by the workers. When the young ants emerge from the cocoons, "they are feverishly licked and groomed" (Schneirla, 1957, p. 110).

In some mammals, licking plays a very important role in maternal behavior. For instance, in rodents such as mice and rats, maternal licking of the anal-genital region of the young is necessary to stimulate normal urination and defecation. In newborn kids and lambs, early maternal activities such as licking play an important role in her subsequent recognition of her offspring (Collias, 1956; Smith, Van-Toller and Boyes, 1966). It has even been claimed (Hersher, Richmond and Moore, 1963) that newborn lambs not licked by the mother fail to rise to their feet after birth, and sometimes die.

Retrieving of the young in some form occurs in most species of mammals. Cats, dogs, and most rodents generally grasp the young by the nape of the neck with the jaws and carry them back to the nest. Retrieving in primates, including humans, consists of the mother gathering the infant into her arms and holding him there.

Maternal behaviors involving the sense of touch, such as cradling, grasping, and other behaviors for maintaining close physical contact with the young, are of primary importance in many primates, including humans. In rhesus monkeys, the infant is held in close contact with the mother essentially all the time for about the first two weeks; in gorillas, it is held for perhaps the first three months. Sometimes the infant may be carried by the mother for many months, either grasping her hair and hanging under her belly or, when older, riding on her back.

Infants of these species actively grasp the mother soon after birth. Van Lawick-Goodall described how an infant chimpanzee grasps his mother's hair (or whatever else is available) when the mother moves; one amusing incident occurred when a mother chimpanzee, Flo, moved suddenly and the infant, Flint, "at once grasped tightly to Flo's body with one hand, but to his own head (which he happened to be scratching) with the other" (Van Lawick-Goodall, 1968, p. 225). Human infants also reflexively grasp when they are suddenly shaken or dropped. This reflex, the Moro reflex, functions to embrace the mother when she moves suddenly (Bowlby, 1969). By a month of age, the human infant is able to grasp well enough to suspend his own weight from a rod for half a minute (McGraw, 1943).

Human infants are also carried, even when mothers are at work. For instance, the infant may be strapped to the mother's back and carried all day, a common occurrence in cultures simpler than in our own. Interestingly, Ambrose (cited in Bowlby, 1969) found that human infants cease crying when rocked at rates of more than about 60 cycles per minute; 60 steps per minute is a slow walk for an adult human. "This means that, when carried on his mother's back or hip, a young baby is rocked at not less than 60 cycles per minute and so does not cry — unless he is hungry or in pain" (Bowlby, 1969, p. 294). Here, both haptic and basic orientation systems are stimulated.

## SEXUAL BEHAVIOR

Sexual reproduction demands the union of an egg and sperm. This most often involves the close association, if only for a short period of time, of a male and female of a species. In some species, tactile stimulation plays a role in the attraction and identification (courtship) of males and females, or to arouse the sex partners. During copulation, it functions to coordinate copulatory movements.

Tactile stimulation perhaps is less important in species where fertilization is external than in species where it is internal. For instance, bodily contact during mating between fishes may be limited to nudging or butting of one fish by the other, or the pair may swim along with their flanks placed together. Male toads and frogs react to all moving objects during the breeding season by jumping on them and clasping them. If the object is another male, it protests by croaking and the other male releases its clasp. If it is a female who assumes the proper position, mating takes place. But in the absence of another of its species, the male will clasp almost anything — the tip of a boot, a human hand, or even an unlucky fish in the pond (Eibl-Eibesfeldt, 1970)!

Among mammals, tactile stimulation is of considerable importance in sexual arousal. Bermant and Westbrook (1966) found the intensity of peripheral (flank, perianal, and genital) stimulation influences the temporal regulation of sexual behavior in estrous female rats. Male rats with surgically reduced sensitivity of the penis show less frequent copulation (Beach and Levinson, 1950). Sexually experienced bulls, when blindfolded, can be induced to mount simply by applying tactile stimulation to the chest (Hafez and Schein, 1962). Other mammals require tactile stimulation for ovulation. For instance, sharp spines on the penis of male cats provide strong stimulation which induces ovulation in the female during copulation.

Analysis of the copulatory behavior of many animals shows that tactile stimulation is necessary for the coordination of particular movements. These tactile synchronizing stimuli have been identified in the copulatory behavior of both cats and turkeys (Schein and Hale, 1965).

The male turkey approaches the female when she crouches. When he approaches, the female raises her head; subsequent mild pressure on the female's back elicits further head raising. When the male mounts, his feet stimulate the female's head. When the female's elevated tail is pressed forward by the male, her oviduct is partially everted. Complete eversion of the oviduct is elicited by further tactile stimulation of the base of the tail. Ejaculation by the male is elicited by contact of the penile papillae with the everted oviduct. Each of these components of sexual behavior in turkeys can even be elicited by artificial tactile stimulation, such as the human hand. Thus, tactile stimulation serves both to elicit specific behaviors and to provide sensory feedback necessary for successful guidance of these behaviors. Without such sensory feedback from the sex partner, attempts at copulation might not be successful, thus reducing the chances of fertilization, and endangering the survival of the species.

## FIGHTING

In many cases, fighting between members of a species is necessary for establishing social relationships. For example, chickens establish dominance hierarchies or "peck orders." If two chickens with an established dominance relationship (one dominant over the other) are separated so that they can see and hear each other but cannot have physical contact, they react like strangers and fight when they are released from their cages (Maier, 1964). Here, actual physical contact for expressing dominance (pecking) is necessary for maintaining the social relationship.

Many animals establish their relative strength during a fight by hitting each other with their tails, butting heads, etc. Fence lizards during a fight alternately grasp each other's neck. The one with the stronger grip is the victor and the loser runs away. Sometimes a smaller lizard will even give up when it realizes, while biting its opponent, that its rival is especially large (Kitzler, 1942). Many rodents, such as rats and mice, will bite each other during a fight; the weaker animal then usually flees. Male rattlesnakes will not bite each other when they fight, but instead engage in a "pushing match" whereby the winner pushes his rival to the ground with his body. This is not at all unlike "arm wrestling" commonly seen in human males. In either case, the conflict is settled without loss of life or limb.

In fighting behaviors, the sensory feedback involved in many cases is pain. However, some of the fighting behaviors described above do not obviously involve pain.

# PREDATOR DEFENSES

Effective defenses against predators certainly contribute to the survival of an animal. Many forms of predator defenses have evolved, and some of them rely on tactile cues for their elicitation. One form of defense is shedding of a body part when it is grasped by a predator. This occurs in several echinoderms (e.g., sea stars) and many lizards; in these cases the arms and tails, respectively, are shed and regenerate after a period of time. The lizard's shedding its tail not only makes it more difficult for the predator to catch it, but sometimes the shed appendage itself attracts the predator by thrashing around on the ground as the lizard escapes. Many fish make escape responses due to pressure changes in the water. For instance, taps on the side of an aquarium will evoke tail flips in goldfish (Rogers, Melzack and Segal, 1963).

Some animals eject toxic or foul-smelling substances at predators; some of these animals so respond when they are touched. Cockroaches fire chemicals from the base of their legs, and Bombardier beetles have flexible abdominal ducts allowing them to aim chemicals at predators. When all other defenses fail and they are grasped by a predator, many animals display tonic immobility and act as if they were dead. Stick insects and beetles show this response when jarred or with loss of contact with the substrate (Carthy, 1958). The opossum is the most familiar example of immobility, but it occurs in many invertebrates, reptiles, and also birds (Rather, 1967). In some animals, grasping plus inversion of the animal is necessary to elicit tonic immobility; in these cases, both the haptic and basic orientation systems are stimulated.

# CARE OF THE BODY SURFACE

The class of behavior which most obviously involves the haptic system is care of the body surface (COBS). It is possible to distinguish between three subclasses of body-surface care. The *individual* care and maintenance of the integument (skin, feathers and coat) is the most common. *Social* care involves an animal preening, grooming, or cleaning another of its species, or even of a different species. Sometimes social care is mutual. Two or more animals groom each other, and in this case it functions also to initiate or maintain group structure. *Symbiotic* care occurs between two different species, one of which is having its body surface cleaned while the other is engaged in another class of behavior, usually eating.

Care of the body surface functions both to keep an animal comfortable or "satisfied" and to insure its survival. Russell (1959) discussed both of these functions and stated that it is necessary to consider the comfort of animals (such as dogs and cats) when conducting physiological experiments because even mild discomfort, such as that arising from overcrowding in living cages, is enough to disturb the physiology of many animals. Of course, animals in their natural environment behave in many ways to eliminate discomfort. These behaviors are also necessary for survival, since proper care and maintenance of the body surface is essential to freedom of movement and freedom from disease. For example, it is essential for birds to maintain their feather covering in good condition, both for the purposes of insulation and flight and for use in display (behaviors which signal another animal). And frogs must keep their skin free from dirt since the skin is even depended upon for respiration!

Individual COBS is important for a wide variety of species. Szebenyi (1969) presents a detailed analysis of preening in fruit flies, showing that they use their legs in either sweeping or rubbing actions to clean the entire body (head, thorax, abdomen and wings). Preening clearly functions to clean the body surface since dusting the fly with fine chalk will increase preening, and dusting specific parts of the body will increase preening of only those parts.

However, more elaborate individual COBS behaviors are seen in birds and mammals. Simmons (1964) has described some of these behaviors in birds, including bathing, oiling, preening, and head scratching, as well as sunning, dusting, and anting.

Water birds, e.g., grebes, *bathe* by ducking the head and shoulders under the water, sending water onto the back, and beating the wings vigorously against the water, splashing it over the plumage. Some species such as geese and swans even occasionally turn somersaults in the water.

Land birds use a number of methods to bathe (Slessers, 1970). Some passerine (perching) birds bathe by standing in the water at a suitable depth and fluffing their feathers, flicking their wings, and ducking their heads until they are completely soaked. Aerial birds such as swifts and swallows bathe "on the wing" by dropping repeatedly into the water and raising a spray of water on their backs. Some other birds bathe simply by exposing their feathers to rain and dew.

*Oiling*, which almost always occurs after bathing, involves the smearing of the fatty secretion of the oil or preen gland on the feathers, particularly the wings. The functions of oiling include the waterproofing and maintenance of the insulating character of the plumage, especially important in water birds. Also, upon irradiation in sunlight, preen oil becomes a source of Vitamin D, which is ingested during preening.

*Preening*, which almost always follows bathing and oiling, is the most important activity in feather care and consists of arranging, cleansing, and maintaining the health and structure of the feathers by the bill, and dressing the plumage with organic liquids (Simmons, 1964).

*Head scratching* occurs either as a reflex elicited by an irritant or as an important behavior in feather care. Scratching in some species also functions as a means of preening and oiling the head.

*Sunning or sunbathing* involves exposing the plumage and the skin to the rays of the sun. The behavior varies in intensity, from a simple fluffing of the feathers, squatting, and drooping of the wings to more intense ruffling (especially the head feathers and the feathers around the preen gland), combined with fanning of the tail feathers and spreading of the primaries.

One explanation for sunbathing is that it increases the movement of ectoparasites, which in turn makes them easier to remove by preening. Many birds sunbathe to dry their plumage after it has become wet. Mousebirds, which have soft hairlike plumage, sunbathe most frequently after rain or dew (Rowan, 1967). Cormorants and snakebirds, which do not have a waterproof plumage but chase and catch fish under water, must dry themselves out by perching in a tree or on a rock and spreading their wings.

*Dusting* in birds consists of squatting in fine dry earth or sand and forming hollows of dust by movements of the bill, scraping the feet, and shuffling the body. The dust is usually driven into the plumage by wing and feet movements. Afterwards, the dust is removed by vigorous shaking. The specific movements of dusting differ between species — a unique example is the White Winged Chough which stands up and applies dust to specific parts of its plumage with its bill.

*Anting* is perhaps the most dramatic behavior involving care of the body surface in birds. This behavior, which is apparently confined to passerine birds, involves the application of the defensive and body fluids of ants to the feathers. The fluid involved is the formic acid produced by acid-ejecting ants that produce a repugnant anal fluid. The species of stinging ants are not used for anting.

One of the functions of this behavior is the removal of ectoparasites, since formic acid and other ant secretions are insecticidal.

Interestingly, while the behavior of anting is relatively stereotyped and innate, birds have to learn which species of ants are "correct" for anting. Some individuals of anting species of birds never learn to ant and others ant with "inappropriate" objects, such as mothballs, cigarette butts, citrus fruits, and other pungent objects.

Individual care of the body surface is just as important for mammals. Everyday observations of household pets, especially cats, gives some idea of the behaviors involved. The fur is usally licked to remove dirt and other foreign substances, the vibrissae are cleaned, the claws are used for scratching and removing foreign material, and the teeth are often used to comb the fur.

*Sandbathing* as a means of caring for the body surface is normally seen in rodents adapted to an arid desertlike habitat. These mammals have evolved methods of reducing water loss through evaporation and, consequently, have increased sebaceous gland secretions which necessitate sandbathing. Chinchillas are unique in that in addition to the other movements they roll over on their backs and roll or spin their bodies in the sand.

An individual COBS behavior seen in primates is *grooming*. Lower primates (e.g., lemurs) use their teeth for grooming the fur, but higher primates (e.g., chimpanzees) use their hands. Grooming in chimpanzees has been described by Van - Lawick-Goodall (1968). Chimpanzees groom the thighs, arms, chest and abdomen, usually with close visual attention. Sometimes both hands are used; one for pushing or parting the hair, the other for picking at the exposed skin with the thumb or fingers. The lower lip may also be used for parting hair. During grooming there are interspersed slow and deliberate scratching movements against the growth of the hair, followed by grooming of this area.

After getting wet, chimpanzees often dry their hair by scratching downward over the body while pulling the hair between the fingers. Other drying movements consist of shaking, rubbing against a tree, rubbing with leaves or licking the water from the hair. Sticky foods (or soil) are usually wiped off, either against the ground, a branch or with a handful of leaves.

Some mammals purposefully expose the body surface to substances other than sand or dust. This type of behavior, analogous to dusting and anting in birds, is sometimes referred to as "self-anointing." Examples are dogs rolling in earth or even dung and cats exposing their fur to aromatic plants.

Perhaps the strangest example of this type of behavior in animals other than humans is seen in the European hedgehog. This animal licks objects while accumulating saliva in its mouth and then "anoints" its spines with the saliva. Alternate licking of the object and then itself may continue for several minutes. It is not known what substances are licked in the wild, but in captivity it has been observed to lick such things as leather, cigar butts, the skin of a toad, varnished wood and a variety of other substances (Burton, 1959). Simmons (1966) also observed this type of behavior in captive capuchin monkeys which spread a mixture of onion juices and saliva over their bodies.

In some primitive human cultures, smearing of the body with substances such as grease and mud is common. For instance, the Dagum Dani, a culture in West New Guinea, grease themselves with pig grease as a preparation for battle or a dance. Often ashes are used to color the grease and various patterns are applied. The grease may help to keep the Dani warm during chilly nights, but it also probably contributes to the general health and healing ability of the skin (Heider, 1970). Painting the body with rouge (usually limited to special occasions) is common in a number of cultures, since red ochre (iron oxide) occurs in many places throughout the world (Hoeble, 1966).

The human animal is the most variable of all in behaviors concerning care of the body surface. Washing at least some part of the body is common in almost all cultures. However, some cultures wash only parts of the body, and then rarely, while the importance of washing in our own culture is illustrated by the many millions of dollars spent a year on soaps, perfumes, and deodorants.

Treatment of the hair in some fashion is common in virtually all cultures; the hair is trimmed and arranged, and treated with a variety of substances. Archeological evidence demonstrates that a great emphasis on the female hairdo extends back even 20,000 years (Hoeble, 1966).

The behaviors included in social COBS are often much

like those of individual COBS. Social care is also seen in a wide variety of animals. For instance, ants lick one another, frequently around the mouth parts, abdomen and limb joints (Wallis, 1962). Licking coats the body surface with saliva which protects it from moisture and may serve to prevent the growth of lethal molds and bacteria (Wheeler, 1910). Also, since differences in odor possibly exist between individual ants in a colony, licking may serve to reduce odor differences by removing exudes from the body surface.

Social COBS in birds, called allopreening, is most characteristic of species which show clustering behavior. Sparks (1965) has described allopreening in the red avadavat, a gregarious species of bird. Red avadavats may spend up to two-thirds of the daytime "clumping," that is, perching in body contact with each other. Ruffling of the head feathers serves as an "invitation" for a bird to be preened by another. Often, the ruffling also serves as an appeasement gesture to reduce the likelihood of attack from another bird. Morris (1955) discusses ruffling of the head feathers as a display or signal soliciting preening from another bird. Mutual head preening in birds has an obvious advantage since a bird cannot preen its own head feathers.

Social COBS in mammals, also called allogrooming, is quite widespread. Cats, most rodents, and primates frequently show these behaviors. Sparks (1969) offers a general review of allogrooming in primates. A characteristic body position usually serves as an "invitation" to allogroom. This consists of approaching a potential groomer and presenting the part of the body to be groomed, or perhaps sitting squarely in front of the groomer. Once grooming has begun, the groomee often makes adjustments and presents other parts of the body to be worked on. The dexterity of the higher primates allows use of the hand in a variety of ways. Fur may be drawn through the forefinger and thumb; raked, combed, and smoothed; or collected or sheathed so that picking movements may be made with the free hand (Sparks, 1969).

Social COBS also occurs between members of different species. Morris (1955) observed Java sparrows, a species with "clumping" behavior, which were caged with a Necklace dove. The Java sparrows were attracted to the dove, "clumped" with it, and preened it. Morris concluded that the dove, which has a rounded appearance as does a Java sparrow with its feathers fluffed, presented a more appealing stimulus than even other

Java sparrows! However, interspecific COBS occurs naturally in other species. The brownheaded cowbird, for instance, is adept at soliciting preening from many other species of birds. An interesting report by Payne (1969) describes a giant cowbird, captive in the Fort Worth Zoo, which solicited preening from humans. Payne said that the bird watched the visitors as they passed the cage. When they stopped, it flew down and ruffed its neck feathers and, with bowed head and tucked-in bill, came up as close as possible to the visitor. Payne rubbed its head; it bent farther forward and erected its nape feathers at nearly right angles to its body.

Van Lawick-Goodall (1968) describes interspecific grooming between chimpanzees and baboons. That chimpanzees will groom other species is clearly seen in a report by Falk (1958) who taught a chimpanzee a visual discrimination using the opportunity for the chimpanzee to groom the experimenter's arm as a reward.

Social COBS in humans includes "flea-picking," a common behavior in primitive cultures, where groups of individuals sit and pick fleas or lice from each other. This type of social activity helps maintain social structure much as it does in other social primates. Included in human social COBS are those behaviors which have a strictly social function (raising the status of the individual) such as tatooing and mutilation. Tatooing obviously is a more permanent decoration than body paint and cosmetics. In Polynesian countries, where tatooing is most common, the more highly decorated a person is the higher his social status. In extreme cases, the tongue may even be tatooed! While in this country it is interesting that tatooing is considered "lower class" by the upper class, it still serves as a sign of masculinity and status within the lower class (Hoeble, 1966).

Decorative mutilations and deformations reveal social status and sometimes have mystical value. Some cultures pierce the nasal septum, ear lobes, or stretch the lips. Some Northwestern American Indian tribes deform the cranium of infants by pressing them against flat boards to make them more beautiful. Some mutilations are believed to ward off evil spirits, and in our culture, circumcision still retains mystical value.

An unusual form of care of the body surface occurs sometimes in symbiotic relationships, whereby one species benefits by obtaining food. Such relationships occur in many invertebrates and some species of fish and birds. Ants, for instance, have parasitic mites which attach themselves to their legs and feed off the secretions which collect on the ants' legs when the ants clean themselves (Wheeler, 1910). Other species, such as a certain small cricket and a specific beetle, lick the surfaces of ants and feed on the cutaneous secretions and the coating of saliva with which the ants cover themselves.

In fish, an interesting symbiotic COBS relationship occurs between fishes of the genus *Amphiprion* and sea anemones. These fishes prefer certain species of sea anemone, frequently defend their anemone as their "territory" against other fishes, and remove organic and inorganic material from on and around their anemone, all without being injured by its poisonous tentacles (Mariscal, 1970). The cleaner-fish cleans other fish of parasites. This fish entices the host to permit itself to be cleaned by a "cleaner dance" consisting of butting its snout against the host's fins to spread them and against the host's mouth to open it so that the cleaner fish can enter. While cleaning the host, the cleaner fish continuously vibrates to signal the host it is being cleaned. The host fish may invite the cleaner fish to clean by opening its mouth. It signals the cleaner fish to leave by closing its mouth half way in a jerky motion and opening it again (Eibl-Eibensfeldt, 1970).

Birds have many symbiotic relationships with other animals during which they clean their host's body surface. A general description of some of these relationships is given by Burton (1969). For instance, the Egyptian plover is said to enter the open mouth of a sleeping crocodile and feed on bits of food lodged between its teeth. This is perhaps the oldest recorded relationship of this sort; the original story is from Herodotus, a Greek historian about 2,500 years ago. The story has been embellished with time and one version relates that the plover pricks the crocodile with a special spike on its head (probably referring to its crest of feathers) when the crocodile attempts to close its jaws. At least it is true that plovers associate with crocodiles and pick parasites from their skin, and since "crocodiles have the habit of sunbathing with their mouth open, it would not be surprising if the birds sometimes entered to take any scraps of food they saw there" (Burton, 1969, p. 33). Another example is the oxpeckers which obtain all their food from the ticks and mites in the hides of big game animals in Africa. Oxpeckers have sharp, curved claws and a long stiff tail so they can climb all over their hosts, up and down their legs, over their backs, and even under their bellies.

# RETROSPECT

It is hoped that the broad range of behaviors described and discussed above will give the reader some idea of the ever-present nature of haptic activity. The haptic system functions within a tremendous range of behaviors and species to insure survival and welfare of these species. Many of these behaviors have not been analyzed from a perceptual point of view. Thus, the nature of the stimulation, the sensory feedback, and often the specific sensory modalities involved in these behaviors are unknown. If nothing else, this essay illustrates that researchers interested in the haptic sensory system have a sufficient number of behaviors available for innumerable years of research. But it also hopefully demonstrates that the haptic system is vital to many important behaviors which occur in everyday life — whether in the everyday life of an ant, a bird, or a human being.

## THE SAVOR SYSTEM

Our environment contains solids, liquids, and gases. Some of the solids and liquids constitute our food. Our contact with these materials is characterized by curiosity as to whether they are pleasant, unpleasant, harmful or harmless. We smack solids and sniff gases.

For a long time sense physiologists and physiological psychologists have been interested in the body mechanisms whereby the sensitivies to the qualities just mentioned are exercised. They have found sense receptors (taste buds) on the tongue and other receptors in the nose and have concluded that there are *two* kinds of sense mechanisms.

Hence, speaking in terms of the experimental laboratory, taste is the quality experienced when the taste buds in the mouth are activated. In common speech, taste is the qualitative experience produced by putting something in the mouth. It is obvious that the first definition is far more restrictive than the second; and that, in fact, the common definition is more realistic and appropriate than the technical one. Since there is another word used for taste, namely *gustation*, it might be better to use this technical term to label the effects of stimulating tastebuds. Experimentation has shown that this leads to the experiences of *salt, sweet, sour* and *bitter*. If we thus choose to label things as suggested, then taste is the word covering any and all experiences resulting from putting something in the mouth.

The receptors in the nose are sensitive to volatile substances (gases). Usually when substances are put into the mouth their volatile component activates the nasal receptors, and we can call this *olfaction*. This nasal component is not always recognized, or at least not recognized for what it is. Once the volatile component is definitely experienced as a unique event, it is a smell, an odor, or a fragrance. To smell something is thus to distinguish it from a taste. Since this does not always occur when tasting and eating, it is logical and appropriate to recognize the integration when it occurs and speak of the combination as savoring. Thus we have a savor system.

We now know very well that when something is put into the mouth, receptors aside from the four types of taste buds — possibly, the olfaction receptors — are activated. Additionally, there is a group of mechanoreceptors which activates the sense of touch. Whether something tastes good depends in part on its texture being soft or hard, smooth or granular, etc. Preference for these and still other tactile qualities in any case depends upon which other stimulus qualities the material possesses. The temperature sense is also activated. Hot and cold coffee are not alike and temperature is thus a factor in the production of various taste qualities. While this thermal factor undoubtedly activates temperature receptors, it may even differently affect the taste buds themselves.

While savoring is, at times, a highly pleasurable and positive act, it is a rather defensive one. Since the organism runs the risk of taking in harmful substances, detection and precaution are involved. One of the outstanding features of savoring is that the individual does it in connection with looking; people want to see what is being placed in the mouth, not simply for enjoyment, but to ascertain whether it is safe. It also helps for becoming oriented or "prepared" for the food.

The old stunt of telling a person to close his eyes and open his mouth evokes resistance. This is often done in order to produce a surprise taste or to have the recipient guess what the item is. The command violates the defensive tendency and will be obeyed only with some reluctance. Various mistaken identifications may be made when something unseen is placed in the mouth. Once the taster is told what the material is, it tastes different. Even when you see a new substance ("food"), you like to be told something about it or told *what* it is before eating it.

The gustatory effect is different when the material cannot reach the olfactory receptors. This is demonstrated by clamping the nose when an item is taken into the mouth.

The savor and haptic systems unite at the mouth. The mouth is just as much a haptic organ as a savoring one, for it provides information regarding *surface texture* (such as smoothness, slipperiness, and roughness), *hardness, softness, shape, size, viscosity, specific gravity*, and *granularity*.

The importance of the savor system is illustrated by the gratifications the individual receives from eating, and by the fact that the question of what to reject and what to accept seems so important to the growing infant and child. We don't know very much yet about what is involved in this rejection and acceptance.

Our concern is with the savor system as a perceptual one and with the role it plays in everyday life. The system presents many interesting and profitable problems. It is both interesting and helpful to consider the role of the savor system in the lives and behaviors of a number of subhuman animals as well as our own. It has been thought by some that we do not properly take advantage of all our savor system has to offer. A better understanding of it would be useful. To provide steps in this direction, the following essays have been written.

# THE ROLE OF OLFACTION IN MAN:
# SENSE OR NONSENSE?
richard l. doty

It is commonly recognized that olfaction, or smell, plays an important role in many vertebrates and invertebrate species, but it is also commonly believed that there are few, if any, parallels in *Homo sapiens*. ". . . We must confess we are miserable dullards when it comes to olfaction," states von Bruddenbrock (1958, p. 114). This popular belief is perhaps explained by overreliance on researchers' experience of their own perceptual capacities and on a superficial examination of the wealth of behavioral and anatomical information available. Whatever its basis, it is widespread, as evidenced by an examination of three current popular textbooks on perception (i.e., Dember, 1965; Gibson, 1966; Bartley, 1969). Although the authors nominally consider olfaction as one of the major sensory avenues and include comparative data from a number of nonhuman animals to broaden their bases of generalization, they devote little more than one percent of a total 117 i text pages, excluding references, to the subject. This "anosmic" orientation to the world of animals all too often leads both scientists and laymen to a misunderstanding of the behavior of other organisms which use olfaction in major ways in their everyday (or everynight) lives. Thus, we see many a psychologist studying learning as a function of vision in various nonvisual (comparatively speaking) organisms, while ignoring olfaction altogether. Fortunately, recent studies have pointed out the possible implications of the influence of odor in a number of traditional learning studies (e.g., Douglas, 1966; McHose and Ludvigson, 1966; Wasserman and Jensen, 1969; Morrison and Ludvigson, 1970).

The present essay, through a composite of suggestions, speculations, and data, attempts to re-examine the interesting role of olfaction in the life of man and presents a few examples of the use of smell in nonhuman vertebrate and invertebrate species.

Hopefully, it will lead the reader to entertain the possibility that man, when given half a chance, is an extremely olfactory organism — but one that goes to great pains to deny it. Kalmus (1958) points out that scientists manifest this indifference to the chemical senses, and that these senses play a much greater role in everyday life than is recognized, while in lower animal forms they appear to be all important.

## USE OF SMELL IN NONPRIMATE SPECIES

Perhaps the best-known highly olfactory animal is the domestic dog, whose keen behavior has long been familiar and useful to hunters and policemen. The average dog's sense of smell has been estimated to be one million or more times as sensitive as man's (Dröscher, 1969).

Bedichek (1960) cites the widely publicized account of the spaniel, Geisha, who was used to help catch coffee smugglers in West Germany in the mid-1950s. Geisha was never known to fail, locating coffee buried under loads of coal, wrapped in gasoline-soaked clothes, and hidden in other odorized and unlikely places. Dogs are currently used in the United States by various agencies to detect the presence of illegal drugs such as marijuana. In Holland and Denmark, dogs are used for finding gas leaks. They are trained to stop when they smell gas, and to bark at the place where the pipe has burst, although this is often a few yards underground beneath unbroken pavement (Droscher, 1969).

Kalmus (1955) demonstrated that one odor doesn't significantly mask another one in the dog's perceptual world, whether they are smelled alternately or not. A well-trained dog can discriminate the odor of armpits from that of hands of the same individual, and can distinguish odor differences between identical twins. Most breeds of dogs can be trained to track human odor, whether the source is airborne or on the ground. King, Becker and Markee (1964) demonstrated that dogs can detect human odor traces (fingerprints on glass) for periods well over a month after their initial deposition. However, when the fingerprinted material was placed outside and exposed to wind, dust and rain, the odor stimuli began to disappear in one week and the dogs were barely able to discriminate the odor after two weeks' exposure of its source to the elements.

The owner of a bitch in heat, as well as his generally unhappy neighbors, knows the important role olfaction plays in the sex life of the dog. The female's odor is so well recognized by males that at least one burglar has been reported to have played roughhouse for a few minutes with his bitch before going on a prowl in order to retain enough of her odor on his clothes to distract male watchdogs. This gives him freedom from attack while ransacking a house (Milne and Milne, 1968).

A less domesticated mammal, whose cautious nocturnal activity has led to few popularized accounts of its olfactory prowess, is the lowly mouse. Recent studies suggest that various species of mice can use odors for such diverse functions as sexual attraction and identification of mates and members of their own species (Moore, 1965; Doty and Levine, 1970; Doty, 1971), territorial recognition and defense (MacKintosh and Grant, 1966), individual recognition (Parkes and Bruce, 1961), food seeking (Howard, Marsh and Cole, 1968), and predator detection. Odors of the urine of unfamiliar male mice have the potential to block pregnancy in recently-inseminated females (Bruce, 1959; Bronson, Eleftheriou and Garick, 1964; Dominic, 1966) and, in extreme instances, may play a role in the population regulation of these creatures (Chipman, Holt and Fox, 1966). Similarly, such physiological regulatory functions as the synchronization of estrus (Whitten, 1956) and the conservation of caloric expenditure have been directly related to smells within the mouse's environment.

In addition to dogs and mice, the number of invertebrate and vertebrate animals that uses olfaction to a high degree is too great to be fairly represented in this essay. However, a few of the more interesting examples have been included to show the breadth of this important sensory system in the animal kingdom. Forms of life as "primitive" as bacteria exhibit attraction to chemical substances — a phenomenon called chemotaxis. At least five different chemoreceptors are present in some bacteria, and the extensive metabolism of the chemicals are not necessary for their detection (Adler, 1969). Amoebae, paramecia, and most other invertebrates also exhibit extreme sensitivity to environmental chemical substances.

Perhaps the olfactory abilities of insects are the most popularized among those invertebrates which have been examined. Female silkworm moths emerge from cocoons in early summer, hang upside-down from nearby perches, and spread their abdominal tips in the early evening, emitting a substance which is detected by male moths of the same species (conspecifics) several miles away. A male moth will journey toward a female who emits this smell, resulting in their ultimate union and the fertilization of her eggs. Various species of bees are able to distinguish between their own hive and another's on the basis of smell. It has been demonstrated that pollen collected on the bee's body communicates to other bees leaving the hive the type of flower for which they are to search. The olfactory sense organs of bees are located on the eight distal segments of their antennae, like most other insects. Some insects, for example, butterflies and the water beetle *Dytiscus*, have smell receptors also located on other appendages of the head (von Frisch, 1964). Bees use sight, in most cases, to detect flowers from afar, and olfaction to determine the species of the flower at close range. For bees the organs of touch and smell are closely related on the antennae, so it is probable that a scented object that is round may have quite a different perceptual outcome from one that is angular (von Frisch, 1964).

## NONANATOMICAL BASES FOR THE CONCEPTION OF NONOLFACTORY MAN

One basis for the popular conception of nonolfactory man comes from our adaptation to a civilization which directly limits the diversity of olfactory stimuli to which we can respond or learn to respond. This mania for sanitation and deodorization is apparent in common clichés used to express hostility toward opposing political, social, or economic points of view — the "dirty-stinking communists" or "dirty capitalists," the "pigs" or "stinking hippies." Big business has reinforced this mania and produced an incredible number of deodorants, sanitizers, cleaners, mouthwashes, toothpastes, after-shave lotions, face creams, bath oils, and room sprays. In fact, several *billion* dollars are spent each year in the United States for toilet preparation and deodorizers.

A jokester recently commented on this matter: "What bothers me is that the streets aren't safe, parks are dangerous and the freeways are impossible, but under our arms we have complete protection." It is of interest that "synthetic" human feces and sweat smell bad only to children after the age of four, with three- and four-year olds rating their odor as pleasant (Stein, Ottenberg and Roulet, 1958). The relative roles of cultural and maturational factors in influencing this classification change have not been determined, although it is apparent, in American society, that the culturalization process is extremely potent around the age of five.

The cultural limitation of natural olfactory stimuli to which we can respond is paralleled by a lack of appropriate linguistic development, thereby limiting the means of communication for the possible gradations of olfactory experience. In the true Whorfian sense, the cultural coding context may result in a lack of perceptual refinement of olfaction, with a resultant overgeneralization and simplification of a few culturally-approved or commonly present smell categories. Bienfang (1946) reports that Polynesian peoples are capable of expressing several thousand shades of meaning through their words for "smell." If this is true, it appears to be the exception rather than the rule, since most ancient and modern languages admit failure in attempting to attach names to specific odors and generally use comparisons and analogies to conceal this deficiency (Bedichek, 1960). As Bedichek points out, the Greek botanist, Theophrastus, was concerned with this matter twenty-two hundred years ago:

> Of odours some are, as it were, indistinct and insipid as is the case with tastes, while some have a distinct character ... But the various kinds of good or evil odour, although they exhibit considerable differences, have not received further distinguishing names, marking off one particular kind of sweetness or of bitterness from another; we speak of an odour as pungent, faint, sweet, or heavy, though some of these descriptions apply to evil-smelling things as well as those which have a good odour (p. 14).

The first observation of Theophrastus is remarkably in line with recent findings (Moncrieff, 1966) that individuals in our culture make sharp distinctions between certain smells, while they respond in a more or less indifferent manner to a great many more. Often we try to tell others about our odor experiences by reference to other odor experiences which must, in turn, be identified by further comparisons. Since we have few words that convey smell experiences exclusively, we have to use words borrowed from other modalities, or adjectives relating to the sensation they arouse, e.g., "pleasurable," "intoxicating," or "disgusting." Smell borrows most of its terms from taste (e.g., "salty," "sweet," "bitter") and a large number from the haptic senses (e.g., "soft," "smooth," "hard"). Bedichek (1960) suggests that when we speak of an odor as "sharp," we are not borrowing this term directly from the sense of touch, but from taste, which had previously borrowed it from touch. If we haven't learned a vocabulary, or even opened the book, how can we be expected to speak the language? It is interesting to note that we commonly describe individuals as bitter, salty, sweet or sour, or as bright, dull, intense, or illustrious. How often do we call them fragrant, putrid, or smelly?

## OLFACTION IN NONHUMAN PRIMATES—
## POSSIBLE HUMAN ANALOGS

In order to understand better our potential olfactory nature, an examination of the olfactory capabilities and practices of a number of modern nonhuman primate groups is of interest. It is generally assumed that the human pattern of reproduction, characterized by the absence of estrous cycles in the female and lack of marked seasonal variations in mating (both of which characterize nonhuman primate reproduction), evolved from patterns similar to those evidenced by modern nonhuman primates (Lancaster and Lee, 1965). Since olfactory processes are intimately related to reproductive behaviors in most mammalian species, including man, such an examination is warranted in the present context. Although our ancestors were not the same as nonhuman or human forms of living primates, the study of the rich behavioral variability of modern monkeys and apes makes it possible to reconstruct the most probable behavior patterns of related past hominid forms (Jay, 1968).

Various primates, including members of both New and Old World monkeys, as well as Prosimians, use olfaction ostensibly in such day-to-day endeavors as territorial marking. Mason (1968) reports that Callicebus monkeys rub a sternal patch of glandular tissue against branches by dragging or pushing the body forward and he suggests that some substance is deposited in this manner. This is substantiated by the fact that the animal often stops and sniffs a previously rubbed area. One function of chest marking, according to Mason, may be to impart to the home range of an odor that is recognized by the occupants, possibly enhancing their attachment to it.

Gartland and Brain (1968) describe scent marking in another group of monkeys, the ground-dwelling Cercopithecus. These monkeys rub their cheeks and jaws against objects within the group's territorial boundaries. They alternately sniff and rub, exhibiting a behavior that suggests complete preoccupation, giving little notice to events that might otherwise elicit their attention.

Some species of Lemurs have specialized forearm and armpit glands which they use for marking. *Lemur catta* rubs its tail on a cornified area of its forearm and may also mark branches with its forearms. *Lemur catta* females often mark objects with their clitoris (Petter, 1965). An analogous territorial scent-marking behavior in man is cited by Hediger (1968). He saw Berbers as close to Europe as Morocco obtaining a tarry substance from the medicine man in the bazaar. The substance was taken home in short lenghts of sheep intestine and smeared on all four corners of the building to ward off the prevalent evil spirits of the region.

We may not like it, but man's behavior is often not far removed from that of many nonhuman primates.

A number of primate groups exhibit conspecific greeting behaviors which include oral-genital manipulations and explorations. These behaviors may provide olfactory and tactual signals for individual identity, as well as response patterns for the acknowledgment of individual recognition (Marler, 1968). Is it possible that backslapping, kissing, hugging, and handshaking are analogous behaviors in *Homo sapiens* which perform essentially the same social functions? Perhaps perfumes, colognes, and after-shave lotions (aside from their possible sexual functions) serve to increase the olfactory cues in informal greeting situations, since social conventions (e.g., moral systems, clothes, etc.) generally don't allow prolonged and intimate contact with each other's natural olfactory stimuli. Kuno (1956) suggested that sexual attraction is the last major frontier where olfaction is important to man. But what about individual recognition? Could it be that our nontactual, uptight, modern social world, as described earlier by Bartley (see "Haptic Mechanisms, Reality and Well-Being") is complemented by an uptight, nonolfactory one?

Among many primate groups, stimuli associated with distance-increasing behaviors are usually related to "strangeness" (Marler, 1968). It seems probable that strange and unfamiliar smells also produce distance-increasing behaviors in man. Most of us know (and keep our distance from) persons whose presence is olfactorily disturbing. Genetic factors resulting in metabolic difficulties are at fault in a small number of such cases. However, there are many other causes of unpleasant-smelling perspiration. For example, travelers often report that people of different "races" or nationalities have distinct smells. The majority of such smells have been shown to be due to dietary differences. The perspiration odor of native Japanese and East Indians is probably due to their preparation of fish (they often eat it raw); similarly, the Eskimo's odor is due to his smoked and salted fish diet. Distinctive odors attributed to Indians are probably the result of their eating sweet relishes and spices. Lean mutton has been suggested as the cause of the odor of Arabs. Northern Europeans have an odor which is due to their consumption of cheese and spicy hor d'oeuvres (Moncrieff, 1965). Pearl Buck has pointed out that the Chinese, as well as other Easterners, often complain that Western people have a bad, buttery smell. Moncrieff (1965) suggests that the influence of food on body odor is greatest in the armpit region, whereas the perspiration odor is generally strongest between the toes, since this odor is aided by mercaptans and valeric acid resulting from decomposition of debris collecting there. It is interesting to note that at one time "armpit stink" was a cause for rejection of would-be Japanese army recruits (Moncrieff, 1965).

Modern man differs from most other species of primates in that he is less prone to remain in one general area (less philopatric). Man loves to travel and has invented a number of conveyances that allow him to do so at his leisure. Is it possible that Western man's insistence upon cleanliness is related to a desire to minimize possible distance-increasing odors between him and men from other parts of the world? Certainly one basis of Western man's wish for cleanliness is to be accepted and liked by his neighbors. We must remember, however, that much of our behavior has been programmed by our culture and, as individuals, such tendencies or desires are rarely realized or examined. In fact, there is much anthropological evidence suggesting that many cultures are less cleanliness-conscious than our own. However, our rapidly expanding culture, with its emphasis upon travel, imperialism, and internationalism may mirror the need for distance-decreasing behaviors in a more direct way than many of the less mobile societies.

## SEX AND SMELL

In a number of mammalian species, a close relationship exists between olfaction and sexual processes. For example, removal of the olfactory bulbs or lesioning of the olfactory tract decreases various measures of sexual activity in the male rat (Beach, 1942; Heimer and Larsson, 1967) and eliminates all male mating behavior in naive and sexually experienced male hamsters (Murphy and Schneider, 1970) as well as in female hamsters receiving androgen as neonates (Doty, Carter-Porges and Clemens, 1971). Male dogs and rats prefer the odor of estrous to diestrous female conspecifics (Beach and Gilmore, 1949; Carr, Loeb and Dissinger, 1965). Apparently, the female rat's olfactory preferences for male-rat smells are influenced by her stage of estrous, since naive and experienced estrous females prefer normal male odors to those of castrates, whereas naive diestrous females show no such preferences (Carr, Loeb and Dissinger, 1965). Male chimpanzees have been observed "inspecting" the genital area of presenting non-receptive females (Lawick-Goodall, 1968). Sometimes the males sniff the females' vaginal openings, while at other times they carefully poke their fingers into the opening, and then smell them. Male chimpanzees have been seen parting the lips of the vulva with both hands while alternately sniffing and looking into the opening. Lawick-Goodall reports that one male inspected 18 times in 10 minutes while the female reclined beside him. Inspections were not common when females had large sexual swellings which are indicative of estrus, although there was a general increase in the number of inspections at the first time of sexual swelling and during the period immediately after detumescence.

Although olfaction does not seem to play such an overt role in sexual behaviors of humans as it does in many other mammalian species, there is still much evidence for its importance in human sexual activity. In human females, the sense of smell is intimately related to the sexual cycle and is influenced by various hormonal factors. The olfactory acuity of women is generally greater than that of men for a number of compounds, with the degree of acuity varying directly with estrogen levels. Thus, the acuity is highest between the periods of actual menstruation (Money, 1965). Women can detect by odor the presence of 17-ketosteroid compounds in urine. Although this ability is lost following ovariectomy, estrogen administration can restore it. The lactone, exaltolide (a synthetic analog of a mammalian sex attractant), is easily perceived by adult women, while men and prepubertal girls smell it only vaguely or not at all. However, a male injected with estrogen can detect its presence. The female's ability to perceive exaltolide is maximal during ovulation and falls to a minimum during the progestation phase, once again implicating the role of estrogen (Le Magnen, 1952; Beidler, 1961). Removal of that portion of the pituitary in humans (hypophysectomy) which suppresses ovarian function also brings about a loss in the sense of smell (Schon, 1958).

There is much experimental evidence showing that males and females have differential preferences for a number of odorous substances, and that these preferences are dramatically influenced by the age and sexual maturity (i.e., pubertal state) of the individual (Moncrieff, 1966). Women generally prefer odors such as camphor, menthol and citronella oil, while men prefer odors of musk, pine oil and cedar wood (Moncrieff, 1965). In summary, demonstration of the important interaction between sexual functions and olfactory factors suggests that smells may be more intimately involved in sexually active men than has been previously believed.

A number of theorists suggest that man's evolution of a standing posture resulted in a lessening of his olfactory powers, since olfaction is generally used by most macrosmatic land species to smell trails left on the ground. Kuno (1956) suggests that the axillary scent of man is more important in mediating sexual attraction than scents coming from the sexual organs and other parts of the body, thereby mirroring this upward adaptation. The findings that apocrine glands in the axillary area develop only a few years before puberty and undergo cyclic or temporary changes as a function of pregnancy and menstruation and lessen their activity in old age are cited as additional support for this theory. However, the extreme importance of cultural influences must be examined before convincing generalizations can be formulated. For example, Davenport (1965) reports on the role of sexual odors in a Southwest Pacific society which contrasts, in part, with Kuno's assertions. Davenport points out that body odors are erotic stimulants, especially those from women's genitalia. Both sexes use odorous substances as means of seduction. One is a certain aromatic leaf worn by men at dances. Another is an odor produced by mixtures of coconut oil and turmeric used in the women's hair on special occasions. Nowadays, pomade and scented talcum have been added to substances that are considered erotic. A form of love magic is exemplified by the supposed similarity of vaginal odors and those of fish. On the basis of this, the men use a red ground cherry attached to a trolling line. When a fish is caught by this lure, the cherry is then believed to have the power of attracting women.

The use of artificially created odors for the attraction and enticement of members of the opposite sex, as well as for escape from "body odor," is not unique to modern culture, although our emphasis upon advertising and propaganda may make us think this is the case. The early Greeks and Romans used perfumes extensively. Solon, an Athenian lawgiver of the Sixth Century B.C., passed legislation forbidding the sale of perfume, although these laws were generally ignored and scoffed at. Emperor Marcus Salvius Otho of Rome carried a supply of scents into battle with him, while the Emperors Caligula and Heliogabalus bathed in perfumes and wines scented with roses. Hundreds of years later, Henry III of France, son of Catherine de Medici, used perfumes left over from the boudoir of Nero's wife, Poppaea, who was reported to have enjoyed bathing in asses' milk. Louis XIV's extravagant use of perfumes resulted in his being known as the sweet-smelling monarch. Louis XV required the wearing of a different perfume each day in his Versailles court. Napoleon is reported to have used as many as 46 bottles of cologne a month, and to have ordered a pair of perfumed gloves from his Paris supplier 30 days before Waterloo (Lardner, 1959).

Within our lifetimes, however, the use of perfumes by men has only been fashionable after World War II, when perfume makers realized the great potential market for these products. In some years, the sales of after-shave lotion alone were much greater than those of ladies' perfume (e.g., 1958, $42 million vs. $34 million, respectively). Madison Avenue recently announced an addition to its large number of scent-products. *Time* (December 26, 1969) reported that other major magazines have been displaying advertisements for a liquid douche concentrate offered in two floral scents (orange blossom and jasmine) and two flavor scents (raspberry and champagne). *Time* reported that *Vogue* magazine banned any hint of the flavors in their ads, allowing advertising for only the floral scents. Apparently, inhibitions toward the role of taste in sexual behaviors in our culture are stronger than those against smell.

## EVIDENCE OF "UNUSUAL HUMAN OLFACTORY ABILITY"

Further evidence for man's potential olfactory nature comes from experimental and anecdotal reports of persons with seemingly unusual olfactory abilities. A number of blind people have apparently exhibited extreme sensitivity to smell. William James (1890) tells of a blind woman employed in a mental institution who was said to be able to sort the linen of the inmates, after it came from the wash, by smell. Similarly, a blind girl working in a laundry was reported to be able to recognize and identify the owners of clothes she sorted by their odors (Kalmus, 1958). Helen Keller claimed to have been able to identify most of her friends and visitors by their individual odors (Hicks, 1965). Gault (1923) reports on a blind girl he tested who was able, in 50 of 54 cases, to distinguish between various-colored yarns of different textile fabrics by smell alone.

Evidence for "unusual" olfactory abilities is not limited only to blind persons, however. Kalogerakis (1963) tells of a boy observed between the ages of two and five who could detect individual body odors, particularly those of his parents, and who was able to differentiate odors from various parts of the body which the adults present couldn't detect. Freud (1959) reports the case of a patient who claimed to have been able as a child to recognize people by their scents. I have talked to several students who claim to be able to tell various people, particularly members of their own family, apart on the basis of smell. It is commonly acknowledged that perfumers and wine tasters have developed their olfactory skills to a high degree, as have some people involved with keeping laboratory colonies of various animals. Hediger (1968) says that a quick shift in scent formation may accompany a momentary change in "mood" in some primates (for example, prosimians) as well as in some rodents. Some men who tend animals report that they can detect changes in animal odor, which may be taken as symptomatic of the animal's internal condition. Certain experts on mice note quite extreme changes which they interpret in this way.

## SMELL AND RELIGION

Both modern and ancient civilizations have used powerful emotion-provoking odors in religious and mystical ceremonies. Much of the following information comes from Moncrieff's (1965) brief, but interesting, discussion of this topic.

In general, odors have been used for one or more of the following reasons in religious ceremonies: to appease the gods, to drown out evil spirits or demons, or to impart to the body the odor of the god. Many early religious ceremonies were probably centered around the use of hallucinogenic compounds to bring forth visions and awakenings, and environmental odors were most likely involved in enhancing the intensity of these multimodal experiences. Odors served both as conditioned reinforcers and secondary stimuli for the gathering place and played the role of enhancing group cohesion, identity, and unity.

Mythologies of the East, as well as those of the Greeks, often announced the presence of the god or goddess with their undiluted odor. Chaldean priests burned incense to Zeus at an altar outside the temple of Bal Marduk over 5,000 years ago, as reported in the Book of Daniel. The Romans filled their tombs with roses, and the Greeks, with myrtle. The funeral fires generally consisted of sweet-smelling woods, e.g., cypress and yew. The Assyrian King Assurbanipal had a funeral pyre built just before his death and was suffocated by aromas of burning wood. Christ's coming was celebrated with the Wise Men's gifts of gold, frankincense and myrrh. A prayer of the Koran states, "O God, make me to smell the odors of Paradise, and bless me with its delights, and make me not to smell the smells of the fires of hell."

As culture advanced from its earliest stages, many of the animals who were once feared became a portion of the ritual and mythology of a number of cultural institutions and traditions. Fear of larger animals may have been replaced by the fear of demons. Historically, demons were often thought to be associated with bad odors, and in some cases were believed to be able to be driven off by antagonistic ones.

## SMELL AND MEDICINE

It is not surprising that the relationship between odors and demons was also conceptually related to beliefs about disease. Early physicians often associated odors with the diagnosis of a particular disease, and attempted to drive out the demons causing the disease with antagonistic odors. Typhus was diagnosed by its "mawkish" odor, smallpox by its "terrible" odor, and the odor of diphtheria was nauseating. An acid smell was indicative of acute rheumatism, and nephritis was associated with the odor of chaff. During the nineteenth century a number of authors wrote on the use of smell in diagnosing diseases, and various odors were commonly claimed to be of use in the treatment of asthma, hysteria and epilepsy.

Less than 250 years ago physicians carried walking sticks and umbrellas with hollow handles forming receptacles for camphor, musk, and other poignant substances which they held to *their* noses when visiting patients to guard against the smells which to them spelled infection. Bedichek (1960) cites an 1853 issue of the Louisiana *Spectator* which tells of the great pains taken to rid New Orleans of the plague:

> The authorities of our city ordered on Thursday the firing of cannon and burning of tar in each district with a view of purifying the atmosphere. For a few hours the booming of the cannon echoing from all parts of New Orleans broke painfully upon the ear, giving us the impression that we occupied a beleaguered town.

Apparently, such remedies were not entirely in vain, however, since even then malaria and yellow fever were linked to the tropical atmosphere, and exploding cannon, burning tar, or a string of garlic worn around the neck were all sufficiently odoriferous to discourage the mosquitoes which were the real carriers of the fever parasites (Bedichek, 1960).

Modern researchers have mustered evidence for the view that schizophrenic patients have a discernible "peculiar" odor that is independent of age, race, diet and cleanliness. For example, Smith and Sines (1960) demonstrated that both rats and men are able to discriminate between the odors from patients diagnosed as schizophrenic and hospitalized nonschizophrenic matched controls. The substance responsible for this odor has been recently isolated and identified (Smith, Thompson and Koster, 1969). At any rate, this and other studies suggest that smell may be useful in the diagnosis and understanding of a number of diseases and that careful future research is necessary to examine this possibility.

## CONCLUDING COMMENTS

The present essay has examined a few of the many possible roles olfaction plays in the everyday life of man. We should remember that we often take the world around us for granted, without realizing that this world is a transformation of our sensory systems if we ignore them, we ignore the diversification and excitement of nature. Our modern world still has enough diverse odors which we can explore if we set our noses to it. The popular use of incense in shops, gardens and homes is one example. Although I could have included a large number of additional everyday situations, hopefully this beginning will help you to start unraveling olfactory insights for yourself. Perhaps it will entice you to go outside and smell the bark of a tree, to take fewer baths, or to sit and dream about a whole new world of experiences you have been missing. Perhaps it will make you think a bit more about your environment. As Hicks (1965) states, "In these days of air pollution, city folk unquestionably are paying through the nose for the dubious advantages of crowded expressways and belching factories." Whatever it does, be sure to keep a sharp eye about you, and keep your nose in the air, for you may be missing something you don't even know about. Well, I'll smell you around.

## LIKES AND DISLIKES IN ODORS

Much of what can be said about odors pertains to whether we like or dislike them. Odors, however, are more than experiences tallying with the chemical composition of substances, despite the fact that the olfactory sense mechanism has played the evolutionary role of detection and defense against chemically noxious substances. Odors involve emotional and other conditioned aspects which may be too varied and diverse to catalog. Despite the richness of connotations there is little in the literature to testify to these aspects in a systematic way. Early dealings with odors attempted to classify them, but the taxonomy has not yielded all the information that might be desired. No rigid correspondence between odors and the chemical composition of substances has been found, and their description is difficult.

Several investigations have gone so far as to deal with qualitative properties of odors rather than developing a simple classification of them. The study by Hazzard (1930) is an example. He dealt with the following: heaviness-lightness, looseness-tightness, smoothness-roughness, softness-hardness, dullness-sharpness, liveliness-inertness, thinness-thickness, brightness-dullness, surfaceness-deepness, and smallness-largeness. Each was treated as a dimension along which any given odor may be located through experimentation. While these dimensions may seem to be artificial designations of odor qualities, remember that the term *dryness* is used to describe wine, which is inescapably wet. Dryness, however, can be detected by tasting the wine. Thus, the experienced aspects of odors, whatever they are, seem best described by terms usually supposed to apply exclusively to sensations in the other sense modalities.

The purpose of the present essay is to deal with odors simply on the basis of likes and dislikes, without describing the nature of the preferences, although it is to be understood that such odor ratings do not actually deal with the unique qualities experienced when smelling them as this would lead into a maze of detail.

Moncrieff (1966) is one of the relatively few who has even dealt with likes and dislikes in an extensive way. We shall give the gist of what he has to say in his book *Odour Preferences.* His subject variables are age, sex, temperament and intelligence.

What he describes cannot be taken as universal, for different peoples and peoples of the same country in different centuries have not had the same preferences. For example, in the court of Louis XIII (1610-1643) it was musk, civet, myrtle and iris that held sway and in the next reign (1643-1715) it was harsh and spicy resins. Later (1715-1774) rose perfumes were preferred. In Napoleon's day, Eau-de-Cologne and rosemary were prominent. After that came lavender and wallflower. Still later, strong musk and patchouli (East Indian mint) odors rose to favor. Availability, novelty and the status of sponsors must have been factors. Nowadays, with the further advance of the chemical industry, both pleasant and unpleasant odors are far more abundant.

In Moncrieff's investigation, he presented large groups of odorous substances to a few people and offered 10 dissimilar odorous substances to many people.

The first method involved 132 different substances given to 12 subjects. Four of the subjects went through the testing procedure twice to determine consistency of judgments. The sessions generally consumed about a day and a-half. The subject's ages ranged from 10 to 77 years.

The 10 odors used in the second type of study were: strawberry flavoring essence, spearmint oil, French lavender oil, musk, lactone, vanillin, Meroli oil (a natural oil that had a very "bright" smell), almond flavoring essence, naphthalene, rope oil (from the seeds of a plant like cabbage), and oil-soluble chlorophyll. All that mattered was the impression gained by the first sniff. The tests were carried out in England and nearly all the subjects were British. We are left to wonder whether a slightly different set of results would be obtained in the United States and whether radically different ones would occur in Asia.

These procedures and their findings, along with the findings of other workers, led Moncrieff to draw up a long list of what he calls *rules,* which are not actual scientific laws, but strong trends in given directions. Since the list contains 124 rules, I do not suppose that a reader would find all of them interesting. Some may almost sound like the same thing stated in several ways.

We have selected a number of these rules and reworded them. It should be kept in mind that they are intended to apply to people in Western civilization or, perhaps, to groups more restricted than that.

## MEN AND WOMEN

1/ Substances found in nature are preferred over synthetics.

2/ When an odorant is diluted, it becomes more pleasant.

3/ All sorts of people are unanimous about some smells—those that are called very bad. Agreement is not as strong about certain odors people call very good. If children are not counted, agreement increases for good odors.

4/ In line with the previous statement, people do not agree nearly so well about odors in the mild-preference range.

5/ Most persons are relatively indifferent to most odors. They do not strongly like or dislike them.

6/ Men and women differ in regard to the certainty with which they like and dislike odors. Men are surer about the moderately pleasant range and women about the slightly unpleasant ones.

7/ When men and women disagree in their preferences and aversions, the differences pertain to those in mid-range.

8/ Both sexes are alike in their preferences regarding fruity odors and most essential oils.

9/ When the sexes differ in their odor preferences, the males tend to have stronger ones.

## AGE RANGES

The next set of comparisons pertains to the factor of age, which was divided into three ranges: (a) persons below 15; (b) persons within the range of 15 to 25 years; and (c) people from this range upward.

1/ Children don't like the oily smells. They do not like flowery smells as frequently as people in the other ranges. However, children accept fecal odors much better than older persons.

2/ All adults are fond of simple flower smells.

3/ Musky and fruity odors are liked by persons over 25 more often than by young adults. Children like fruity odors better than the adults, however.

4/ The smell of onions and chives is liked best by young adults.

All in all, age is a more decisive factor than sex in classifying odors into good and bad.


## TEMPERAMENT FACTORS

Introversion and extroversion were the factors studied here.

1/ Temperament is not very effective in determining what odor is liked or disliked.

2/ When extroverts differ from introverts on the pleasant odors they prefer, their choices tally more closely with those of children. In choosing among unpleasant odors, introverts, when they differ from extroverts, tend to resemble the children in their choices.

3/ Strange odor qualities are more acceptable to introverts than extroverts.

4/ When extroverts and introverts differ on an odor, the introverts probably like it better.


## RELIABILITY OF PREFERENCES

Reproducibility in odor preferences from time to time is best in the 20-to-40-year range. Males are more reliable than females. No temperament differences were found.

Males seem to be a little more stable in their preferences than females. The factor of introversion-extroversion does not seem to produce differences in reliability.

Not all odors are alike in stability of preference. Some preferences change very little with the subject's age, whereas, for example, the preference for lavender was found to increase greatly from 15 to 18 years of age. Odors which have a sexual significance undergo two changes with age—at adolescence and at the end of the reproductive period.

In general, intelligence is not a factor in odor preference. The one exception was that the more intelligent children at a given age manifest preferences which resemble those of older normal children.

Earlier experience with a given odor seems to play a part in whether it is preferred or not.

To experience separately two odorous substances—for example, one pleasant and the other unpleasant—that are present simultaneously, a shift in attention seems to be necessary so that one is smelled at a time. However, the odor and the unpleasantness evoked are experienced simultaneously.

Recognition of an odor was found to enhance its pleasantness. Strangely enough, Moncrieff concluded that old people tend to become indifferent to odorous substances, even those that are unpleasant or possibly dangerous. He found that a few people were very sensitive to odorous substances. Odors evoked very emotional reactions, sometimes upsetting subjects and sometimes tending to elevate mood.

The rules we have just listed are, of course, only some of the many given by Moncrieff. To learn of the others, the reader is referred to Moncrieff's book.

## TASTE

Studies of taste (as I have defined it) and of gustation have been of the following sorts.

The early studies established four essential classes of taste quality, namely, salty, sweet, sour, and bitter. The next attempt, one that was continued, was to relate these qualities to the chemical composition of the substance tasted. Early in the sequence, one doctrine was that all the complex tastes of food were simply combinations of the four essential qualities. Somewhere along the line, it was agreed that taste experience includes more than these qualities, taking in temperature, mechanical (haptic), sense-of-smell, and even pain effects.

It also became a doctrine, at least in some quarters, that when gustation and olfaction are both involved, the result is experienced as taste, not generally as taste *and* smell.

A few studies were made of temperature effect, both on infants and adults. One type of temperature study was made on soft drinks and it was found that temperature differences had to be great to evoke differences in liquid acceptance by early infants.

Studies were made on infants to determine whether very young subjects were able to distinguish between substances that result in the four taste qualities in adults. Some differences in reaction were found.

Some studies were made to determine the ability of totally anosmic (unable to smell) subjects to distinguish food substances they were not allowed to see. In many cases substances that were quite unlike could not be distinguished.

Studies were made by investigators interested in food processing to determine what leads to maximal acceptance of foods. While these were quite detailed, they did not result in a clear picture of human preferences.

During a great part of this time, studies of the discriminatory activities of gustatory receptors by means of neurophysiological experiments have been going on. Instrumental means have greatly improved over the years, leading to more definitive studies which have brought about an understanding of body mechanisms. These studies have not provided material for our purposes here.

All of these investigations have provided various kinds of textbook information, some of it quite detailed. But my search has uncovered very little of the kind of human-interest material that this book is meant to present.

I have looked for studies that would portray what taste means in the daily life of the human subject. Each of you can say something about your own taste preferences; I had hoped to provide you with more general insights—to tell you something that could be classed as organism- rather than environment-centered. For some reason, I have not found the material. I can imagine that case histories of clinical psychology patients might contain material of this sort.

Taste is determined by a number of factors that we could attribute to learning from specific past experiences and to general attitudes, beliefs and the like. This makes any study from the organism-centered standpoint quite complex, and the drawing of general conclusions rather difficult but, nevertheless, it is not to be avoided.

The fact that gustatory receptors adapt quite noticeably and that all do not adapt at the same rate makes the enjoyment of extended ingestions, such as a meal, quite subtle to analyze. The results of the many scientific studies of the kinds just listed do, however, provide guidelines for the investigations that would result in the kind of insightful description of human behavior we have looked for.

Hollingworth and Poffenberger (1917) wrote a small book on the sense of taste. Much of the book is as worthwhile today as when first written. The authors say that taste is in many ways the most paradoxical of all the senses. Books on esthetics and art have little or nothing to say about it, despite the fact that taste can afford the strongest feelings of pleasure. Though many people "live to eat" and thus to taste, proficiency in compounding tastes and flavors brings the expert neither artistic recognition nor the social eminence achieved by painters and musicians.

Strangely enough when figures of speech are used, "vision" has to do with the seer's intuition, and is removed from sensation. "Touch" expresses intimate and personal reactions such as sympathy, pity and agreement. "Odor" as a figure of speech refers to the undesirable. "Warmth and coldness" refer to affectional states. "Taste" refers to the choice of the appropriate and harmonious. Thus, the word for what many people refer to as one of the lowest senses is used to designate one of the most critical functions of behavior.

# THE AUDITORY PERCEPTUAL SYSTEM

Hearing, like our other senses, is so common that it is taken for granted. Despite its familiarity, many of its aspects are not well known. In this subsection, we are interested in the role hearing plays in the life of the human individual. We are interested in discovering whether hearing can be analyzed in an analogous way to the treatment given the haptic system.

Observation of the haptic system has shown it to be indispensible in producing a well-ordered and balanced personality. It plays a number of roles, one providing for the most fundamental and effective interrelations between people. It is a vehicle for preventing the individual from feeling alone and unwanted. It provides for the fulfillment of basic desires and for essential balance and security.

We can ask whether the auditory system does the same thing for the individual. In observing and studying the haptic system, the consequence of the system's minimal stimulation and use in the development of infant and child, and in the personalities and capacities of adults, was assessed. We will report in the same way on the auditory system.

The atmosphere around us is of such a nature that microvibrations can be set up in it. Some are propagated quite long distances and, when this is the case, it may be said that the organism can respond to distant events, in the same way that it can respond to distant objects by vision. Thus, first of all, the auditory system is a detector of distant events.

By being sensitive to these microvibrations, organisms can detect the existence of the originating sources. They can also detect the direction, distance, movement, and even other things about the originator of the vibrations.

Some of these acoustic sources are other people and the acoustic patterns then form means of communication. Man can discriminate between very subtle differences in the patterns of the propagated acoustic effects and can produce a very large number of patterns himself. These, along with possible brain endowments, have provided for the development of true language although the patterns other animals send and receive are often broadly called language.

In this subsection on the auditory system, three terms will be used. *Acoustic stimuli* will apply to the effective energies reaching the ear. If no effect is produced on behavior or nothing is heard, the more appropriate term is simply *acoustic impingements*. Sounds are what are heard; they are responses, not stimuli; hence, the word *sound* will not be used to indicate the action of an acoustic source.

Sounds have many qualities, some of which can be closely related to the wave patterns of the vibrations that form the acoustic input. But there is much beyond this. Some sounds are heard as speech, which is a kind of higher-order information that other humans convey to the hearer. Another form of sound is music, which produces several kinds of effects. Its rhythms induce muscular activity—swinging and swaying, clapping the hands, and tapping the feet. It seems to require a certain amount of inhibition or training for such results not to occur.

Sound heard as music can symbolize highly abstract cognitive matters and create attitudes and moods. It can function as a kind of language. It can motivate to action or substantiate belief in ways even beyond words.

Many attempts have been made to relate specific forms of music to definite moods. While this can sometimes be done, some of the factors involved in determining response lie behind the immediate occasion and are difficult to deal with.

While a great deal may be said about the role of hearing in the life of the individual, it is not the whole story. The results of absolute *deafness* form another part of the story.

# WHAT HEARING MEANS
susan c. brainerd

The present essay is concerned with hearing as a form of perception (getting meaning from the environment), with the mechanisms that provide hearing, and with the role it plays in human life. This is a huge subject and we can hit only the high spots.

Hearing as it occurs in most people will be dealt with first. It enables several things, namely: (1) localization of acoustic sources (what "makes the sound"), (2) echolocation, which is a means of localizing objects by acoustic reflections from them, (3) identification and information about the nature of the acoustic source, and, finally, (4) human communication. In addition, descriptions of distorted hearing and the psychological isolating effects of deafness will be discussed.

## LOCALIZATION

For the majority of animal forms that have hearing, localization is only two dimensional, i.e., it involves only a horizontal plane (e.g., the direction of an approaching automobile). What lies above or below is not well distinguished. Man takes advantage of his ability to separate acoustic sources through the invention and sale of stereophonic instruments. Many prefer the results over those of monaural recordings. Frequently, animals that are either predators or victims of animals of prey possess movable external ears that provide increased localization ability. Owls have asymmetrical ear canals which provide them with the unique ability to localize efficiently in *three* dimensions (DeReuck, 1968). Since owls hunt while in flight, this unique ability is vital to their survival. In contrast, man's relative inability to localize in three dimensions may be demonstrated by clocking the time required for him to find an airplane in flight. Of course, jet planes can have left the point at which they produced the acoustic waves by the time the waves reach the listener's ear. But the human disability is shown even when planes are flying in line with the direction of sight.

## ECHOLOCATION

Echolocation refers to identification of the presence of objects which produce no sound of their own. The signals consist in echoes reflected from the surfaces of these objects.

Echolocation or auditory navigation is used by sub-humans such as porpoises, birds and rats which need to travel in environments that are not conducive to visual navigation (Riley and Rosenzweig, 1957; Novick, 1959; Kellogg, 1961). Bats also navigate via echolocation (Griffin and Galambos, 1941), producing ultrasonic squeaks (at a frequency near 50,000 Hz) which are reflected from surrounding objects. Based on the time and quality differences of the returning echoes, bats are able to infer the size and position of surrounding objects.

Man also employs the technique of echolocation; his sonar systems are based on identifying underwater objects by bouncing sound waves off them. Likewise, echolocation is used by blind persons (Griffin, 1944) when they are taught to tap a cane as they walk. After extended practice, they can respond appropriately to changes in the reflected sound waves produced by the cane.

Possibly even men who have normal vision use echolocation daily. Solov'ev (1969) conducted an experiment where the subject was required to detect an approaching object without viewing it. He used two groups of subjects (blind subjects and blindfolded subjects who possessed normal vision). He showed that both groups were able to detect the approaching object at equal distances. He concluded that this equality in performance could occur only if the normally sighted subjects also employed echolocation in their daily lives.

## IDENTIFICATION

In addition to localization, auditory perceptions also allow organisms to identify unseen entities. Therefore, organisms can use audition passively to monitor the environment which is

external to their visual field. Audition thus broadens the organism's world.

Information received through the auditory system
allows the organism to identify and therefore react to relevant
unseen environmental occurrences. For example, through his
auditory perceptions man can respond to an infant's crying,
water boiling over on the stove, a ringing telephone, an alarm,
a thunderstorm, a passing parade, a neighbor's argument and
countless other nonvisible occurrences. Moreover, a man frequently identifies malfunctions in machinery merely by the
sou..ds produced by the machine.

Subhumans such as crickets and frogs, who inhabit
environments where visual contact among group members is
impossible, rely on auditory identifications to keep the colony
in contact (Mathews and Knight, 1963). In fact, the continuation
of their species depends upon the ability of the females to identify the location and availability of males through auditory
signals. In these species the call of the male directly reflects his
ability to mate. When the long-horned grasshopper is at his
prime mating potential, his call is strongest (Milne and Milne,
1962). Following a successful mating, however, this grasshopper
loses up to 40 percent of his body weight and his signalling stops.
Signalling returns when he again is physically able to mate.


## COMMUNICATION

Possibly the most important function of audition is that it provides an efficient channel for the exchange of information among
organisms. Auditory signals used by insects to provide relevant
communications among group members were described. Other
animals, including fish and birds, also use differential auditory
signals to communicate distinct messages (Fish, 1956; Milne and
Milne, 1962). The purposes of these communications include
territory proclamations, warnings and mate invitations.

The most complex auditory signal system, however,
has been developed by man. Unlike the languages of subhumans
the human language does not consist merely of a limited number
of differential signals which are appropriate for only a small number of situations. Rather, man's signal system allows him to
develop an endless number of signals for use in countless situations.

In particular instances, all four functions described
above carry a high survival value for man. His life may depend

upon his localization ability when he is on a battlefield; his underwater navigational ability strongly depends upon echolocation. Survival in a fire or storm may depend upon his identification of the auditory warning signal. And, finally, man's ability to function and progress as a human being depends upon his ability to communicate with other men. Distortions in auditory perception are common and carry certain significant consequences.

## AUDITORY RECEPTION

Auditory stimuli are produced by vibrations. These vibrations are propagated through elastic media such as air or water and reach sense receptors in the form of waves of particle disturbance. The sound waves impinge upon auditory receptors and result in auditory perceptions, provided they are within the organism's threshold levels for intensity and frequency reception.

The auditory system of most vertebrates, including man, is composed of three ears. The dynamics of auditory perception for these vertebrates are as follows (see Zemlin, 1968): Sound waves are gathered by the *outer* ear and funneled into the ear canal where they impinge upon the eardrum. At the eardrum the acoustic energy is transduced into mechanical energy. This mechanical energy is transported across the *middle* ear via three bones (the ossicular chain). At the window separating the middle ear from the inner ear the mechanical energy is transduced into hydraulic energy. This hydraulic energy travels through the fluid systems of the *inner* ear and is transduced into electrical energy at the hair cells of the true end organ of hearing (the Organ of Corti). The nervous impulses then travel by way of the eighth cranial nerve to the temporal lobe of the cerebral cortex. At this point the impulses are interpreted subjectively.

## PERCEPTIONS FROM
## PATHOLOGICAL OR
## MALFUNCTIONING RECEPTORS

The functions of location, echolocation, identification and communication can be executed adequately only by normal auditory mediation. If there is malfunction or pathology in an individual's auditory sense organ, the neural signals it sends to the cortex are distorted. This distorted signal may result in greatly misunderstanding the *acoustic* signal. Therefore, the ability of the system to fulfill its normal functions becomes limited.

The characteristics of the peceptual outcome mediated by a pathological or malfunctioning auditory system are correlated directly with the location of the involvement in the system. The components of the auditory system can be divided into two categories on the basis of their functions. The outer and middle ears function merely to conduct the sound stimuli to the inner ear (or cochlea). The inner ear and central auditory pathway, however, function to analyze the incoming signal. Therefore, from a knowledge of the locus of involvement, the types of perceptual distortion an individual experiences can be predicted. Likewise from a description of the distorted perceptions an individual experiences, the locus of involvement can be identified.

Auditory distortions arising from malfunctioning or pathological receptors normally involve either loudness and/or pitch.

*A perceptual distortion in loudness* may result from a malfunction or lesion located anywhere in the auditory system. The effect of a distortion in loudness is that the individual perceives sounds as being either softer or louder than the same sounds perceived by persons with normal auditory systems. The degree and direction of loudness distortion depends upon the location of the involvement in the auditory system.

Malfunctions involving the conducting mechanism of the auditory system produce loudness distortions which are well defined. Individuals who have conductive hearing impairments perceive sounds only as being softer than the same sounds perceived by persons with normal auditory receptors. The average conductive impairment is quite marked.

Malfunctions involving the analyzing mechanism of the auditory system produce impairments referred to as sensorineural hearing losses. The result of any sensorineural hearing impairment is an increase in the threshold of reception for auditory stimuli. Therefore, in order for a sound to be heard at threshold level, it needs to be presented at a higher intensity level than normal. Any degree of loudness distortion may accompany the perceptions experienced by the individual with a sensorineural hearing impairment.

Individuals with cochlear pathology, moreover, experience a unique type of loudness distortion referred to as *recruitment*. Recruitment involves an abnormally fast growth of loudness when an individual is presented stimuli of increasing intensity. The person with recruitment, therefore, can tolerate only a reduced range of auditory intensities. In some instances the recruitment may be so severe that the individual experiences pain when exposed to acoustic stimuli of moderate intensity.

*A perceptual distortion in pitch* also may result from a malfunction or lesion anywhere in the auditory system. Moreover, the relative degree of loss at each frequency is dependent upon the location of the involvement in the auditory system. Pitch distortion affects identification and communication most noticeably.

Conductive malfunctions produce a minimum of pitch distortion. The conductive impairment is characterized either by an equal loss of hearing at each frequency or a slightly greater loss of hearing in the low than in the high frequencies. Normally, the relative loss across frequencies due to a conductive impairment is not large enough to affect either the identification or communication functions of audition, provided the individual is presented with a sufficiently intense auditory stimulus.

A significant amount of pitch distortion results from sensorineural impairment. That is, the relative difference in thresholds for varying frequencies is large. Normally in a sensorineural hearing loss, the thresholds for low-frequency sounds are much better than those for high-frequency sounds. Thus one of the frequent results is that although the individual can perceive the presence of speech he cannot understand or interpret it. The English language is made up of approximately forty phonemes—individual speech sounds. Each of these phonemes is produced by a unique complex wave set. The formants of energy for each phoneme vary in their location along the audible spectrum of frequencies. For example, energy for the sounds "m," "d," and "b" is found mainly in the region below 400 Hz; while energy for the "s" or "th (thigh)" is found above 3,000 Hz. In relation to speech reception, this means that a man without hearing above 3,000 Hz will be unable to discriminate between the words "sin" and "thin" and, in fact, he will probably respond as if the speaker had said "in."

The amount of difficulty an individual has in understanding speech is related directly to the amount of hearing loss he has for each frequency contained in the speech signal. When a person has an inner-ear pathology, his discrimination ability is predictable from his thresholds for pure tones. On the other hand, if the hearing loss is due to a lesion in the central pathways or to neural degeneration (frequently a contributing cause of presbycusis, hearing loss that accompanies the aging process), the individual's discrimination ability will not be predictable from his relative thresholds for pure tones. Rather, the individual with a central lesion will have more difficulty understanding speech than would be predicted from a consideration of his pure tone thresholds.

Another perceptual characteristic associated with a cochlear pathology is referred to as *diplacusis*. A person with diplacusis perceives the presence of two distinct tones of different pitches even when a single frequency is presented to both ears. Music which is pleasant to a normal-hearing individual sounds discordant to the person with diplacusis because the music contains inappropriate tones.

Under normal conditions, *conductive hearing impairments are not permanent losses*. In some pathologies, normalcy will return spontaneously. A good example of a temporary hearing impairment is the loss that occurs when the Eustachian tube is blocked by congestion. When the congestion problem is remedied, the Eustachian tube opens and the middle ear regains its normal pressure. When the middle ear pressure returns to normal, the thresholds for auditory stimuli also return to normal. In various other pathologies recovery will not be spontaneous but will require medical attention. Abnormalities in hearing associated with conductive malfunction are potentially removable.

On the other hand, sensorineural hearing losses normally produce permanent impairments of auditory sensitivity. In a select number of instances, however, recovery of normal auditory functioning, and likewise of normal auditory perceptions, may be seen. Temporary sensorineural hearing impairments are associated with both noise exposure and excessive aspirin consumption. Unfortunately the relationship between temporary threshold shifts and permanent hearing impairment is not well defined yet.

The hearing impairment that accompanies either Meniere's Disease or syphilis mediates a unique sensory experience for the afflicted person. The thresholds of hearing fluctuate significantly in the early stages of both diseases. They will vary spontaneously from normal hearing levels to moderate or severe hearing-loss levels. In the final stages of both diseases, however, the auditory thresholds stabilize, leaving the individual with a permanent sensorineural hearing impairment. In many cases the individual completely loses all auditory sensitivity.

## DEAFNESS

Deafness, the total loss of auditory functioning, has profound effects on the life of the individual. It isolates him from a very important avenue of information about the world around him. Even when not deaf, the human cannot make use of certain ranges of vibrations that are employable by certain other animal forms.

Man's hearing normally lies within a range of frequencies from 20 Hz to 20,000 Hz. Many sybhumans, on the other hand, such as rodents, birds and marine animals rely on ultrasonic auditory signals. Mice, for example, produce and respond to frequencies up to 100,000 Hz (Ralls, 1967). Their area of greatest sensitivity is from 60,000 Hz to 90,000 Hz, compared to man's area of greatest sensitivity at 3,000 Hz. In effect, normal-hearing man is deaf to the communications of many animal species.

Although the deaf individual cannot hear, it does not mean that he cannot make use of what others try to convey to him by speech, or of acoustic vibrations. He has certain compensatory possibilities.

Whereas the auditory system of the deaf is of no use to him, he can make use of graphic representation of acoustic echoes. He can thus see what otherwise would produce something heard.

The deaf can learn to make tactual use of acoustic impingements.

Here, two results of deafness are to be considered: the compensatory actions taken by other sensory systems in terms of the normal functions of auditon; and, the isolating effects of deafness.

It is not possible for an individual who is deaf to identify the presence of sounds through auditory interpretations of reflected sound waves. The deaf individual can, however, make use of manmade sonar systems which provide a visual graphic representation of the echo. In this way the deaf individual can use vision to compensate for auditory dysfunctioning.

The tactual sensory system, like the auditory, is sensitive to vibrations. The special circumstances required are that the vibrations either be of an extremely high intensity (such as the pressure wave following a bomb explosion) or propagated through a more efficient medium than air (such as wood). For example, an individual who is deaf may learn to identify the location of an object dropped on a wooden floor on which he is standing via tactual perceptions. However, for most purposes the individual who is deaf is unable to localize sound sources efficiently.

Tactual awareness has classically been utilized in order to help the deaf feel vibrations from unseen entities. For example, the rhythm of music can be experienced efficiently by individuals who are deaf through the tactual sense. The most effective manner of transferring these vibrations is to have the rhythm played on a piano that sits on a wooden floor upon which the deaf individual is standing.

Current researchers are investigating the possibility of having speech identified through tactual experiences (Pickett, 1963). Subjects are being trained to associate different vibratory frequencies perceived tactually with the corresponding acoustic phoneme.

The major effect upon communication depends upon the time of onset of deafness. Individuals who develop speech before losing their hearing have less of a handicap than do the congenitally deaf. The text of this presentation is concerned with the majority of the congenitally deaf.

The processes a human infant employs in order to develop the human language are not well understood. There are a number of theories as to how language develops. However, all of the current theories recognize the importance of the child's perception of the spoken language of his culture. For example, the behaviorists suggest that language itself is produced through parental shaping of infant vocalizations (Skinner, 1957). The psycholinguists also suggest that although the rules for language may be innate, the child needs to perceive the speech of his parents in order to determine which grammatical structures are appropriate (Smith and Miller, 1966).

The child who is congenitally deaf, however, is unaware that a verbal language system even exists. He needs to learn that the facial gestures and accompanying laryngeal vibrations made by those around him have meaning. Until the child can recognize a need for the verbal system, he will not be motivated to develop the compensatory activities required in order for him to learn verbal language.

Provided that the child can be motivated to learn a spoken language, he is trained to receive speech mainly through use of his visual system. The printed word serves as the most effective symbol for representing a concept to the deaf child. In certain circumstances the verbal symbols for the concept may be recognizable on the lips of a speaker. However, since only about one-third of the phonemes of English are visible when produced, lip-reading does not provide a very efficient avenue for speech reception.

The child who is deaf is able to develop a sizeable receptive vocabulary. This vocabulary is developed through repeated pairing of the object of concern, its printed symbol and the spoken symbol. The inherent flaw in learning language in this fashion is that generally only the verbal symbols for concrete objects or actions are well understood. Therefore, the receptive vocabulary of the deaf child tends to consist mainly of nouns and verbs—those words which represent visible objects and actions (Brannon, 1968).

A vocabulary that consists mainly of concrete representations is normally not sufficient to understand thoroughly what people talk about. Due to his language deficiency, the deaf child is frequently unable to understand abstract concepts which hearing persons learn through language mediation. Likewise, his lack of linguistic experience prevents him from understanding complex grammars (Goda, 1964). In addition, the child who is deaf cannot understand words which have auditory connotations, or, in other words, refer to hearing as such.

Solov'ev (1969) reported on the responses given by deaf children when they were asked to identify the sounds made by objects. Solov'ev indicated that the object made no noise. Examples of these answers included the following: "A brook does not make a noise which is either loud or soft. Snow does not shout and does not make a noise. Paper does not make a noise and does not ring; it is soft."

Solov'ev also reported that when the children did identify a sound their answers were generally erroneous. Examples of the answers given when asked what sounds inanimate objects make include: "A brook hums or knocks. Thunder shouts. The sea crackles. A saw shouts or chatters. Grass crackles, makes noise, or murmurs." Examples of the answers given when asked what sounds animate objects make include: "A fly shouts. A beetle sings or howls. A crow howls. A dog shouts."

Solov'ev suggests that the answers given by the deaf children reflect erroneous generalizations. He indicated that, based on these misunderstandings, it would be very difficult for the deaf child to understand much of what he reads. How these erroneous generalizations would naturally affect his thinking process is unknown.


## EXPRESSIVE LANGUAGE DEVELOPMENT

The individual who is deaf can learn to speak by using his kinesthetic and tactual sensory systems as compensatory systems. Early training in tactual awareness focuses on developing the concept of causation of vibrations. The child is taught that vibrations are caused by mechanically activated systems. He is shown that when the mixer is mixing, he can feel its vibration—likewise with the washer, dryer, automobile and countless other entities. Through this continued association, the child eventually understands that when he feels vibrations from a person's throat they also are activating some system. Hopefully, he then learns that he has the ability to produce the same vibrations with his vocal cords.

Once the deaf child produces a correct sound, he needs some feedback system to allow him to repeat the production. Whereas hearing individuals auditorily monitor their speech, individuals who are deaf need to rely on kinesthetic feedback. The deaf child needs to learn what it feels like when his tongue and other articulators are in the proper position to produce a particular phoneme. He needs to learn the feel of the proper tension in his vocal tract for producing speech which is appropriate in pitch and quality to his age and sex. Likewise, he needs to learn the proper muscle tension in the thoracic region for monitoring the loudness of his speech.

Needless to say, only the most persistent among the deaf are able to master expressive and receptive oral language to any degree of proficiency. Most individuals who are congenitally deaf learn to read and write at a minimum level of complexity. The major part of their communication takes place by a manual method of communication, either signing or fingerspelling. The manual method of signing consists of a group of specific actions which are made with the hands. Each sign represents a different concept. The signs are combined into a language system which is not a copy of the spoken language of the culture (Tervoort, 1961). The manual method of fingerspelling, however, is merely an orthographic form of the spoken language of the culture. That is, the finger positions used in fingerspelling are associated with the alphabetical letters of the language. Use of manual communication is one factor that helps isolate the deaf individual from the rest of society. This and other factors involved in isolating the deaf are considered below.

## ISOLATION

When an individual is deprived of auditory functioning, his *experiential world is narrowed*. His social contact with hearing individuals, moreover, becomes extremely restricted or non-existent.

A deaf individual is in contact only with that part of the environment he can see or feel. This reduces his ability to react to changes in the environment that are relevant to him. The consequences of this disability are most significant when the unseen occurrences take the form of auditory warning signals. For example, the deaf individual cannot take cover in response to the tornado siren, nor can he evacuate a building in response to the fire alarm.

The deaf individual needs to monitor his environment through an *active* visual process. For hearing individuals environmental monitoring is a *passive* process. These differences in monitoring systems can be illustrated through the following comparison. A hearing mother proceeds with her daily chores while her children are sleeping or playing since she is confident that she can respond to their needs any time they cry out. On the other hand, the deaf mother must repeatedly watch her children in order to respond adequately to their needs.

Deafness also prevents the individual from completely understanding many of the environmental occurrences he witnesses. It prevents the individual from knowing the cause of the occurrence. For example, assume an individual observes a group of people running down a street toward him. If the individual is deaf, he may hypothesize a number of reasons for their behavior. One of his hypotheses may include the possibility that the group is pursuing him. If, however, the observer is a hearing person, he also hears the explosion behind him and the observation would pose no uncertainty at all.

## DEAFNESS GREATLY AFFECTS SOCIALIZATION

Only during the preschool years when language is not important may the average deaf child develop satisfactory social relations with hearing individuals. As the child grows older, however, he becomes different from the normal hearing child. He fails to develop language spontaneously and, therefore, he also fails to learn the rules of socialization.

The segregation between deaf and hearing individuals increases if the deaf individual attends a residential school for the deaf. In this environment the deaf child will meet other children like himself. He will learn that through manual methods of communication he can efficiently interact with his deaf peers. The need to communicate with the hearing world may disappear almost completely. The deaf individual may even become bitter toward the instructors who insist that he learn a system of language which is almost impossible for him to acquire.

The majority of deaf adults live in subcultures within the hearing society. This physical separation increases the misunderstanding between the two groups. Moreover, since most deaf adults cannot communicate efficiently via the spoken language and since most hearing individuals do not know a manual form of communication, the segregation flourishes.

Hearing individuals do not understand deafness. Because it is not a visible handicap such as paralysis they may even tend to fear the abnormality. Frequently hearing individuals assume that all deaf persons must necessarily be mentally retarded, but this has been shown not to be so (Furth, 1966). Hearing persons are hesitant even to employ an individual with whom they cannot easily communicate.

Likewise, deaf individuals do not understand the actions of normal hearing individuals. Due to their verbal language deficiency the deaf adults frequently are unable to comprehend the rules of society, such as taxation. Many deaf adults believe at first that their employer is cheating them when he retains part of their salary. Likewise, they frequently don't understand why the clerk charges them more money than is listed on the price tag. Misinterpreted interactions such as these reinforce the deaf individual's choice to remain separate from most of the hearing society.

The nature of deafness itself forces these individuals to be isolated from the social activities occurring around the world. Hearing individuals receive news broadcasts over television or radio. The deaf individual, however, cannot make use of these informational sources. In many instances, the deaf individual cannot even benefit from newspapers or magazines because of his verbal language deficiency. Contrary to common belief most deaf individuals are not able to read and write normally. The average deaf individual of age 10.5 to 11.5 reads at a 2.7 grade level, whereas the average deaf individual of 15.5 to 16.5 reads at a 3.0+ grade level (Wrightstone, Aranow and Muskowitz, 1963).

A major result of deafness, therefore, is that the individual exists in an environment foreign to the one inhabited by hearing individuals. The adult individuals from the two environments do not appear to be socially compatible.

# THE CONTEMPORARY
# ACOUSTIC ENVIRONMENT

There are similarities and differences between the overall patterns
of the visual and auditory environments. Very often it is the
similarities in the two that are described. In the present article
we wish to discuss a marked difference and the consequences that
stem from it. In the photic environment "light" reaches the eye
from all directions. There is an angular limit over which the eye
is able to receive photic radiation while in one position, but with
the motions of the eye, head and body, we see an environment
fully illuminated from all directions. We so thoroughly expect
this that we would be horribly startled if we looked out the window and saw part of the sky its usual bright color and just next
to the lighted part a pitch-black section or, let's say, "nothing."
Thus, the visual world, though made up of very complex patterns
of "light and shade," is essentially a continuous domain of illumination.

The acoustic world is generally somewhat different.
It is not an environment completely filled with stimuli, although
it can be and sometimes is practically that.

In vision we have for our puposes a universal source,
an astronomical source of *photic* radiation, our sun, but we do
not have for our senses a similar universal source of *acoustic*
radiation. The stimuli for sound are much more local. The usual
net effect is that we hear sounds coming from localized sources
in specific restricted directions. In between these specific directions we may hear nothing originating. The gaps do not disturb
us. In fact, we feel better than when strong sound comes from a
great many directions. Vision is a space sense and we are depend-
end upon it for appreciating the overall pattern and the details
of our three-dimensional environment, but hearing is a localizing
sense. It tells us where *specific* things are in this visual three-dimensional space rather than giving us a filled-in area effect such
as we obtain in vision.

Visual and auditory stimuli can both be reflected.

Not all photic and acoustic radiations come to our sense organs directly from the original sources we have just described. The reflection in acoustics is called reverberation. Orderly reverberations are experienced as echoes, but these are only one kind.

Present-day man lives in an environment of physical constellations which he senses as *surfaces*. Surfaces reflect both photic radiation and acoustic energy.

A great deal of effort is made to minimize reverberations. Many public rooms and other spaces are surfaced by acoustic absorbing materials—acoustic tile in the ceilings (and sometimes walls), drapes, and carpeted floors.

Reverberation, of course, depends mainly on the nature of the walls of an enclosure (room), but its magnitude is governed also by the energy of the acoustic source. Of course, small enclosures differ from large ones in the energy of the reverberation reaching the ear. Some reverberation is recognized as such by the listener and if the enclosure is large enough, he hears it as an echo. Thus primitive man may have heard canyon echoes but was not the recipient of the kind of reverberation we shall discuss here.

Because you now live in enclosures (buildings) and because artificial acoustic sources have become so potent, a new pattern of acoustic input, which we shall call *encompassing*, pervades today's living. Via reverberation acoustic waves are reaching the ears from all directions (barring the "sound shadow" made by the head). The question is how does the auditory system handle this kind of an input and does it produce a fuller spatial quality to hearing than an environment in which acoustic waves reach the ear from narrowly restricted directions? Or, does this sort of an environment present an input unfavorable for the listener?

Many environments produce only small amounts of reverberation. In fact, those providing small amounts aid the listener to perceive the distance of acoustic sources.

Let us consider what happens in a room. In Figure 12 it can be seen that an acoustic source sends vibrations to the ear in two ways. Some of the vibrations reach the ear directly as indicated by the solid line from S to E. Other vibrations given off in other directions reach walls, floor and ceiling before reaching the ear (E). We say they are reflected off these surfaces. The nearer the acoustic (sound) source is to the ear, the greater the proportion of the total acoustic energy that will reach the ear directly. As the acoustic source is varied in distance, the listener

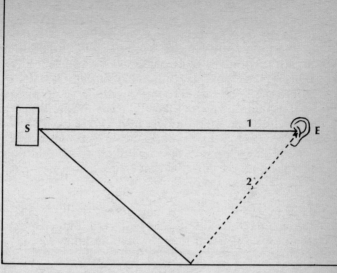

Figure 12/ Acoustic energy ("sound waves") reaching the ear in two ways—directly as shown in line 1, and indirectly by reflection (reverberation) from walls, floors, and ceiling as shown in dotted line 2.

hears the variation in the ratio of direct-to-reverberated energy reaching him. As a net result, the listener who does not even see the acoustic source perceives a sound originating from a specific distance. If the listener is put into an *anechoic chamber*, a room from which reverberation is eliminated, the result will be different.

An anechoic chamber is shown in Figure 13. The walls, ceiling and floor are made of wedges the apexes of which jut out into the room. The wedge material absorbs acoustic vibrations, but those that may not be fully absorbed when they first strike are bounced back and forth from the wedge surfaces till absorbed rather than being sent back into the room.

The working floor of the anechoic room is a wire grid for supporting the workers and their equipment above the floor wedges.

When a blindfolded listener is asked to pay attention to a sound, he will report that it remains stationary even when the acoustic source is being moved farther away. He does however experience the sound growing weaker. Hence, without the reverberatory component in the ear's acoustic input, the reduction in the energy reaching it (because of greater distance of the source) will be heard as reduction in loudness. In showing what happens in the absence of reverberation we have a good demonstration of its role in the usual situations.

A very definite effect is produced in a room with "acoustically treated" walls, ceiling and carpeted floors. For example, if you are in such a room in a building that faces a traffic-laden street, you can hear the traffic when the windows are open, but as if it were out on the street. The sound is not bothersome at all. People talking to you in the room can be heard very well. Were the surfaces of the room not made of acoustic tile and the floor not carpeted, the traffic noise would be bothersome and you would not be able to hear the other people in the room too well.

What is the basis for the difference? In the acoustically treated room, reverberations are not permitted to occur. The acoustic energy that reaches your ears directly from the outside sources is almost all that you receive and thus the input is

Figure 13/ An anechoic chamber. Such chambers or rooms can be quite large. This one is shown looking outward to the man at the entrance. Note the wire-mesh floor. The wedges which line the whole chamber absorb the acoustic energy reaching them. (Courtesy of Industrial Acoustics Co., Bronx, New York.)

"clean" and specific. The acoustic input thus is not largely determined by the reverberations in the room. As far as the street input is concerned, the room more or less doesn't exist acoustically.

In the untreated room the incoming energy is reverberated ("bounced") off the walls and thus the usual pattern produced by an enclosure is added to what reaches your ears directly. This enclosure pattern of stimulation is one that produces the perception of sound sources near at hand; hence, the outside (street) noises seem to be nearer and they intrude. With this eliminated, the traffic noises are heard as occurring out on the street where they belong.

We come now to the *intensive* factor in acoustical input and the sources we are still discussing are those within enclosures where, naturally, there is generally some reverberation.

As the intensity is raised at the source, both the energy reaching the ear directly and the energy in the reverberations are increased. Whereas with low-intensity levels of acoustic output, the amount of reverberation may be little enough to be negligible, with increased intensity the reverberation may begin to count. The levels of tolerance for these two inputs to the ear need not go hand in hand. For example, if there were no reverberation, one might accept a high sound level without too much annoyance. But because reverberation is raised along with the energy of the stimulus, one may come to the limit of tolerance for reverberation before reaching the other limit.

When listening to a radio program, one often finds the volume control setting to be crucial. There is a setting above which the sound is too "loud," and below which it is still appropriate for a quiet range; below that it is too low. Possibly the settings that are experienced as too high begin to produce too much reverberation as well as too much *direct* stimulation. Below these levels, the acoustic input arriving directly from the instrument itself is far above the effective level of the reverberatory component which reaches the ear at the same time. Hence it functions as more nearly the exclusive acoustic source. The input pattern is pleasing and acceptable. When the crucial level is exceeded, aversion of one form or another sets in and the input becomes noxious. Beecher (1959) has pointed out that people respond to noxious stimuli in several ways: (1) by skeletal muscle responses, (2) through reactions mediated by the autonomic nervous system, and (3) by processes in the central nervous system.

We have already described the nature of the reverberatory input to the ear as one coming from all directions, producing an impression of *encompassment*. What one hears "comes at" him from all directions; its effect is confusing and, for some, overwhelming.

While possibly this sort of input may be used by some people, at some level or another it produces annoyance.

The level at which one wishes to set the volume control on a phonograph or radio depends upon a number of factors. Some of these pertain to one's activity and mood at the time, as well as to the factors just mentioned.

It is generally only when we actively respond with body movements that encompassment is tolerable. It is useful to understand the factors just described.

There are a number of reasons why some young people tolerate or even enjoy the acoustic conditions just described as unpleasant, obnoxious or intolerable to others. No doubt all of the reasons are not known. Several of the reasons, however, can be mentioned: (1) Very often the intense acoustic environment involves what is music to them. When enjoyable music is heard, even much older persons can stand or even want it to be intense. (2) The acoustic stimuli that you actively respond to can be far more intense before becoming annoying. (3) Much more of young people's lives are lived in an active fashion and this calls for the intensity we have just been describing.

No behavior of the young that I know of belies what I have described regarding the effects of reverberation and encompassment.

An example of encompassment and the elimination of the visual factor in listening to sound is given in the following description.


## THE AUDIUM

In a studio in San Francisco there is a room called The Audium, in which there are sixty-one loudspeakers distributed on all sides and above and below the people who can assemble to listen to a demonstration (see Strand, 1970). This takes place in the dark and from every direction one can hear clicks, swooshes, gurgles, spatters, voices, running water, running engines, and sounds that are electronically produced and called music by some people.

The Audium is regarded in various ways by different groups. Its producers were musicians, and it would seem that they sought this means to expand and intensify the effects of sound experiences.

Some visitors to The Audium might see the demonstrations as simply thrill producers, for unquestionably the effects are potent. There are still other interpretations of the endeavor. But one of my purposes in mentioning The Audium is to illustrate sound encompassment. Acoustic sources are located all around him and thus the listener is made to hear sound coming to him from all directions. The encompassment discussed earlier involved *reverberation* from many or all directions. Here the actual original sources are distributed in all directions.

In encompassing reverberation there is no articulation in the sound and no distinctions to be attributed to different sources. In The Audium there is potentially the possibility of articulation—i.e., one kind of sound coming from one direction and another from a different direction. It is more like what the conductor or a player in an orchestra would get in hearing different instrumental sounds from different directions. The audience receives much less of that effect.

The second reason for mentioning The Audium is that the demonstration is given in the dark. The absence of visual stimulation changes the effect of acoustic input.

This brings us back to a situation familiar to all of us—listening to an orchestral number, either produced at the time by a live orchestra or heard on records or via radio or television.

Obviously, this is a stimulus situation that can be manipulated so that certain components are omitted or added. In listening to a record, you can keep eyes open and allow the appearance of the room to be a part of your awareness at the time, or you can close your eyes. You can even lessen your level of haptic input (feedback from muscular tension) by lying on the divan with eyes closed.

On the other hand, you can go to a concert and hear the same number rendered by a live orchestra. When you do, you are bombarded with various other stimuli. You see the people; you watch the players in the orchestra. You follow the behavior of the conductor—all in addition to hearing. Thus it is apparent that the sensory input can be highly varied and can involve several sense modalities instead of the supposed single modality of audition.

The listening also involves a personal orientation which we may describe in terms of likes and dislikes. For example, some people greatly enjoy going to the music hall (or auditorium) to see and be seen. They like to be a part of a social gathering and this has enough value in itself for them to prefer to hear the music in such a setting. Other people don't care a great deal for such gatherings. Hence hearing music there has no advantage. When two people take opposing stands on the conditions under which the music seems best, this factor may unwittingly be the one that determines the preference. If so, the one person may be giving his answer on the basis of a broad preference not limited to what is heard and including factors that are not strictly auditory. The other person might be reporting on how music itself sounds.

One of the best ways of getting at the issue is to listen to a musical number first with eyes open, and then with eyes closed—in both cases attempting to concentrate on the music and disregarding other things. For some people, the music heard with eyes closed is richer, fuller in tone and melody, if not more significant in its temporal characteristics such as beat, accent, etc. Some people can alternately open and close their eyes in a slow sequence and have the quality of the music change back and forth accordingly.

We can take the usual listening to music to be an example of a figure-ground situation. Awareness of what is *figure* is qualitatively different from what happens to be *ground*. Most textbook examples of figure-ground lie within a single sense modality as, for example, in *vision* alone. But the figure-ground principle also operates when two or more modalities are involved. In the situation above we have a description of how these senses are related to each other in the overall experience or response at the moment. In some cases what is visual is figure and other senses are involved in the ground. Or, what is auditory may be the figure. It would seem that this is illustrated in listening to an orchestral number.

Now, back to The Audium and other examples. Another of its features as a producer of sensory input is the acoustics it generates. The intensity of the energy reaching the ear is enormous and this is a considerable factor in emotionally moving people. A very common example of this can be found in visits to steel mills and other places where the acoustic stimulation is intense.

This same potency is inherent in the acoustic output

of many big engines or let's say, "noisy ones" such as sports cars. From the experiential standpoint, noise is power. Noise of this sort is a good example of the causality principle that is dealt with in the subsection on vision.

Another example occurs when watching a crack express train pull into the station. Unfortunately, this experience is becoming very rare, but older readers will feel it to be a good example. The rumble of the heavy engines, the sound of the cars, and the exhaust of the airbrakes (and, of course, the sights along with it all) make it an emotionally moving experience, a thrill that may actually bring tears to the eyes of a railroad buff.

## PROS AND CONS OF NOISE

A number of things that are being done about noise these days are of interest and significance in this chapter on audition.

Noise has intruded unwanted into a great many situations in our everyday life. The power devices that have been put on the market all seem to involve the production of considerable noise. Motorcycles, sports cars, lawnmowers, snowplows are good examples. As a consequence, various groups of people wish to do something about it.

It has been assumed by some that it would be desirable to reduce or eliminate the noise produced by typewriters. As a step in this direction, Sperry-Rand has produced a very quiet model of their Remington typewriter. It must have taken considerable ingenuity and involved some expense to do this. It is reported, however, that secretaries and stenographers do not like the machines. At least, they complain that the machines are stiff and slow. The makers say this is not so. This complaint must have been quite a surprise and disappointment to the manufacturer. As a consequence of the complaint, he is engineering noise production back into his typewriter.

In another essay (on visual perception) we deal with what is termed *causality*. In the examples various items such as blocks are seen to move and come into contact with others, at which instant the others move. The impression given the viewer is that the first items *cause* the second item to move. If at the instant that the two items come into apparent contact, the viewer hears a click or other abrupt sound, the impression of causality is intensified, i.e., made even more convincing.

In the case of the typewriter that is almost noiseless, it can now be understood that the typist is being deprived of the full action of the auditory sense to enhance the impression that she is doing something. Most typewriters produce rather abrupt

A drip-dry shirt will wake him up!

and sharp sounds which are natural signs of quick action. What we are saying then is that the auditory component is a natural aid to giving the impression of something happening (causation), and the very fact that the sounds are clicks is a further advantage for the impression of quickness and speed of the action. The problem then is how loud must the sound be to become annoying to the typist.

A new problem enters when several typewriters are being used simultaneously. The noise heard from the other typewriters doesn't function for the typist the same way that her own does. She does not perceive herself as causing the other noises, so they are irrelevant, out of her control and may be bothersome. But, generally, she apparently learns to pay minimal attention to them.

NOISE AND SLEEP

Supposedly there are people who cannot sleep amid too much quiet. It is not certain that this is a common happening. Be that as it may, a certain company has marketed a device to help such people. It is said to produce a sound like breeze in trees. There is still another product, namely, a phonograph record which, when one side is played, produces the sound of the ocean surf. The other side produces tropical bird noises.

Perhaps it is not so much the acoustic production

itself as the monotony that is effective. Going to sleep is partially based on what the would-be sleeper *does* or doesn't do when he intends to go to sleep. In monotony, not boredom, the individual may relax into sleep.


## WHITE NOISE

In a later essay we talk about some of the effects of "white noise." White noise is what is heard when the acoustic source produces a wide variety of vibration frequencies heard more or less as a hissing sound. Devices that produce white noise are now being made for the purpose of "masking" intermittent sounds. Some individuals, for example, those who have tinnitis (ringing in the ears), simply turn their radios fairly low to eliminate hearing the ringing. They need to hear, if anything, something that they localize outside their own heads.


## NOISE AND STUDY

I have incidentally asked students to tell me why they like radios playing while they study. Many older people are puzzled by it. One answer is that it is an ongoing sound which eliminates incidental transient sounds. Whether this is the actual reason is difficult to determine. The use of noise here may bring out a difference between people of low and high thresholds for irritation. Possibly the same individuals, when they are ill or even merely have a headache, do not want the so-called constant sound of the radio because under these circumstances they are more sensitive to it. There are those individuals who are plagued by conditions such as allergies to pollen, dust and molds who are in a more or less constant state of irritation from stuffy noses or smarting eyes. These individuals could be expected to belong to the group that does not like radio. They would prefer conditions which do not raise their level of excitation.


## AN AUDIO SIGNAL IN CAR OPERATION

Noise can be used as a signal. Sometimes this is recognized as a possibility and is utilized; sometimes, not. Actually, what we have just said about noisy and quiet typewriters is apparently a case in which noise is a signal to the typist she is working effectively.

A good example has appeared recently in connection with the device that activates the turn signals in an automobile. It is the electrical component that makes the turn lights act intermittently ("flash"). It makes a noticeable clicking noise as it closes and opens the circuit to make the lights flash. This click is easily heard by the driver above all other incidental noises around him. As a consequence, he naturally relies on it to tell him that the flashing turn signals are working. The driver thus has two ways of knowing about the signals—the visual green intermittent light on the dashboard, and the click. The click informs him without his having to glance away from watching traffic. Recently, some of the new electrical switches have been made quiet. Whether this was intentional or incidental is not certain. Be that as it may, it has been a step backwards as far as the driver's operation of the car is concerned. He now has to reassure himself by looking at the dash-signal to see if his directional signals are working, and this reduces the safety factors in operating the car. It involves learning a new habit. The same principle works here as in the case of the typewriter. The audio signal is a causality enhancer. It is an informer (feedback) as well. When the signal makes a sound, it is more convincingly real than when it is perfectly quiet.

In the examples just given the role played by certain kinds of supposedly incident noise was discussed. It has generally been supposed that any noise we do not produce on purpose has no useful role in everyday affairs. The typewriter example showed that this is not always so.

We would be badly distorting the general discussion if we were not to emphasize that much noise (many intense incidental sounds) is detrimental. Bierrien (1946) and others have studied the effects of noise, particularly in work situations. Under many of the conditions studied it slowed work and produced fatigue.

## WE OFTEN HEAR BETTER
## AS WE BECOME INVOLVED

The following is a phenomenon that one does not read about in the usual textbook. It is a shift in the quality of what is heard as time passes. Since it has not been studied as far as I know, it is difficult to tell to what to attribute this. The phenomenon shows up quite well at times when listening to a speaker. The result we refer to here may thus stem from a change in the speaker's articulation or other speech quality. It may simply lie in a change in the hearer. It may be both.

One morning I showed up in a conference room in a new building to take part in a Guidance Committee discussion of a proposal for a doctoral dissertation. I had never been in this room before and, as usual, was quite curious and observant of its acoustic qualities. It was a room 16 by 25 feet. The ceiling was of acoustical tile and the walls were of plaster on a non-lath base. The room was supplied with one tall narrow window and the entrance door. Otherwise, the walls were unbroken, smooth, bare surfaces. Visually, the room was rather empty, although the color of the furniture and walls was relatively rich and fairly pleasing.

For some reason, I didn't think the acoustics were very good. I seemed to hear a slight reverberation and the speech of the four other people was not as intelligible as I would like.

I became absorbed in the topics of discussion and when, in about an hour and a half, the business of the meeting was completed, I took occasion to remark about the room's acoustics or, one might say, to report upon my auditory perceptions.

They were as follows. After I had been in the room for almost the whole period of the discussions, I became aware of my hearing being a great deal different. I could now hear distinctly every word that was being said. The experience of the room being "noisy" or reverberatory was gone. It was now quiet and the words came to me out of this quiet background. It was a very different room, so different that it was hard to believe and for this reason I was impelled to say something about it, particularly since the phenomenon showed up while I was among those interested in and knowledgeable about acoustics and hearing. The meeting was in the Department of Audiology and Speech Science. My observations provoked some interest and discussion, but no pat answers came out of it.

This phenomenon can hardly be considered rare in every way. The setting simply turned out to be a very suitable one inasmuch as it consisted of a preliminary period during which I made a definite observation and then an extended period during which my attention was more or less occupied with other things and, finally, a check period when I made the second observation. I am assuming that a great many of the features of the stimulus situation remained the same. It could possibly be that once the door to the room was shut and the room constituted a specific though new environment for the discussants, the participants began to speak differently and more effectively as time went on. On the other hand, this may be a demonstration that as a person goes from one acoustic environment to another, he is at first not likely to be auditorily adjusted so well to the new one as he will be after a short stay. Whether or not this occurred here I began to hear better and more comfortably. It may be that, once the conversation got into motion, I began to hear better because I was not trying so hard to hear. If so, the change may have included an adjustment in the middle ear reflex. Incidentally, it was a middle-ear reflex problem that was being discussed as the thesis topic. It is possible that I was unknowingly putting into action some form of auditory posture which included the crucial participation of the middle ear reflex. This reflex is described elsewhere in this subsection by Sue Brainerd, but to make the present story more meaningful, I shall give you some idea of what the reflex is.

In the inner ear there are two tiny muscles, one of them the smallest muscle in the body. These muscles have to do with the way that the acoustic mechanism of the ear functions. The muscle behavior is called reflexive, for apparently under certain conditions of acoustic input, these muscles, unbeknown to the person, contract. Some contraction may be produced by an anticipatory attitude on the part of the individual. Actually, the factors that bring the muscles into play are by no means all known and understood. Hearing, like vision, is accomplished partially by a muscular process of the sense organ to posture it properly for action.

## LISTENING AND HEARING

When we go to sleep, we close our eyes and thus shut out stimulation, to a fair degree. Added to that we prefer sleeping in a situation devoid of all but small amounts of illumination. We want to be in semidarkness. But we still are somewhat alert to acoustic stimulation for we cannot preclude acoustic energy from reaching us. Whether we accept or wish for acoustic stimulation in order to go to sleep depends upon factors mentioned in a preceding essay.

But what about hearing while we are awake and going about our daily routine? There are many things we do not hear. This does not mean that the ear is not activated. It simply means the brain does not utilize the input. As we say, we "pay no attention."

For example, some people do not like to have the radio on except when they specifically want to listen to it. Such people may be rare these days, but they do exist.

One of the reasons why they do not want the radio left on all the time is because they have developed the habit of listening to the sounds they hear. Thus, the radio is often a distraction when they wish to do something else at the time. Many of the older generation were very emphatically taught when young to "listen." This applied to what was being said by their parents. To listen to the human voice was thus a habit. Persons with this habit are therefore more distracted by talk than by other sorts of radio programs when they do not want to listen to them.

It is possible, however, for such persons to develop a habit of not paying attention to the radio. They then are likely not to pay attention to the human voice in certain other situations also. To communicate with such a person one has to make sure that the person's attention is definitely directed toward you.

As individuals grow old, the habit of not listening often becomes quite pervasive. One of the things it very definitely includes is the practice of not listening to one's husband or wife. This is particularly true when one of them happens to be talkative.

We know that as people grow older they may become hard of hearing. Deterioration of attention is a bigger factor than is often recognized in this loss. First there is the habit of not paying attention just described, and second there is the need for stricter attention than ever when the hearing mechanism itself is less sensitive. It is extremely difficult to evaluate these factors, but surely the attention factor is crucially involved. Orientation is a large factor in perception.

## WHAT DO OR DON'T YOU HEAR?

When listening to a voice, it may not be the only thing heard.
Several sources of sound may be acting at the same time. When
this is the case, certain unexpected results occur—hearing the
voice is quite different from what one might expect. One might
anticipate that the other noises, if louder, would prevent one's
hearing all that was being said. This can happen, but many times
something else happens instead. The listener hears every word
that is spoken as if there were no interfering sound sources.
Such results have aroused the curiosity of certain investigators,
and they have gone into the laboratory to find out more pre-
cisely what does happen. In what follows, I refer to Warren and
Warren (1970).

To begin with, they taped a sentence and then cut
out a certain small section, replacing it with a blank. Next, they
used the same sentence, but replaced the delected section with a
cough instead of the blank (silence).

When subjects listened to the tape with the cough,
they heard the complete sentence with the missing speech sound
as clearly as the rest of the sounds of the sentence. The authors
gave this the name of "phonemic restoration."

When the subjects were presented with the tape the
second time, after having been told that a sound was missing, the
subjects again heard the complete sentence and could not tell
which was the "illusory" sound.

One might have supposed that the missing verbal
sound to be where the cough was located. It was found, however,
that the cough had no clear location in the sentence. It simply
seemed to exist along with the speech sounds without interfering
in their intelligibility.

Other sounds were also used in place of the cough.
These were simple sounds such as that of a buzzer, for example.

They also failed to be heard in place of the syllables for which they were substituted.

There is a very close parallel to this in vision. For instance, a missing letter in a written sentence is obvious whereas an inkblot over a letter will not interfere with the subject's perceiving the complete word.

However, the experimenters did find a condition in which the missing sound was not "restored." For instance, in the sentence, "The state governors met with their respective legislatures convening in the capital city," the "s" in legislatures when omitted in the tape was not restored in what the subject heard.

A still more complex and interesting example occurs when a sentence is so constructed that the verbal context provides no certain clue to the omission.

The example given by Warren and Warren is the following: "It was found that the —eel was on the ———." If the last word were supplied in the sentence, the listener was able to hear the omitted letter in the first word. When it wasn't supplied, the word was simply *eel*. If the last word in the sentence was axle, then eel became wheel. If the word supplied was shoe, the restoration made eel into heel. If it was orange, the word eel became peel. If it was table, eel became meal.

Apparently, some storage can take place until the necessary context is supplied.

At times you, no doubt, have been briefly spoken to and at first had no idea what was said. Either most of the sentence was a nonsense garble or some part of it was unintelligible. In some cases, you asked the speaker to repeat. In others, you said you didn't understand ("didn't hear" him). At still other times, you didn't bother. But, in possibly a minute, the voice sounds as you remembered them shifted from a nonsense pattern to an articulate word or words.

This shows that given enough time often the acoustic input is finally processed in an effective way. For a quick response, either the speaker's articulation was too poor, or the listener's attention was inadequate, or both.

To summarize, you may either hear more or less than was given. In the latter case, a little delay in asking what was said may suffice for you to make sense out of it without asking for repetition.

## THE VISUAL SYSTEM

By the essays in the previous subsections you have vicariously
been brought face to face with examples of the ways that various
sensory mechanisms develop and operate in the individual from
infancy to adulthood.

        Now we come to the last perceptual system, the
visual. In many ways we are more familiar with it to begin with
than the others. Perhaps it is only that we are more familiar in
detail with its products. Be that as it may, there are some very
interesting features of vision of which the typical person is
totally unaware. What we want to describe in this subsection
are situations that will enable you to understand and appreciate
vision in ways not heretofore the case. Again, no pretense is made
to cover the whole gamut. We give only some illustrations to help
indicate what vision means in life.

## PEOPLE WITH AND WITHOUT SIGHT

One of the best ways to understand vision as a human accomplishment is by making comparisons between the behavior of the sighted and the blind. This comparison brings the haptic sense into the description and much that will be said would seem to belong as much in the subsection on haptic perception as it does in visual perception.

The common notion of the sighted regarding blindness is well put in the nonsensical statement that "the blind are sighted persons who simply can't see." This implies that they are like the sighted in all other ways but this one. Nothing could be farther from the truth, for the blind are people living in a world that is different from our own. Some of them started out in infancy in this different world. Whenever a sense mechanism is absent or functionally obliterated, the world is different.

The purpose of the present description is to point out a few of the differences and similarities between the sighted and the blind.

Thomas D. Cutsforth in his book, *The Blind in School and Society*, had some very important things to say about the blind. Dr. Cutsforth was blinded in childhood and his adult life was partly spent in the study of the blind and partly as a clinical psychologist. His insights regarding child development in the blind and the personalities of the adult blind are unsurpassed. His book was first published in 1933. Later, The American Foundation for the Blind republished it. What Cutsforth said forms as insightful a picture as any in existence today. He came nearer to describing what blindness is like than any other writer. Many things he said are relevant for our present purposes.

Vision is the primary sense by which form and dimension are perceived, and when it is absent, tactual perception is retarded and restricted. When vision is absent, an enormous amount of detail is lacking in what is perceived by touch. The true shape of objects cannot be recognized until finger movement becomes well coordinated. Cutsforth believed that the body of the blind when very young must feel nebulously massive and extensive. In fact, it is even probably inaccurate to describe the child's experience in as articulate terms as these. As he says, only later do smaller masses such as head and limbs emerge as entities. As this occurs only size—not form or shape—can at first be distinguished. As finger exploration proceeds, the child becomes more and more aware of detail, but this is definitely limited.

Sighted and blind infants differ greatly in what is available to them in the environment. While the one learns the environment by watching moving forms, the other is totally unaware of these. Nothing comes into its experience that lies beyond hands and feet.

Although voices come to be recognized, they emerge out of and disappear into nothingness. What stimulation and urge to action the blind receives come largely from within himself. He lacks the tremendous stimulation that the seeing child gets from moving objects around him. Even voices cannot be reacted to as objects as they are for the sighted. Motor behavior thus lacks connection with what is heard.

While the objects touched and manipulated are the only ones the child knows, he needs a plentiful supply of them. But they must not be too complicated in form otherwise the child cannot follow their complexities. When this is so, understimulation exists in the face of what might be supposed as plenty. Objects can, on the other hand, be too simple, in which case there is too little invitation to manipulate and explore. A rubber ball that by its nature is not too complex but still is something that doesn't hold still is far more instructive to the congenitally blind infant than a doll, for the latter's form is beyond comprehension.

This principle was illustrated in the case of Laura Bridgeman, born in 1829, the first deaf-blind child ever to be trained. She constantly nursed and played with her father's boot. This she preferred to the family cat. The boot was something whose contours, form and size could be followed easily by touch.

Cutsforth pointed out that hearing becomes an active sense before the hand becomes at all skilled in tactual manipulation and exploration. While the cogenitally blind may not, at least at first, be able to make very fine spatial discrimination, they have been observed to make quite fine discrimination in pitch. Response to voice and the repetition of rhyme forms the most tangible avenue of interplay with the environment in the congenitally blind child. Despite this, however, what the child gets out of this qualitatively is far different from the sounds heard by the sighted infant. Case studies show that it is a long road to where the blind child makes direct connections between the acoustic source and what he hears. Free locomotion must be reached before this is achieved. One blind child even age six, was unable to distinguish the direction of sound sources. This child had never been allowed to move around freely. Space beyond the position of his body at the moment was virtually nonexistent.

Cutsforth has some things to say about what he calls the discrepancies between sight and touch. As an example he tells about a blind visitor to the Perkins Institute some years ago. The person was interested in the problem of tactual perception and was shown a miniature reproduction of the more or less well-known statue *The Appeal to the Great Spirit*. The statue was that of an Indian on horseback, with his face uplifted. Throughout his inspection of the statue he was completely unable to identify it as statuary he had ever heard anyone describe. He did recognize the horse as a horse and the Indian as an Indian with full headdress of feathers, having lived in the West for many years. But the meaning of the statue eluded him. By touch, the visitor was only able to derive *posture*. Recognition of attitude and movement failed to emerge. Movement in awed reverence and in a drunken lurch are fairly similar to the blind, while vastly different to the sighted. Cutsforth points out that the subjective (i.e., the perceived) contribution in the blind is often more significant than the objective situation. Therefore, the blind visitor totally missed the conventional interpretation and appreciation typical of the sighted because of the form of his imagery and the organization of his memory.

The blind, who depend most on tactual contact and haptic perception, are less able in many ways to derive meaning out of touch than the sighted. Perceptual systems do not function alone, just as the various senses do not act independently. The contributions made by each aids the others. Vision and touch, in the main, are two distinctly different forms of experience; they serve different ends; they make contact with two different aspects of the environment; hence, the worlds of the blind and sighted are different worlds.

Tactual perception, no matter how developed by practice, is a form of literal, realistic meaning which does not allow for grasping abstract and ideal meanings. Cutsforth says that the most perfect piece of taxidermy is far less a real animal in the tactual perception of the blind than the most ordinary two-dimensional drawing is visually for the sighted. No only this, but the stuffed animal for the blind differs more from the live animal than it does for the sighted. It is a form of reality all of its own. For the blind, all of the tactual qualities perceived, except static form and some of its texture, are not what they are when a living animal is tactually examined. The stuffed animal is hard, stationary, stiff, and without pliability. Even its posture seems unfamiliar and thus provides a new meaning rather than the recognition of something previously experienced. Even the fur is dead and cold. The skin is rigid. While it may be called the animal, it is tactually something different and a bit strange.

The blind, who do not have visual imagery, display a different set of preferences for object forms than the sighted. For example, Révész (1950) presented sighted persons with a series of rectangles varying in their proportions, and asked them to choose the one most pleasant in appearance. He found that a majority preferred a rectangle with a ratio of 1:1.6. Others picked even more extreme ratios.

However, when the same series of rectangles was presented to blind subjects, the proportions most preferred were in the ratio of 1:1 (the square). The sighted and blind differed in still another way. The blind found that picking the most pleasant or agreeable form was somewhat nonsensical. Their choice, to them, was somewhat "arbitrary." This led Révész to conclude that no genuine esthetic judgment is possible in pure tactual perception.

On the other hand, Cutsforth (personal communication) says that setting the blind to making brooms and other things of the usual rough materials is atrocious, for the roughness is abhorrent (ugly) to them. I have mentioned the occasion when Cutsforth (who was blind) made himself a desk. He worked hard and long to produce it, and one of the achievements which pleased him most was the very smooth and polished surfaces. He emphasized that smoothness was most pleasing to the blind.

After all, smoothness can be thought of as primarily a tactual quality. Visually we can see whether an object is smooth or rough but it is possibly an achievement that derives its meaning from tactual contact and exploration. While this can be said about perhaps all visual meaning, smoothness is in some respects less of a broad space quality than are certain other visual qualities. For example, some surfaces could look untextured but when touched may be found to be "sticky," though this was not apparent by sight. The touch experience was the final and absolute criterion.

Often when "incomplete" visual forms are presented to the sighted, they *complete* them when asked to draw what they saw. For instance, an incomplete ring or circle will be drawn as a full circle.

When blind subjects are provided with solid three-dimensional objects which have missing parts and are told to describe them, they do not supply the missing parts. Of course, the procedures are not comparable since the presentations to the blind cannot be made so brief as for the sighted.

This brings up the fundamental difference between the perception of the sighted and the blind in all cases, namely, that which is *seen* can be a global or extensive affair as far as space is concerned. In the blind using haptic perception, apprehension is piecemeal and sequential. The blind can touch only a limited portion of anything that occupies much space; hence, they must resort to exploration, bit by bit.

Von Fieandt (1966) points out that the blind often try to objectify odors by using touch. They try to touch what they believe to be the source of the odor. Touch seems to make odors more real and satisfying and is used by the sighted, under some circumstances, to make what is seen seem real.

Tactual mechanisms can be used for symbolization just as audition can. Items touched can function as do words heard to carry meaning. The use of the Braille alphabet is an example. Thus, three sense mechanisms—vision, hearing, and touch—can very definitely be used to carry symbolic meaning.

If a congenitally blind person lies completely motionless, an egocentric organismic space exists. It is a *body space* which in its phenomenal attributes is extremely restricted in all its dimensions. Subjects blinded later in life would have their visual imagery to fall back upon. They exist in a visual world. But as far as we know the congenitally blind do not have a context, which we know as space.

If the person moves, the body space changes into *movement space*. It is more extended than body space, and the individual feels rather nebulously located and oriented. We must admit, however, that some form of integration of haptic experiences (performances) must take place whereby even the blind are able to get around fairly well in restricted environments which are stable and in which they have had considerable practice. No sighted person can fully comprehend what this integration is like.

The nearest we may come to demonstrating the existence of a spatially functioning integration in the blind is illustrated by how one feels when he has learned a finger maze. This maze is a complex set of grooves in a metal plate with the usual blind alleys into which the learner inadvertently goes as he traces the maze under blindfold. After sufficient trials, one is able to trace through the maze faultlessly even though he has never seen the maze and the correct path. If, at this point, he introspects, he can say that in tracing the maze he makes one move after another in sequence and all that guides him in correct moves as he goes along are simply his muscular (haptic) feelings. He is not able to visualize the pathway even though he has visual imagery. So, we might well suppose that the world for the congenitally blind is a truly haptic (muscle-and-skin feeling) world. It possesses integration, otherwise the maze would never be learned, but it does not possess overall content at any given instant such as a visual image of a room. Hence it cannot be compared to what sighted persons experience as space.

Let us illustrate the situation by asking a sighted person and a congenitally blind person to imagine a stairway. The sighted person "sees" it instantly and completely. That is, he can take a passive visual "look" at it in imagery. The blind person has to relive the act of going up or down a pair of stairs. It is a sequential (step-by-step) affair rather than a full-fledged complete thing on the instant.

The bodily postures and movements of the blind are different than those of the sighted. The head tends to be held rigid, that is, in a more constant relation to the gravitational field than is the case with the sighted. This head posture often involves a slight tilt upward—at least it seldom, if ever, is a tilt downward—as if to watch where the person is going. The blind maintain more of a listening than a looking head posture, despite the fact that they may be rapidly walking along probing with their white canes.

Blind pianists make, in general, movements that are different and more exaggerated than those of the sighted. Remembering some of the extreme movements of certain well-known sighted pianists would tend to belie this statement, but it nevertheless stands. To the sighted the movements seem to relate, though somewhat awkwardly, to the task at hand.

The blind use more "visual words" (words pertaining to visual experiences and objects) than the sighted do (Cutsforth, 1951). Along with this, one might suspect that a socially adjusted blind person might be more talkative than a sighted person. This is not a very easily tested statement for even the sighted vary greatly in this respect. The statement might better be reworded to indicate that the blind might rely on words and his auditory mechanism in a different way from the sighted. Possibly more confidence is placed in words by the blind than the sighted. Even this would be difficult to test.

The sighted person's world so dominates even the blind that he refers to seeing things and people. A blind person would not say that while downtown he touched or felt a friend. He would say he saw him. On the other hand, it is customary for everyone to talk in haptic terms by saying that we *make contact* with friends when we don't even touch them, or we may not have seen them.

Blind people, in getting to know new people, are dependent upon touch and haptics. They want to run their fingers over the other persons' faces and feel their bodies. Lacking this sort of information, other people are not very real or, shall we say, not nearly as real as they are when this haptic exploration is permitted.

A very insightful blind person whom the author has known for many years mentions some differences between the blind and the sighted in eating a meal. He says that when the sighted take food onto their plates they do so with vision as a guide. We see what we are going to eat and choose amounts according to their visual magnitude which is somehow related to appetite. We also most usally identify beforehand what we bring to our mouths. There is a kind of visual preparation to receive it. The blind often take onto their plates too much food. Regardless of how it gets onto the plate, they tend to keep on eating till it is all gone. While the sighted are sometimes taught to "clean their plates," the sight of food often forms a deterrent and causes us to leave some of it. Just to look at food after we have been eating awhile may stall the appetite, but this deterrent is absent for the blind.

Perhaps if the blind could handle their food in their fingers, the gauging of the amount to eat would be easier than with the use of silverware. So, we can say that the blind person is not merely a "sighted person who simply cannot see."

# DEVELOPMENT OF VISION
# IN THE CHILD

The full understanding of vision is not to be derived by analyzing adult behavior in which the phenomenological details of form vision are likely to be the main point of interest. Instead one needs to take at least a brief look at the many bodily activities that are part of the acts of looking and seeing. These become noticeable in examining infant behavior when these activities emerge for the first time. It is there that it becomes apparent that seeing is an active postural affair involving many processes which have to be organized and integrated before seeing as we know it is achieved.

The one who has followed this sort of development most carefully, consistently and extensively was Arnold Gesell, assisted by his co-workers at the Yale Clinic of Child Development. What Gesell did was to observe infant and child overt behavior. A review of some of the observations of the Gesell group are appropriate here.

Vision is anything but a static affair. Seeing is the result of a number of delicately coordinated active motor processes within the eye, coordinated postures of the two eyes, appropriate ever-changing positions of the head and the body, plus the appropriate prehensile use of the limbs in reaching and holding. All of this has led Gesell to speak in a number of places of seeing as a prehensile activity. This term is ordinarily used for the arms and hands in *reaching out* to grasp, *pulling* in, and *holding* objects. In a way this is what is represented in the component parts of looking and seeing.

All of this is very different from the descriptions of laboratory scientists who concentrate on discovering the nature of the receptor activities of the eyes, who deal with the photochemistry of the rod and cone receptors, and who record the neural action currents in the optic pathway. Truly, seeing involves all these processes, but it is more directly described in terms of a person doing something, particularly when one is dealing with infants and others who cannot make experiential descriptions of *what* they see.

In observing the infant and young child using his eyes one sees the development of attention, the specific orientation of head, body and limbs, the growth in the use of memory, and the initiative in the search to obtain visual stimulation. Piaget, another famous investigator of child development, provides us with descriptions of the role of the sensory and perceptual apparatus in the achievement of cognition and thinking. Thus the works of Gesell, Ilg and Bullis (1949) and Piaget (1954) nicely complement each other.

The Gesell group studied five aspects of behavior, four of which we shall review briefly. The first was *eye-hand coordination*. The newborn was seen to immediately move and stop his eyes, an activity taken to be an endeavor to adjust to circumstances around him. Pursuit movements of the eye and evidences of fixation appear during the first four weeks. The child can follow an object through 180° of the field by 12 weeks. By 16 weeks, he occasionally observes what is in his hand. By 24 weeks, he seems to distinguish between strangers.

By two years he can use his eyes independently from his hands, and thus may examine items with the eyes alone. At two and a-half years he can see analytically enough to deal visually with an item held by another child without attending to the child himself. By three and a-half years the child adjusts his viewing distance to look at a page in a magazine. By four years, the child achieves a free and fluid eye-hand relationship.

The second aspect of visual behavior singled out for study was *fixation* of visual regard. At 30 weeks the infant's eyes definitely show convergence, as for example in fixating a dangled bell. From this he is able to shift his eyes to look at the examiner's hand.

At one year, the visual attention turns to the examiner, in a fairly expert fashion, with the eyes working nicely together. At two years an object can be picked up, using merely a rapid glance to spot it in doing so. At the same age the child draws back when an item is moved close to his face.

As children approach three and a-half years they differ more from each other than before. Some can obey a command to "just look" or to "just point," whereas others cannot. The eyes, even at four years of age, perform changing fixations better when the hand is used to hold or touch the moving item than when it is not.

The third aspect of study was what has been called the *retinal reflex*. This is what an examiner observes about the inside of the eye when he examines it with a hand-held retinoscope. What is observed is actually the focusing of the eye. Supposedly the focus of the eye is a pretty well-fixed process depending largely on the distance of the visual target ("object") from the eye. Gesell and his associates, in observing what children do in this respect, adapted the retinoscopic procedure so that the instrument did not need to be held close to the eye, but rather far enough away so as not to interfere with the child when he looked at a target. The eye did not always focus a fixed amount for a target at a given distance. That is, it focused in some cases as if for a target further away than it actually was; in some cases, just the opposite occurred. This focusing oscillated back and forth. The shift from one to the other was found to be related to the child's perceptual and cognitive activity. Visually, the child reached for things, and at other times he rejected them. The perceptual, cognitive and attitudinal activity of the child were in part demonstrated in what the eye was doing in focusing. This is the prime demonstration of the prehensile nature of vision.

From the age of 30 weeks to four or five years, the changes in the "retinal reflex" activity of the eye were observed. These changes corresponded to growth in the child's comprehension of the visual world. Some have regarded this retinoscopic technique as a nonverbal way of potentially measuring intelligence in the very young. In fact, it has been claimed that the technique works for older subjects. However, so many precautions have to be observed that it has never come into general use.

The last aspect of visual behavior we shall describe was called *projection*. This had to do with the child's comprehension of "where" the items he saw in stereoscope were.

If a three and a-half year old is asked to tell where the object he sees in a stereoscope is, he may simply say it is "out there." If he is asked to touch the object, he declines because he says it's too far away. Some may try by reaching out into space.

At seven years of age, the child explores the instrument (stereoscope) and finds it interesting to discover that the "picture" he sees when using the instrument is two pictures on the stereogram itself. It is said that only at eight years of age does he fully recognize that he sees the stereogram as one picture in the instrument.

At eight years of age he now recognizes that another person can see a scene differently than he does, and he begins to like to see the scene from the other point of view as well as from his own. At this age he begins to evaluate his own performance, as evidenced by his asking whether his eyes are good.

## PIAGET AND OBJECT PERCEPTION

Piaget (1954) points out that the first contact or interaction between the child and the environment (even when we see him touch something) does not actually imply awareness of an object as such. This is the case when he finds his mother's nipple, and when he rediscovers his thumb and wants to suck it. These and other occasions are not examples of true object perception, as yet because nothing induces him to regard his "experiences" as pertaining to something detached from the activity itself. Just so long as his activity succeeds, the child's objective and his awareness involved in desire or in effort are identical. Piaget goes on to explain what finally constitutes object perception.

Baldwin (1955) has listed some criteria that have to be met before we can say the child has attained a full cognitive representation of the external world. The first of these is that certain stimulus configurations have to be reacted to as continuing ("permanent") items, existing external to the child even when the items are momentarily not directly perceived. Items have to be treated as independent of the come and go of stimulation. Second, the properties of a configuration must be distinguishable from its position and movement. One of these movements, for example, is the rotation of the item about its own axis. Third, the child's behavior must be organized so as to cope with a single external reality. That is, the child must act as if he is in one physical world, not many. The child must realize that items and their movement may occur outside himself. Finally, the child must recognize himself as one of the items (objects) in his "cognitive map."

Piaget has distinguished stages in the development of object perception. In the first two stages, none of Baldwin's criteria for assuming that the child possesses a cognitive representation of the external world has been reached. In these stages the child does not search for an item that has been removed from sight. All he may do is to continue to look at the place where it disappeared. Likewise, during this period, the child has no realization of what he can or cannot cause.

When Stage 3 is reached, the child still does not search for an item that has disappeared. Some progress, however, is shown by the fact that when an item which he has been holding is pulled away from him and he loses his grasp, a grasping movement in line with the direction of withdrawal will be made. Still, however, when an item is suddenly jerked away from him or screened out of sight, he will not yet search for it. However, the child by now seems to recognize an item when part of it protrudes from behind a screen. Despite this he does not yet seem to miss a vanished item.

Searching for a vanished item marks the beginning of Stage 4. In this stage the child begins to understand the disappearance of an item. He will search at the point where the item vanished. If we now let the child find the item at this point (Point A) and have it disappear at Point B even while the child is directly watching the disappearance, he may search for it at Point A. Piaget states this as a conflict between what has been *learned* and *search* based on what has just been perceived. This conflict becomes resolved in Stage 5. The child soon comes to search for the object where he just saw it disappear rather than where it disappeared previously and was retrieved. The child's appreciation of object movement has now become greatly developed. This is exemplified by the child's being able to throw an object behind himself and then turn around to look for it (in a direction originally oppositely related to him). He can likewise visually follow the path of a moving item part way and look for it at the point at which it probably landed.

Stage 6 marks the achievement of full object cognition. Here behavior evidencing the recognition of absent items and events that have come and gone is manifested. The age at which this occurs is earlier than one would expect from the work and observations of Gesell and his associates, which probably means they are not actually getting at the same aspects of behavior.

In Stage 6 "pretending" shows up, manifested when the child repeats the behavior of others. When the child repeats the behavior in an inappropriate context but shows he realizes this, this sort of repetitive behavior is called "pretending."

# WHAT DO WE SEE WITH?

When you look about you, you use your eyes, and it is easy to suppose that seeing is nothing but the consequences of the reception of patterns of photic radiation ("light") on your retinas. Seeing is the combined result of using ears and body muscles and even the skin as well as the eyes. Such statements are often made, and it may be that many people accept them as fact, but it is a great deal more convincing and satisfying to have at least some of this participation spelled out.

First of all, it is to be expected that if one were totally paralyzed from birth, seeing would be something very different from what it is in normal individuals. Whereas we can often tell the difference between smooth and rough surfaces just by looking at them, we would not have been able to tell if we had not used both the visual and tactual (haptic) mechanisms together to begin with. Whereas we can often tell by sight the difference between what is soft and what is hard, we could not have done so had we not had tactual experiences. These and other properties that are essentially and primarily mediated by sense mechanisms other than vision become fully visual as a result of several sense modalities being used together.

There is still another way in which vision is contributed to or made possible and that is by the way things look as various tensions are applied to skeletal muscles. The prime involvement of skeletal muscles is in maintaining static posture, or in changes in the kinesthetic feedback to the central nervous system as body movements are made. These tensions are the result of static or changing patterns of skeletal muscle activity that position you with relation to the earth and the gravitational field. Two things are involved, namely, patterns of muscle tension and geometrical orientation to objects around you including the earth itself. These two factors are not independent of each other but are lawfully related. For example, if you bend over and look backward between your legs to the horizon, you are seeing the "world upside down," and are producing a particular pattern of tension in most if not all of your skeletal muscles. If the tensions were suddenly relieved, one would experience a different overall reality. The assurance that what you were looking at is upside down would lessen or cease.

Two novel sets of conditions can be brought about, wherein the muscle, tendon and joint (kinesthetic) contributions to the sensory input are radically changed. This one case is the artificial application of tension to a group of skeletal muscles, and the other is by the production of weightlessness. The latter set of conditions is very difficult to produce. It is reached by certain stunt conditions in aviation or in rocketry which carry man far enough from the earth and other planets to make their gravitational effects negligible.

Application of artificial amounts of tension to muscles such as those of the neck can be made without a great deal of trouble. The following is a description of such a case. Schneider and Bartley (1962) built a device which enabled the experimenter to apply a twist to the neck of a subject in a darkroom as he looked at a luminous upright bar pivoted in the middle. The subject was able, by using a remote control, to rotate the bar so that it looked perfectly vertical. The experimenter could set the bar off-perpendicular and have the subject adjust it to what appeared visually to be an exact perpendicular. The subject's head was held in a stanchion which could rotate the head horizontally. Naturally, if the subject allowed the tension of the stanchion to rotate the head, he would be looking "out of the corner" of his eye to see the bar. The subject was to resist the tension that was applied. The apparatus showed whether the head was kept oriented in the original position or not. The actual result that was wanted was simply a rotary tension applied to the neck muscles either to the right or to the left, without the head being moved.

The task of the subject was simply to put the bar into the visually vertical position. Since the room was dark, the only object seen was the bar, which was surfaced with paint that made it glow in the dark.

It was found that the apparent vertical differed from the true gravitational vertical more and more as tension was applied and increased.

Changes in the appearance of the bar itself were also

reported. The experiment demonstrated that visual space perception is partially determined by the pattern of muscle tension in the neck.

Another type of observation that links space perception and muscle activity is to be found in golf stance. Individuals who change from handling clubs left-handed to right-handed note this especially. Obviously, as you view the fairway off your right shoulder, you are looking at it differently from when you view it off your left. The shift from the one stance to the other emphasizes the intimate relation between the feel of the one posture and the other. The one posture places the elements of the scene somewhat differently in front of you than the other. Proper driving of the ball involves making a connection between how the fairway looks and execution of the proper motions. It can as well be said that executing the proper motions depends on how the fairway looks. One of the most conspicuous features of it all is how you feel. Once you become a good golfer, it is possible that this self-consciousness disappears, but it is there to begin with.

Many other examples of muscle involvement in the act of looking and seeing may be found, all illustrating that we see with the whole body.

## THE EYE IN VARIOUS SITUATIONS

The pupil is the aperture through which illumination enters the eye. Its diameter is determined by the muscles of the iris. The best-known routine activity of the pupil is its regulation of the level of illumination of the retina. When illumination is scant, the pupil opens up. Its diameter increases. When illumination is intense, it closes down. The pupil can vary between about 2 and 8 millimeters in diameter.

When photic energy activates the iris, its action is called a *light reflex*. Although iris activity is reflexive and occurs without any intent of the individual himself, it is far from being just a routine light reflex. Definite pupil reactions occur as a result of other influences, some originating within the body and some in the environment.

Pupillary activity is part of the response to illumination. It in turn is a factor in determining the amount of illumination admitted to the eye. The most interesting thing about pupillary activity is that it is an indicator of the way the person uses the input or the way the person is oriented at the time of stimulation.

One of the best examples of this is the following. Figure 14 is a double Maltese cross, simply a design made up of a disc with black-and-white sectors. The viewer is able to look at this design and see the black sectors as constituting a black cross. In such a case, the white sectors are a white background. The viewer is also able, at will, to see the white sectors as a cross. In this case the black sectors are a black background. Thus, the viewer can choose either cross to be the "figure," and the other one to be the "ground." In both cases the target itself sends the same amount of photic energy to the eye. The difference is what happens at the eye and in the visual system.

The significant thing is that the pupil diameter is not the same under the two conditions of viewing. As the viewer sees

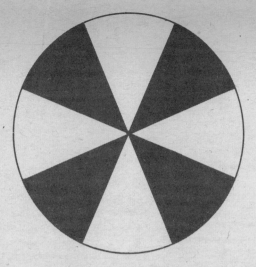

Figure 14/ Double Maltese cross which can be seen either as a white cross on black, or a black cross on white.

the white sectors as a white cross, the pupil diameter becomes less than when he sees the black sectors as the cross. These adjustments result in different levels of retinal illumination in the two cases and has an effect on perceived brightness. The important point for us here is that perceptual response is not passive, but active, and that this action involves motor adjustments as well as features you would most usually expect.

The pupil changes in keeping with the shift in meaning. While reactions of this sort have not traditionally been extensively studied by experimental psychologists, certain people in other occupations have routinely watched people's eyes to gain clues regarding their attitudes. Chinese jade dealers, for example, watch customers' pupils to tell when they are delighted by a specimen and may pay a good price. Magicians in card tricks are also said to watch the other person's eyes to see his pupils enlarge when a certain card appears.

Some of the most varied and interesting laboratory experiments have been made by Hess and Polt (Hess, 1965) on pupillary responses.

One of their experiments involved men and women looking at the same picture while a special camera photographed their eyes from instant to instant and registered the particular objects fixated. Men's eyes dilated more at the sight of a pin-up than the women's did. The items inducing most pupil dilation in women's eyes were pictures of babies, mothers and babies, and male pin-ups. These responses were, of course, interpreted as evidences of the viewer's *interest*. Pupillary responses were thus nonverbal indications of some of the same reactions (attitudes) we more commonly gain from subjects' verbal reports.

Women's pupils constricted when pictures of sharks were viewed. This was taken as an example of *aversion*. Other pictures, such as those of crippled children, elicited constriction of women's pupils. The same constriction reactions were made when some subjects were shown pictures of abstract paintings. Curiously, such reactions occurred consistently in some individuals' pupils despite the fact that they declared they *liked* modern art. The constrictions here may possibly be explained by the fact that the subjects could not succeed in achieving satisfactory meaning. For example, one psychologist had found that pupils constrict when his subjects viewed "unfamiliar" geometrical patterns..

Hess and Polt (1964) also determined pupillary effects associated with working mental arithmetic problems. It was found that as the problems were increased in difficulty, pupil dilation became greater.

Whereas it was typical for the subject's pupils to constrict back to normal after the answer to a problem was given, some subjects manifested a subsequent return of dilation. This was interpreted as evidence of an effort of anxious subjects to work the problem to check the answer given them.

Kahneman and Beatty (1966) obtained pupillary results consistent with the ones just described when they studied the effect of "load on memory," the attempt to remember what was read so as to use it in a task solution.

## "LOOKING STRAIGHT IN THE EYE"

We all are familiar with the difference between looking straight at people when we talk with them, and not being able to do so. There are conditions under which looking into the other person's eye is easy, and others in which it is difficult.

I was told of a high school class which made some objections to their teacher wearing dark glasses while lecturing in the classroom. When asked what their objection was, he was told that, with the glasses on, the members of the class could not see where he was looking. I might put the matter a little differently.

It would seem that since they could not see his eyes, they lost the usual full contact with him. They could hear his voice and see him as a human figure, but despite this he was not as fully present as when they could see his eyes.

This same thing holds true when a human looks into the eyes of a dog, for instance. His direct gaze has an effect that, indirectly observing, the dog does not have. Many dogs act as though they do not like to be looked directly in the eye. When this happens, few will stare back at the human, but will either drop or shift their gaze or even cringe and move away.

Even differences in the coloration of the eye are important to some species. Certain species of gulls differ from each other only in a slight but detectable difference in their eyes. These gulls inhabit the same region, but do not interbreed because they are able to detect this difference.

## SEE IT, TOUCH IT, DO IT

It is common knowledge that an object one looks at can be
changed in its visual shape by use of lenses or prisms. Various
kinds of experiments have taken advantage of this fact. One that
would seem to be of interest to most anyone will be described
here.

Rock and Victor (1964) determined the outcome
when vision and touch were involved in perceiving the shape of a
small three-dimensional object. It had to be something fairly
simple in its geometrical form so that the use of a distorting lens
would change its visual appearance in an easily reportable way.

The object chosen was a white one-inch square of
plastic, about one-twenty-fifth of an inch thick. This square was
set vertically on an upright stem so that it could be explored manually with ease.

The lens arrangement used compressed the visual
appearance of the square to the shape of a rectangle one by one-
half inch. The subject was allowed to see the "rectangle," and
then to explore it manually while not viewing it. The experimenters used three different methods of determining what the
subject's impression of the item was. The first was to have the
subject pick out a comparison object that was identical in shape
to the object as viewed. The second task was to pick out a comparison object identical to the one felt. The third was to draw a
picture of its shape.

Of course, different groups of subjects were used
for each of these tasks. And, in no case were the terms "felt
like" or "looked like" used by the experimenters. The subject
was asked simply to select or draw the comparison object in
accord with his "impression" of the object.

The results of the three different tasks were that,
with few exceptions, the visual impression dominated the tactual
one.

Vision and touch were again compared when a lens was used to alter the visual impression of the object's *size*. In this experiment, also, the "conflict" between vision and touch was resolved in favor of vision.

As a final test, the subject was told to grasp the standard object and to close his eyes and then open them. When the subject did this, he was asked whether the object "felt" any different under the two conditions. Twenty-three out of the 38 subjects said that it "felt" larger when their eyes were closed. The others could not report any difference.

As a result, the experimenters concluded that vision is so powerful in comparison to touch that it alters the very touch experience itself.

I would say that as one grasps a small object and looks at it at the same time, it is vision primarily that is used to perceive size and touch to perceive texture. If one definitely tries to "feel" the size, it is one magnitude while looking at it, and another magnitude when vision is eliminated. When vision is not present, tactual qualities become different.

It is for the different and added qualities other than size that one wishes to touch an object in the first place.

One of the beliefs among those who study vision is that it is based on touch. The exact way in which this dependence occurs has not been made clear. Rock and Harris (1967) report experiments performed in their laboratory that bear on this matter and cast doubt on the belief.

They had subjects look through a right-angle prism that acted like a mirror, reversing the visual field from right to left. This prism was supported by a rigid frame. The first part of the experiment consisted in having the subject watch his hand while drawing and doodling for 15 minutes on each of four days. The only thing that was not to be written or drawn was *letters*. Neither was the subject allowed to see any letters while looking through the prism. The reason for this will be apparent later.

For most of the subjects, of course, when they moved their hand in one direction, they saw it going in the opposite direction. The hand they felt and the hand they saw seemed to be two separate hands. However, it was only a few minutes until most subjects no longer experienced any discrepancy. They began to feel and see the hands moving in the same direction and soon had no trouble drawing or reaching in directions asked for by the experimenter.

Later, in order to detect any possible aftereffect of

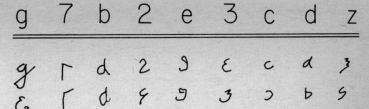

Figure 15/ Shows the kinds of letter and number reversals described in the text.

this visual "capture," the subjects were then asked to write promptly the 10 letters and numbers dictated by the experimenter.

While doing so, they were prevented from viewing their writing hands. The subjects had been previously told that the adaptation procedure they had gone through might make them write some letters backward, so that they must be sure to tell the experimenter when they thought they had done so.

Obviously, the subjects could believe that a letter was properly written when actually it was reversed and a letter could be believed to be written backward when it was properly written.

Both kinds of mistakes actually occurred. The subjects reversed about 30 percent of the letters and numbers they wrote, as illustrated in Figure 15.

The experiments were believed to show that when the haptic senses convey information that conflicts with what you see, the visual information determines the perception. After sufficient encounter with an intersensory disagreement, there is a change in haptic perception. It is now transformed so that it agrees with visual perception.

## VISION AND CAUSALITY

All perception involves the matter of causality in some form. For example, certain tactual experiences are thought to involve causality. They are experienced as something touching the skin and perceived as having a mechanical cause. Sometimes the tactual experience is of an insect walking across the skin. When one looks, he does not see any insect. In essence, in this case, one does not find support in vision for the causality he vividly experienced tactually.

Our purpose here is to describe briefly an investigation made some years ago by the well-known Belgian psychologist Michotte (1946). It is written up in his book, *La Perception de la Causalité*. The investigation about to be described had to do with visual causality.

In general, when we see an object A move up against an object B, if B, without delay, moves away in a direction that is the continuation of A's prior movement, it looks as though A has set B into motion. In other words, it appears that A caused B's motion. This need not be the case at all even though the whole event is perfectly convincing as a visual experience.

Michotte had an arrangement consisting of a blank perpendicular screen bearing a narrow slot. What was to be seen to move acted behind the screen and appeared through the slot. The observer was made to see a colored "block" (A) move along the slot on the screen (Figure 16). The rate of motion of this block could be varied by the experimenter. A could be made to move from left to right and stop midway along the slot. At that point B, another item seen as a block behind the slot, had been motionlessly waiting. As A moves up alongside B, B is made to move, not by A having actually bumped it, but by the experimenter starting the device carrying B to the right. Visually, A

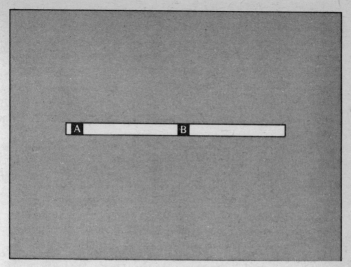

Figure 16/ Michotte's slotted screen which presents blocks A and B. A moves toward B and, as it reaches it, B moves away. It appears that A causes B to move.

is seen to *cause* B to move. While most people might be amused and simply say that this is an illusion, we do not stop there for it does not clarify the matter one bit. Michotte and I both see causality as something to be studied.

Michotte's arrangement permitted varying the time elapsing between A coming to a stop and B beginning to move. Also, the arrangement allowed for A continuing to move immediately behind B, in which case a new causality emerged in which B was seen to *carry* A along with it.

Michotte announced several factors necessary for the cause-effect impressions: (1) There must be two objects, for when there is only one object, cause and effect are not distinguished (isolated). (2) The movement of one object must visually dominate, as is the case when one object moves first. (3) The "impact" of one object on the other must be seen in foveal vision. If the event is seen out of the corner of the eye, the two objects are not clearly distinguished, and the impression is merely that a single object was involved. (4) Fixation on B is best for the impression of causality. (5) For the clearest causal impression, there must be sufficient unity (continuity) in space, time and direction. However, slight discontinuities will not entirely obliterate the impression of causality. The interval between A stopping and B beginning to move may reach a tenth of a second before causality disappears. Also, a slight space between where A stops and B is located will not obliterate visual causality. Likewise the direction of B's motion can be somewhat other than in the straight line of A's motion. As soon as causality disappears, the behavior of A and B are separate events. Michotte does not believe visual causality is a transfer from the mechanical (motor-kinesthetic) sense, but this is not a necessary conclusion.

Visual impressions of causality, while pertaining to items apprehended visually, are certainly not always to be relied upon. In traffic situations, the same form of impression could lead us into error. This form of causality is, however, very entertaining, and to understand the nature of perception it should be studied more in detail. That is, a variety of diverse situations should be investigated, including cross-modality interaction. For example, one may present a visual target and in connection with it an acoustic stimulus. Will the visual target (seen as an object) cause the sound one hears? Many such combinations could be tried in the hope that some general principles can be derived. If they are, then we would have a further understanding of the nature of perception.


## INTERSENSORY CAUSALITY

This type of experimentation leads into the question of ventriloquism. Ventriloquism is the art of speaking in such a manner that the sounds seem to come from somewhere other than the speaker. Ventriloquism is simply a special case of a much more general fact, namely, that sound localization is poor and that the causality principle we have been describing is involved.

To the human, sound doesn't just happen, it is *caused*. Conditions can be manipulated whereby false causality, veridically speaking, can be produced. This is taken advantage of in ventriloquism. The speaker talks with two voices. One is attributed to him; the other must come from somewhere else, particularly if the *visual* conditions are set up appropriately. This is accomplished by use of a mannikin (Charlie McCarthy) whose mouth and gestures are made harmonious with the sounds heard as speech.

Ventriloquism can certainly produce enormous entertainment for young and old. We see it as more than that, however, because it is but a special example of a broad set of principles; we therefore regard it as an object of experimental study. One might well want to set up very simple sets of conditions for the production of false sound localization. False sound localization enters into daily life in a number of ways. Now and then one hears sounds at night in the house when all is quiet. These arouse curiosity or even fear. Two things are involved—identification and location. *What* is heard, and *where* was it produced? It is obvious from what we just said about causality that we are talking about a case of it. Here it is auditory causality, but since in investigating the source (cause) vision is most always used as the final sensory modality for determining cause, we shall discuss it here rather than in an essay on audition.

Even in ventriloquism, the visual modality is involved in a dominant way. The verisimilitude that is produced depends upon *seeing* what it is that is producing what is *heard*.

Bartley provides a rather interesting and casual example of intersensory causality, or rather as far as the principal actor in the story is concerned, a *search* for *cause*.

The story is this. One hot summer day after hours of cross-country driving in an Old Model T Ford, in the 1920s, B had pulled to the curb and stopped in a little town to rest. The engine, as might be supposed, was very hot. As B sat in the car, he began to hear a click. This occurred at slow regular intervals and evoked considerable curiosity. B tentatively supposed it to be the noise of the heated engine slowly cooling down. This, of course, is a well-known sound when certain metal structures cool. But the supposition did not fully satisfy B, and he began to check to verify it. When he looked down at the floorboards of the car (no nice rubber mats those days!), the sound originated from that direction. But still he was not fully convinced, so the search went on. The sound did arise somewhere in the car. So B got out and looked under the hood and under the car. The sound continued. In B's estimation, there was no doubt that it came from the car, but since no pinpointing of the sound seemed possible, he was greatly puzzled. After moving around to find the cause of the click, he looked up and saw some youngsters in a porch swing. The houses were above the street, separated by about a six-foot bank. The porch swing was the old type, suspended from the ceiling of the porch by chains. B watched the children swing and soon found that the timing of the clicks coincided with the back-and-forth motions of the swing. Now he had found via vision the *cause* of the clicks. This was another case of visual causality, the action of something seen producing something heard. B searched no further; he was entirely convinced.

Visual causality is also exemplified in present-day sound movies (talkies as they used to be called). In producing convincing ("natural") effects an experimental investigation of the conditions sufficient for making the sound seem to originate at the places it should, according to what is seen in the visual presentation, had to be undertaken. While some latitude in setting up conditions for this is permissible, it is certainly true that verisimilitude will fail to be produced under some conditions. We do not intend to go into a detailed description of the visual and acoustic factors. They can be found in both editions of Bartley's *Principles of Perception*. The factors that are critical and that can be manipulated to suit are focal length of the camera used to photograph the scene and the reverberancy of the walls of the rooms, etc., that constitute the set and the distance of the microphone from the camera to the scene. Some photographing is, of course, done close up, and some from a distance. A problem is where to place the microphone in relation to the camera and the actual source producing the acoustical output. Various formulas have been worked out. One of the significant findings that cropped up was that even if the formulas would predict under what conditions the sound would be heard as originating quite close to the listener in the audience, it generally, if not always, was heard to be no closer than the plane of the screen.

Another example of cross-modal perceptual causality is the following. Frequently, I go down to the basement and pass by an ironing board on which an electric iron is standing in the usual nose-upright position as when left after ironing. Being a very cautious person, I am habitually concerned as to whether the iron has actually been turned off. On the evening in question, as I saw the iron I chanced to pass under the ceiling register which was putting out considerable heat from the furnace, and this struck me in the face. The very realistic impression I received was that the iron had been left on and I was feeling the heat from it. Momentarily the iron looked hot. Of course, I walked over to the iron to test it. By that time, I had passed from under the blast of heat and no longer felt it. Although I reached out my fingers cautiously to check the iron, it no longer convincingly *looked* hot. I then realized where the heat had actually come from.

In this illustration we have the requirements stated by Michotte, that there be two objects or two separate sensory experiences and that they are not seen as unitary. One seems to cause the other. Furthermore, in this case, the one experience was mediated by one sensory mechanism (temperature sense), while the other was visual. The heat was felt on the face, the causal item seen at a distance. This was a cause-effect perception that had been learned. Perceptual causality of a more general sort would be expected even if the iron had not been seen, for heat in the form just described is experienced as coming from some source (being caused). All that was necessary was to see a source which on many previous occasions had been a source of heat. Again, this is an example that would be labelled by many as simply an illusion, a mistaken perception. If we hold that every perception must have a set of lawful conditions for its production, otherwise it does not occur, then the reaction we have described is not explained by calling it a mistaken perception or an illusion. The discovery of necessary and sufficient conditions is what is called for.

## HOW THINGS LOOK UNDER WATER

Vision in water differs from vision in air. One of the numerous visual problems annoying divers under water is the distortion of the image on the retina produced by the refraction at the face mask. This is, of course, the result of rays passing from water as an optical medium to air inside the mask as another medium. This refraction involves a number of consequences. The rays arrive at the eye as if coming from a point three-fourths the actual distance. Hence, a diver is in error in perceiving distances. An object looks much *nearer* than if seen in air.

Second, the retinal image is larger than it would have been if the rays had arrived unrefracted from the visual target ("object"). This may cause the diver to see objects as too large. Third, the refraction is dependent upon the angle at which the rays reach the mask interface (the greater the angle, the greater the refraction). This works toward dislocating the objects. They are not in the direction they appear to be. The refraction factor influences perceived *size* as well.

Hand-eye coordination is disrupted as a consequence of this discrepancy between physical location and apparent visual location.

Kinney, Luria, Weitzman and Markowitz (1970) studied eye-hand coordination under water by using a table two feet square on which several points were marked. The diver was asked to touch the underside of the table at the points designated on top of the table. In air a person can do this quite well. But the divers were not able to perform this task accurately. In general, the points touched were displaced toward the edges of the square and toward the diver himself. The discrepancy was a matter of inches even at arm's length.

Visual acuity, the ability to distinguish fine details, is generally poorer under water than in air. This is also true for what is called stereo-acuity, or the ability to distinguish the differences in distances of various objects from the viewer. It is thought that this impoverishment may be enhanced by the fact that there are generally fewer clearly visible objects under water. Underwater scenes often approach the condition known as a *Ganzfeld*. This is the German name given by psychologists for a completely un-structured (objectless) visual field. This kind of field has been found to be the basis for special deficiencies in visual behavior in air. It impairs object detection and degrades reading, a task which one might suppose involves only the center of vision in-stead of the whole field. To test this reaction, the authors system-atically restricted the extent of the visual field and found that as it was contracted, depth perception became progressively poorer.

The color of objects under water is a matter of prac-tical importance. The manipulation of factors that control the color of objects is employed as a means of either increasing the chance that objects will be seen or, on the other hand, for camo-flauging them.

Scuba divers were used to test color perception under water. These men were tested in various bodies of water ranging from those that were clear to those quite murky. Three forms of illumination were used: natural (solar), tungsten, and mercury lamps. The visual targets used were spherical and were painted black, gray, white, blue, yellow, orange or red. Some were coated with ordinary paint and some with fluorescent paints. It is well known that fluorescent paint has been used to increase visibility of targets in air.

Incidentally, it is interesting to note how fluorescent-painted targets function. They convert short wavelength energy to longer wavelengths. The eye is less sensitive to the shorter wave-lengths, hence the targets are made to seem more intense (brighter) than one would expect.

Under water the targets coated with the fluorescent paint were much more visible than those of the same color coated with nonfluorescent paint. In turbid water the longer wavelengths (red, orange, yellow) were the most visible, but as clearer and clearer water was involved, visibility shifted toward the shorter wavelengths, toward the blues. For example, in Morrison Springs water, green was seen most easily and red targets, which were the easiest to see in the Thames River (Connecticut), became invisible. Blue targets which were invisible in the preceding tests became vis-ible, second to green.

Fluorescent paints produced a result many people might not expect. The exciting energy for fluorescence is in the short wavelengths. In clear water the transmission of these is good. Good fluorescent orange colors result. Targets of longer wavelengths are poorly seen. The result is that orange targets are brilliant to the eye but this brilliance decreases rapidly as distance is increased.

With the artificial photic sources used, the results are more complex. To activate fluorescent paint, these sources must contain the wavelengths which produce fluorescence and these wavelengths must get from the source to the target. It happens that with a mercury source fluorescent paints are far better than the nonfluorescent in all kinds of water. In turbid water the tungsten source loses its effect.

Another thing to remember is that white targets, although visible, take on the color of the water in which they are submerged. Hence they are very poor targets to use when several different colors are to be distinguished from each other. It happens then that for color coding (using distinguishable colors) it is best to limit the number of different ones used to two or three at the most. One from each end of the spectrum and possibly black would be the best choices.

The same authors studied the effect of amount of underwater experience on the accuracy of vision. They found that the visual performance of men under water was greatly influenced by the amount of experience they had. At first, their visual-motor performance was greatly disrupted. This is to say that perception, to begin with, was based on the habitual utilization of the retinal image which, of course, was distorted under submerged conditions. Some perceptual adaptation was achieved fairly quickly, but the ideal response (complete adaptation) was manifested only after extensive underwater training.

## WHAT IS A STAIRCASE?

In describing the difference between the blind and the sighted I have often used an example of what the two classes of persons can imagine. Of course, what they can imagine is derived from what they can directly experience in the first place. Imagination is thus an indicator of what their direct experiences (sensation and perception) are like.

Take the example of imagining a staircase. The sighted, of course, will imagine how it looks. When he does so, he can "see" the whole staircase instantaneously. He does not have to imagine it, part by part. This is because he was able to look at a staircase in the first place and see all of it at once.

The blind person can walk up and down a staircase, but he cannot see it. The sensory contact he has with the staircase is haptic (tactual and kinesthetic). To imagine it, he must go through some sort of a sequential remembrance of what his actual contacts with the staircase have been like. From the sensory standpoint, to the sighted, a staircase is mainly what he can see. In a secondary way, it is also what it is to him in climbing and descending it (something haptic). It could be that if the subject of stairs comes up in conversation, his impression of stairs is expressed in imagery of muscular exertion and shortness of breath. In this respect he would be much like a blind person who has the same exertional limitations.

In any case, a staircase is to a person what it is to him sensorially and perceptually.

Recently, in a penetrating conversation with a congenitally blind man, I brought up the question of how the blind can imagine a staircase. In what constituted a surprise remark, he said to me that a blind person might imagine what the stairs felt like if he laid down on them so that various parts of his body would touch different steps. Truly enough, he had given me an example in which the person was using the maximal possibility of experiencing a large part of the total staircase simultaneously. While the blind could do this, the more typical imagery would have to do with his usual experience, namely, climbing and descending the stairs.

The experience of lying on the staircase would, as the blind man said, give the person a feeling of the structure's tilt from the perpendicular. It would tell him its slope or "steepness," hence he would be exercising his basic orientation system.

The blind person could extend his tactual and haptic exploration of the staircase by manual exploration, going from one step to another and by sitting on successive steps, and so forth. But, here again, sequential rather than simultaneous and comprehensive experience is involved.

The typical sighted person at this point is likely to think that this exploration would provide for an overall image of the staircase, such as the visual image that he has, but this is not to be expected.

I think one of the best examples of the sequential nature of tactual experience is to be found in the experience of the sighted in learning a *finger maze*. A finger maze is made of grooves in a metal plate which can be followed by a blindfolded person with a hand-held stylus. Of course, this maze can be learned with eyes open whereby the learner can see and avoid blind alleys and, finally reach the point of tracing the maze fairly quickly and faultlessly. It might seem that once learned he could trace it faster than a blindfolded person, but this is not so.

Let us now ask what the blindfolded person's image of the maze is once he has learned it. It is not something that encompasses the whole maze at once, but a set of haptic feelings (images) of tracing parts of it.

What the blindfolded person has learned is how to proceed turn after turn in the maze. The feeling of one segment in the maze leads to the direction to turn at the next portion. Were he to begin tracing somewhere in the middle after he had learned the maze, he would be at a loss as to what the correct first turn would be. After a tiny bit of exploration, he would discover "where" in the maze he was and then make correct turn after correct turn from there on. At no time are *all* the "correct turns" at once in his imagery, yet we know he can run the maze successfully.

Thus we can suppose that the imaginal life of the blind and the sighted are very different in this one essential feature—

their sensory content. In the sighted, it covers a comprehensive portion of externality and in the blind it covers externality more nearly piecemeal.

The stairs or the maze are only what they can be experienced or imagined to be.

## DISTORTED VISION REVAMPS REALITY

Much of the study of vision is made to discover how its body mechanisms operate. Careful experimentation has disclosed a number of precise optical details. Much of this information, though indispensable, is not, in effect, the description of a person going about his daily affairs by the aid of vision. Certain descriptions can be made, however, to show how seeing is part of a person's reality. The circumstances that can be best used for this are often cases in which, for some reason, vision is anomalous, or as we would most often say, distorted. The purpose of the present exposition is to present such a condition in a way to show that vision is not simply a restricted process of *sensing,* but that it reaches into all aspects of living.

The anomaly about to be described is not a very common one and it has been clearly isolated for only a little over three decades due to the invention of appropriate instrumentation. It is a peculiar form of distortion perception and is called *aniseikonia.* Since the optics of the condition have become understood, it can be produced experimentally by wearing special glasses. This is, of course, only done to study the anomaly.

Aniseikonia is a condition which includes distorted perception of the location, size, and shape of objects and certain pervasive forms of personal distress. Aniseikonia is based on several different forms of optical anomaly and the consequences show up in greatly differing ways and degrees from case to case.

A rather simply described case is illustrated in the vision of a journalist, now deceased, who saw horizontal surfaces somewhat tipped. As a consequence, he used a book under one side of his typewriter to make it appear level. In certain other cases the symptomatology is not as frankly expressed in visual terms. Headaches, gastric disturbances, and other nonvisual symptoms often form the major distress. This may seem strange since in most people's thinking vision is simply vision, and symptoms of the malfunctioning visual systems should be manifested primarily in visual terms. That this is a misconception is one reason that we are describing aniseikonia. What we shall have to say should form a demonstration that when one is dealing with sensory mechanisms and perceptual phenomena, he is dealing with *people* as people, not with isolated entities such as "vision."

Aniseikonia (not yet named and clearly described) came to the attention of Adelbert Ames as a consequence of his studies in vision at Dartmouth College. The Dartmouth Eye Institute was a later consequence of these studies.

Before describing aniseikonia and its personalistic consequences, a very brief partial description of one of the instruments for detecting and measuring it will be given. We shall avoid many of its details for we only want to indicate it as a way of disclosing some of the aspects of visual distortion. As a general rule in vision, precise instrumental conditions can disclose anomalies that may not show up otherwise.

One part of the instrument consists of two perpendicular strings suspended behind a rectangular opening. Since they are equidistant from the eye, they should look equidistant, but for some viewers they don't. In fact, a casual glance might result in almost anyone's saying that they look equidistant, but when called upon to make a careful observation very small differences become observable and relevant. The observation is made through an adjustable optical system in front of one eye which can be varied so as to make the two strings look equidistant. The amount and direction of adjustment to accomplish this is taken as a measure of the optical imbalance which in some cases is the basis for the anomalous perceptual syndrome. It happens that some people have a slight optical imbalance without consequent symptoms. But no one with symptoms is found without imbalance.

Another situation (an experimental one) in which aniseikonic symptoms become manifest is called a *leaf room*. It is simply a room (cubicle) about seven feet in each dimension. It has one open side, and it is at this open side that the observer (patient or whoever) stands and examines the interior of the room, the ceiling, floor, back wall and both side walls of which are covered with artificial leaves (Figure 17). These leaves simply preclude the otherwise flat surfaces from being seen as such, and also preclude seeing the linear junctures between walls and ceiling and between each other. When a fully normal sighted person stands halfway between the two side walls and examines the room,

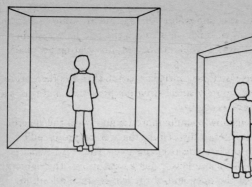

Figure 17/ A diagram showing a cubicle room (a "leaf room"). On the left, the viewer stands at the threshold of the open side and looks in. The room is rectilinear and appears to be so. On the right, the same person sees the room very differently while wearing a size-lens. The room is now greatly though realistically distorted.

he finds it a normal rectilinear room. That is, its walls and ceiling join at right angles. The back wall looks oriented at right angles to the observer's line of regard. All features of the room look as they would be expected to look. But some observers do not see it that way. One side of the back wall may appear further away than the other. Other features of the room also may not be symmetrical. One of the immediate results of viewing the room when it doesn't appear normal is a feeling of surprise and uneasiness.

Years ago, Professor Ames pointed out in conversation with me that children, women, and men tended to react somewhat differently from each other when they saw the room as being distorted. The typical children were amused and delighted. It was a surprise, but fun. Men generally couldn't quite believe their perceptions and wanted a chance to make exact measurements to see whether they would correspond with the room's dimensions as perceived. Women often became disturbed and wanted to get out of the situation. If the visual distortions were being produced by wearing the special glasses just alluded to, they wanted to take the glasses off quickly.

Even with the brief examples just given, it should be realized that what was visual was at the same time fully *personal*. The visual experience was encompassing. It described a form of reality, even if surprising or even if weird. It often called for escape, but escape was impossible if it was due to some form of inherent asymmetry of function between the two halves of the visual system. It was possible if due only to wearing peculiar glasses.

This visual perceptual situation thus has the encasement effect that a purely social situation possesses, and this is a significant thing to recognize.

Let us now become more familiar with the specific nature of a typical set of distortions that can be produced by wearing the appropriate lens over one eye. The lens is what is known as an "axis-90 size lens." Let's wear it over the right eye, and then stand at the open end of the leaf room and look in.

The lens just mentioned simply magnifies the retinal image in one axis. Thus the two eyes, the naked one and the one with the lens, are not provided with images that are the same. They differ in size in the one direction, and this slight difference produces pervasive visual effects.

The viewer now sees the room as distorted. The back wall is farther away and the ceiling is higher on the right side, and the right wall is farther off the side of the viewer than the left one. The floor slopes down toward the right. All of this is perfectly real to the viewer and if he were to walk into the room, he would begin to act as though he were walking on a sloping floor. If a marble were placed in a grooved board and the board tilted slightly to get the marble to roll in a given direction, it would appear definitely to roll uphill. If an object were suspended on a string, the string would not hang perpendicular, but at a definite slant. What would otherwise have been taken to be a string (a nonrigid item) is now taken to have the properties of ar rigid wire. The example, although an experimentally produced one, is paralleled in many respects by clinical cases in which the optical and neural systems of the two eyes are in imbalance. Thus the example is not just a "parlor trick," but is a real condition which sometimes occurs in people.

The condition is not simply one in which strange optical effects exist or are produced experimentally, but it also involves general consequences throughout the organism. In the clinical form of aniseikonia the individual may have nausea or headaches or feel maladjusted in various ways.

These are symptoms that psychologists often find in clinical patients who don't have aniseikonia. The supposition is that some social conflict or maladjustment, such as a phobia, is the basis for the distress the person experiences. In fact, the implication sometimes is that all one's anxiety-producing troubles are social.

Aniseikonia demonstrates that this is not the case; the distress it produces and the distress a social situation may produce are identical in terms of symptoms.

Psychologists sometimes find that the help they give their patients may be only temporary. The patient seems all right for awhile, but soon develops other forms of distress and needs help again. In some patients with aniseikonia the same thing is true. They are given what appears to be the correct optical prescription and are relieved of their distress. However, it may return, in which case a new examination and a slightly different prescription for their spectacles is given. Again, they are all right for awhile. This is not the rule, however, for many patients experience maintained relief for years.

While what we have been describing may seem to be an optical matter when first considered, it is to be seen in our context as a matter of perception. It is another example of the pervasiveness of perceptual processes and the fact that what one perceives is a part of one's reality. In a space world perception can be an effective response or just the opposite. It is not apart from the individual; it *is* the individual in action in relation to his environment.

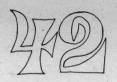

## SYMBOLISM AND COMMUNICATION
## IN VISUAL PERCEPTION

What one sees includes not only material that can be defined in terms of space, color, form and brightness, but also something abstract or symbolic. One is able to perceive meaning. We have an example of this when we see cause and effect involved in objects in action. This was discussed in the article on vision and causality.

Our purpose here is to discuss the role of visual perception in obtaining various forms of meaning and also in communicating when pictures and paintings are involved. It so happens that the visual (photic) environment differs from certain other environmental forms since it provides for recording and preserving meaning in relatively natural ways. Whereas one can produce and preserve records of sight and sound, he cannot do the same for other senses, except by preserving the original situation itself. This is to say replicas are not made and preserved.

This distinction between the "real" or original stimulus situation and something that functions as a replica or facsimile is not the main issue of what we want to discuss, although distinctions are sometimes made in the study of vision between scenes and pictures of them. Paintings are visual targets which we can study in their own right.

The common question evoked by the typical viewer of certain kinds of paintings is, "*What* is it?" This question implies that a painting is expected to resemble some literal thing or scene familiar or understandable to the viewer. It must have the properties that make it a *picture* as naively or narrowly defined. That the painting may represent some other intent is not universally countenanced, even when the possibility is recognized.

A painter may have purposes other than the one implied by the expectation of the viewer. A painter may produce a work for any one or more of the following reasons. (Note, however, that the classification contains overlapping items, and it is not exhaustive.)

1/ To document—to *picture* so as to inform of literal details and preserve a record.

2/ To represent. This is the term often used when documentation is meant. One meaning of this term is to copy. Literalness is the objective, but representation may go beyond literal copying. Actions and abstractions may be represented, although this is stretching the common use of the term.

3/ To create mood.

4/ To create atmosphere. Mood pertains to the viewer, and atmosphere is projected into the painting or drawing.

5/ To create sensory impact. This is to produce something that is directly pleasing in color, form or arrangement. Perhaps it could be called the pure esthetic effect. The beauty seems to reside in the painting or drawing and not in what it represents or symbolizes.

6/ To convey abstract ideas. To produce something quite different in kind from the painting itself, to symbolize. This, in part, is similar to 2.

7/ To compose. To create something visual that produces satisfaction by the mere arrangement and distribution of its components. (To produce for the composition's sake.) This is largely like 5, but refers more to spatial arrangement than color.

8/ To show the play of light and shade. To make light tangible, to give it substance (see Rembrandt). This is a depiction that shows a sensuous appreciation of some feature of nature. This is a form of 5.

9/ To depict action, force, or motion. In this category belong rhythm and velocity.

10/ To elicit auditory, tactual or other imagery. For example, to produce textural effects. Texture is apprehended tactually as well as visually. The painting of texture may be effective and pleasurable mainly as composition, or it may suggest or represent something that excites *tactual* imagery.

This list should indicate that two things are involved in the actions of the artist: his own satisfaction, sensory and otherwise, and his wish to convey sensory pleasure or abstract meaning. The list implies that painting is a language. Its "vocabulary" is commonly much more personal than is a vocal one. Each artist may have, to some sizeable extent, a language of his own, and this is where misunderstanding between him and the viewer of his painting comes in. Not everybody is prepared to understand. Actually, there can be many languages for each production. Three languages stand out, however: the artist's, the art critic's, and that of the viewer of the painting. The artist may be little able to verbalize, but feels he is expressing himself in visual terms; whereas the critic is verbal and can interpret but may inject much of himself. The viewer learns something by the critic's report but still may wonder whether what he says is "authentic."

The viewer typically possesses one standard for what he sees outside of paintings and another one for what he sees in a painting. From the spatial standpoint, paintings subtend restricted visual angles and therefore occupy limited portions of the visual field. Since paintings exclude much of what is perceived outside of them, the visual end result differs in the two cases. Paintings require their own *spatial contexts* and are incongruous or ineffective in others. The only apparent exception, at least from the painter's standpoint, is the nonobjective work of huge dimensions. Such paintings are their own contexts. Many of them are large enough to be murals. Framing of large abstracts is not always thought appropriate, whereas the framing of most smaller paintings is. Not only is framing appropriate for many of these, but the form is crucial for the more representative of paintings. The choice of a frame is actually part of the problem of making the painting say what the painter wants it to say. The subtle and symbolic effects involved in our list are either produced, enhanced, or destroyed by the frame used.

What we have just been saying may resemble an essay on art or painting and thus may be out of bounds, but it is meant simply as a brief statement of what can be perceived in visual targets and what someone conveys who wishes to communicate. While communication is not a synonym of perception, it is something that occurs only through perceptual mechanisms.

The things we have said about paintings and what they may convey is another demonstration of the great part that visual perception plays in life.

One of the most concrete ways to demonstrate a characteristic of visual perception involved in viewing pictures or paintings is illustrated in the differences between material seen in their right and left halves.

The differences are of several kinds. Some have to do with perceived distance or nearness; others lie in the realm of more abstract meaning. Under many conditions items in the left side of the picture look nearer than they look when the mirror image

Figure 18/ A representation of the way Rembrandt grouped the subjects in his "Return of the Prodigal Son." Note that the father and prodigal are most prominent.

of the whole scene is presented. This is an easy test to make when scenes are photographed because one print can be made in the usual way, and a second print can be made by "flopping" (reversing) the negative. Thus, items that are in the left in the normal print are now in the right in the second print. These two scenes are spoken of as mirror images of each other. Using the original scene as the reference, the second is a mirror image of it and will be so designated as we continue our description.

While the measurement of differences in apparent distance is quite concrete when using the arrangement to be described, the measurement of abstract meanings is not. Nevertheless, these differences exist depending upon the right-left position of the items in question.

One of the very best illustrations of abstract meaning being regulated by lateral position is to be found in Rembrandt's "Return of the Prodigal Son." In the Bible story, there are at least five persons involved: the father, the prodigal son, the mother, and at least two brothers. The return of the prodigal son who went out and wasted all his inheritance was a special event. The father was overwhelmed with delight in having the son back again, but the brothers were jealous and irked at the attitude of the father and the stir he was making. Rembrandt pictured the five persons so as to show who was central to the occasion and who was secondary or accessory. This simply involved the spatial arrangement of the members of the family. How did he do it?

He positioned the persons as seen in Figure 18. Look at it on the opposite page and then inspect the mirror image (Figure 19). Which drawing does what? Would you have arranged the persons as Rembrandt did, or would you have done it differently? Is the mirror image better, just about as good, or less satisfactory than the way Rembrandt composed his picture? What is the basis for judging good or bad?

Naturally, he wanted the father and the prodigal to have the most prominent position perceptually. It is to be remembered that Rembrandt used other devices besides position. He was a master of light and shade and so what was not to be prominent was kept in shadow. This was the case here with the mother. This factor was what primarily put her in the "background" of attention.

The scene as Rembrandt composed it, with the father and son on the left, happens to be the arrangement to capture the focus of perception. Naturally, in addition to putting them on the left, they faced each other and this adds appropriate meaning for

Figure 19/ A mirror image of Figure 18. Note that now the two sons are "focal" or more prominent. Actually, the whole meaning of the picture is changed from what it was in Figure 18.

the viewer. We could change the scene with the father and son not facing each other but the viewer, and with the other persons in about the same position, but all simply facing the viewer. Even in this arrangement, the two on the left side of the scene would possess some sort of perceptual significance lacked by the others.

Thus we see that pictorial arrangement with reference to lateral position involves consequences that are unique and are dependent upon a characteristic of perception, not inherent in geometry as such.

An additional example is included here. It is a photograph taken at the south entrance to the Mackinac Bridge. In this print, the bridge is not in a position to be entered upon by a more or less straight-ahead approach from the viewer's position. In the mirror image, the entrance to the bridge *is* straight-ahead (Figures 20 and 21).

The second example is a scene in which a distant building can be seen through some trees. It cannot be seen with as little "obstruction" when the trees are on the left as when on they are the right side of the print.

Various other kinds of examples can be shown to express the specific and unique properties of visual perception. Still

Figure 20/ South entrance to Mackinac Bridge.

Figure 21/ Mirror image of Figure 20.

others can picture action which they lose with slight composition change (a different stage of motion).

# THE ROLE OF THE VISUAL SYSTEM
# IN REGULATING BASIC BODY PROCESSES

It is not usual to think of the visual system as performing functions that do not have to do directly with seeing. Despite common unawareness of it, the visual system relates the human organism to the environment in certain nonvisual ways. Of course, we know that seeing involves certain motor processes which have to do with positioning of the eyes in relation to what is looked at and to controlling the amount of photic radiation entering the eyes by regulating pupil diameter. Since these are motor (muscular) activities, one might speak of them as nonvisual. They are, in a way, visual functions after all. But there are still other activities that are mediated by the visual system. These are too important to overlook.

The optic pathway, i.e., the nerve fibers that make up the pathway from retina to brain, contains four groups. Only one of these groups ultimately forms the pathway to the visual cortex of the brain. It is the group that most people think of when the optic pathway is mentioned. One of the other groups of fibers goes to a motor center of the brain and has to do with the motor functions just mentioned. Two other groups go elsewhere. One of these constitutes the *accessory optic tract*. Actually, this tract has three subdivisions in some species; hence, one generally hears of *tracts* instead of a single accessory tract. It is these tracts that we are going to discuss. The information regarding the function of these tracts is interesting but scattered. It comes from many sources, and all of it has not yet been put together in a full and well-established description.

In the preceding essays, we have been dealing with man's relation to photic radiation in the form of complex optical arrays which result in the perception of the shapes and surface qualities of objects. This seeing has included higher-order meanings and the satisfaction of intellectual and emotional needs. Now we are going to deal with the organism's relation to the photic aspect of the environment in other ways. Here, photic quantity—not patterns—will be the crucial factor. Here we discuss various internal body processes for which *presence* or *absence* of "light" will make a fundamental difference.

Even so, we are still dealing with discrimination, the very discrimination that is pointed to in our definition of perception. We should realize, however, that some discriminations have to do with basic adaptive or adjustive relations to the environment, while those that mostly gain our attention as students of behavior are the highly transient and subtly structured activities involving consciousness and feeling. In principle, there are common denominators between the two levels of reaction to photic energy. Marg (1964) has put forth a number of suppositions regarding the functions of the tracts. For example, he supposed that the accessory optic system is a pathway from the eye to the midbrain for alerting and arousal actions. This implies a connection to the reticular system which will be described in Part V. He also supposed that the accessory optic system concerns the organism's estrual, circadian (diurnal) and other internal rhythms. The suppositions, of course, have some support in experimental findings and are not simply armchair imaginings. Since all higher animal forms are not equally rigidly tied to environmental rhythms such as the seasons and the diurnal light-dark cycle, what may be said about one species may not apply quite the same way to others.

Jöchle (1964) has concluded that the eye functions as a photocell that correlates the organism's internal processes (internal clock) with the external clock of night and day. The hypothalamus is considered to be the most important means of connection between the organism and the environment in doing this. The connections between the accessory optic tracts and such structures as the hypothalamus are present. Feldman (1964) has recorded electrical responses in various portions of the anterior hypothalamus to photic stimulation of the retina.

Ortavant, Mauleon and Thibault (1964) concluded: (1) That photic radiation influences the release of gonadotropic pituitary hormones, that photic radiation influences the hormonal system, particularly the production of gonadal hormones. (2) That there is an optimal number of hours of daylight for spermatogenetic stimulation in various animal species. There is an optimum amount of illumination for the production of sperm and sexual activity in animals.

This is to say that organisms are definitely affected by sunlight. We know certain effects occur, but most of us do not concern ourselves with how they occur. Generally, we suppose that all such photic effects occur by affecting the skin. Sunbathing is part of this recognition, as well as a pastime for other reasons. It is not generally known that some of the basic effects of sunlight are mediated by the visual system (optic pathway), rather than through the skin.

## THE THIRD EYE OF THE LIZARD

There is a structure in lizards called the "third eye" which will serve to emphasize the fact that all eyes are not used for the purpose of "looking and seeing" as ordinarily defined (Eakin, 1970). The question of what an animal does with a third eye would be a very natural one. This third eye may seem bizarre or it may seem simply like a fairy story, or even a bit of science fiction. In fact, in certain fairy tales some giant creatures, the Cyclops race, had only *one* eye in the center of their foreheads. Nature has actually gone in the other direction. The third eye of certain lizards is located on the front of the head, slightly posterior to the level of the two lateral eyes. What is the function of such an eye? It had to be tested to see whether or not it actually functioned. When tested, it was found to respond to the general level of the illumination. The same was found to be the case with several additional species of lizard. Because of the difference between the activity of those lizards with the eye covered and those that were left unhampered, it was suggested that the eye served as a *dosimeter of solar radiation* (an instrument for measuring the quantity of radiation from moment to moment). It was also found that the amount of glycogen in the animals with light-adapted third (parietal) eyes was greater than in those with dark-adapted eyes. Removal of the parietal eyes also raised the functional level of their thyroid glands (Stebbins and Eakin, 1958; Eakin, Stebbins and Wilhoft, 1959).

In general, it was concluded that the parietal eye of the lizard, *Sceloporus occidentalis,* exercises an inhibitory influence on the animal in relation to daylight. It functions as a brake and with other neural and hormonal mechanisms acts as an adjustor of the animal's circadian rhythm. While the findings regarding the parietal eye of the lizard are no direct proof as to the function of the accessory optic tracts in the human, they are a demonstration that photosensitive receptors in vertebrate do function for purposes other than what we usually call seeing.

# SUNLIGHT AND MAN

Certain conditions in man have been attributed to lack of photic radiation reaching him by way of the eyes. One of these is illustrated by the metabolism of the blind. Jöres (1933), for example, assigned the deviation in water excretion curve to insufficient photic stimulation via the eyes. Raab (1939) found a relationship between a form of hypoglycemia (low blood-sugar level) in the blind and insufficient photic stimulation. Other investigators have attributed vegetative disturbances during winter (less sunshine) to lack of photic radiation, although it wasn't certain whether or not this lack was brought about via the eyes. Hollwich (1964) found deviations in water balance in his blind subjects. Nycturia (frequent passage of urine during the night, or passage of more during night than day) was more definite in those who became blind early. Still other workers have found comparable results, although the explanations were not all alike. Studies in carbohydrate balance show some differences in the blind and the sighted. The greatest deviations were found in those who became blind early.

The accessory optic nucleus, the brain center into which the accessory optic tract feeds, is a part of what is called the *limbic system*. The limbic system is a group of brain centers described in Section V.

The limbic system is sometimes called the nose brain because the olfactory tracts enter it, but animals with poor olfactory systems still possess a limbic system. This system actually has two parts, the olfactory and the nonolfactory. The nonolfactory part is concerned with what might be called "substitutional response." Substitutional response is a group of internal activities that occur when response cannot be overt. In general, these are the central nervous and other bodily activities that emerge when the organism for any reason cannot act out its response. It is in such situations that strong feeling arises in the human. This is the feeling we call emotion. So we can say that the limbic system has to do with emotional response.

If some of these portions are stimulated directly under experimental conditions, certain responses connected with the upper segments of the gastrointestinal tract are evoked. These include sniffing, biting, licking, retching and gagging. Another class of reactions that such stimulation evokes includes throwing back the ears, snarling and protrusion of claws. A third group of responses has to do with respiration and with the autonomic system.

It is apparent then that if the accessory tract links with brain regions evoking the reactions just mentioned, the accessory tracts are connected with something quite basic to the general economy of the animal. Photic radiation is more than a guide for a space sense; it exerts influences upon fundamental body processes, and the sensory mechanism for the former is also the mediator of the latter.

## AN ATTEMPT TO IMPROVE
## DIRECT EXPERIENCE

Perception is the immediate result of contact with the environment.
Part of perceptual response is awareness, but another name for it
is "direct experience." In our society, direct experience is played
down in many ways in favor of intellectual activities which, of
course, vary in their remoteness from actual contacts with the
environment. This bias has been inherited both from the Greeks
and from the early church fathers. Much has been made over
man's prowess over other animals in his intellectual achievements.
Our formal education from kindergarten through the university
minimizes direct experience. For example, pupils and students
spend most of their time in classrooms looking at blackboards or
green chalkboards instead of experiencing directly the matters
being dealt with. We hear *about* and see *representations* and dia-
grams instead of seeing, hearing and touching directly. The world
we *sense* is overshadowed by the world about which we *think*.

According to a view now being put forth in certain
circles, not all classes of individuals are equally able to have effective and satisfying direct experience. Part of this view supposes
that individuals attempt effectiveness and utilize those means
they happen to discover which will improve this contact with what
is around them. Alcohol is used by some for this purpose.

Thus, instead of alcoholism being a result of excessive
use of alcohol, an illness or expression of a condition of "allergy"
to alcohol, it is taken to be a condition detectable before excessive use of alcohol. It is taken to be a condition characterized by
the inability to deal effectively with direct sensory stimulation.

Hamilton (1968) insists that a diminished capacity
for direct experience has serious consequences for living. He thinks
it is the basis for most forms of human psychological aberration,
alcoholism being one of them. He points out that the world the
child in our society encounters involves surrogates or substitutes.

It is essentially a translated world involving varying degrees of remoteness from his world of direct experience. We have constantly
increased the amount of time in which the individual in school
deals with surrogates. He thinks as a consequence that it is not
surprising that there is an increasing interest in agents that *heighten
direct experience.*

It is not my purpose here to plead for this view. I
would rather like to put forth some experimental evidence that
has been obtained and interpreted by those holding this view.

At present there are various investigations in progress
bearing on the question of the alcoholic's ability to have effective and satisfying direct experience. One of these studies, dealing
with *perceptual memory,* is a study made by Nelson (1968) at the
University of Alberta in Edmonton, Canada.

Although some people can distinguish about seven
and a-half million different colored surfaces, we know the memory
for colors is far from being correspondingly accurate.

Perceptual memory is not confined to colors; it applies
to all forms of comparing what one sees at the moment with what
one has seen previously. One can never rely upon memory in going to the paint store to buy paint to match paint on the wall at
home.

The study about to be described was based on twin
suppositions. One was that alcohol taken in certain amounts changes one's contact with the physical environment (changes direct experience). No one seriously doubts this. The second supposition
was that the alcoholic belongs to a class of persons who obtain relatively profound effects from the use of alcohol. Such a supposition is not easy to demonstrate. One way is to compare the perceptual changes induced by intake of alcohol in samples of alcoholic and nonalcoholic subjects. Another is to study these two
groups in the sober state. Nelson chose to make a study of the
second sort. As a result, he found the ability to remember color
samples differed greatly in the alcoholics and nonalcoholics even
when sober. The alcoholics were in an institution so it was known
that they had not used alcohol for thirty days.

The alcoholics were very much less able to remember
than the other group. Furthermore, their errors were in a different
direction than those of normals. Patches *seen* as yellow are *remembered* as more green by the alcoholic, and as more red by the nonalcoholic. When blue-green is viewed, it is remembered by the alcoholic as more blue and by the nonalcoholic as more green.

The findings were interpreted that the memory decay

seems accelerated in the alcoholic, and that it is likely that he makes a "less successful and perhaps qualitatively different contact with the physical world about him than do the nonalcoholics."

The findings fit in with the novel belief held by Nelson that the alcoholic drinks to get more effect out of direct contact with the environment, to heighten direct experience. This would be curious for the achievement is not all that it might be; the frustrating consequence of drinking soon sets in. That is, alcoholic intake soon dulls sensory appreciation.

# part
# FIVE
# some
# general
# considerations

Up to this point we have been describing various features of perceptual response and its immediate consequences. Our main objective has been to provide as intimate a picture as possible of the way we human beings relate to our surroundings to show that we are a part of Nature. The several perceptual systems were dealt with one at a time. However, we have not covered all that is pertinent and interesting about our relations to the context we live in, nor everything we might well like to know about the mechanisms within ourselves.

We can now deal with these matters, the first being is what happens when stimulation is lacking or withheld. This is spoken of as *sensory deprivation or isolation* and has concerned experimentalists for only a relatively short time. Now enough has been learned to provide some important insights. Human beings (no different from other organisms) require a stimulating environment.

Associated with this need for stimulation is another topic, a consideration of the class or classes of chemical agents that *suppress sensation and awareness*. This class includes analgesics (the agents that reduce sensation), narcotics, soperifics (the agents that produce sleep), or we might say in general, sedatives and anesthetics. Such agents are closely allied to those that distort sensation and consciousness—the psychomimetics and hallucinogens. We shall avoid going into the complex subject of the latter. Any description given is likely to seem socially biased and, in fact, many other authors and lecturers are canvassing that topic quite extensively.

Many readers might be interested in, and profit by, a description of what goes on in the body due to the activation of sense organs. We shall very briefly describe the neural systems that are involved in transforming the input into perceptual behavior.

There is a subtle relation between what we have found the physical or external world to be like and the way aspects momentarily seem to us. This will take us into *illusion, perceptual constancy,* and certain distinctions between *truth* and *reality.*

These topics, along with others of a general nature should form a helpful and interesting climax to the whole presentation which we have called "Perception in Everyday Life."

# THE SUPPRESSION OF AWARENESS

The suppression of awareness can be dealt with from two stand-points: (1) reduction of consciousness as in sleep, the obliteration of consciousness as in surgical anesthesia, and (2) the alleviation of pain.

For the most part we have been dealing elsewhere in this book with the positive aspects of awareness, the major excep-tion being the effects of sensory deprivation. No understanding of consciousness is complete without some understanding of the con-ditions which preclude, lessen, or abolish it by doing something to bodily processes. Of course, one agent for reducing or abolishing awareness is drugs. The results produced by drugs are not simple, and all drugs do not affect the organism alike. Their effects do, of course, help science and medicine to understand the human or-ganism, but they hardly help the layman much in this respect, for he is unable to interpret them on his own. Sophistication regarding perception necessitates knowing something about the effects of sedatives and anesthetics and about the body mechanisms affected by use of narcotics and hallucinogens (substances producing hallu-cinations), but that topic will not be included here. This essay is meant for a very different purpose from what seems to be us-ually involved in the mention of drugs. The purpose here is to de-velop a general and serviceable understanding of sensory mecha-nisms and perception. The present discussion is not intended to be a medical treatise but rather a psychophysiological one.

The suppression of awareness has several purposes: (1) alleviation of pain; (2) relief of a general state often called ten-sion; (3) relief from general bodily discomfort including the feel-ings in illness; (4) relief from worry, a state analogous to what is meant by tension; (5) production of sleep; (6) anesthesia in sur-gery. It is not our purpose here to discuss all of these at length, but rather to say that everything just mentioned involves reduction or change in the central nervous system's utilization of inputs from sense organs and, in some extreme cases, possibly the reduction of the activity of sense organs themselves.

*Pain.* Pain we shall define here as the uncomfortable experience which is localized at some specific or general area of the body. It is difficult to distinguish pain so defined from the aversive effects that go along with it. At least it is a bodily-based or localized experience. In a subsequent essay, I shall deal more at length with pain and *anguish.* The expectation of the average, and even somewhat more sophisticated, person in this area has been that pain can be attacked separately by certain agents such as medicines, leaving other forms of discomfort little or totally untouched. The truth is that the agent used often changes the individual's general state of awareness, making it more easy and comfortable, and the specific complaint called pain disappears as part of the general relief. This is the result often produced by analgesics such as aspirin.

*Tension.* Several things may be called tension. One is an experience of tightness and/or rigidity in some muscle group, such as those of the limbs. Here again the separation of this specific form of tension from a general feeling of tightness and/or irritability is often difficult, even if possible, to make. Quite often it is this latter state that is of focal concern and various means are employed to lessen or alleviate it. In the haptic subsection, I discussed the Jacobsonian technique of relaxation and another technique known as transcendental meditation where tension is relieved by direct means of producing skeletal muscle relaxation on the one hand and by preoccupation with certain specifics of attention in the other. In the one case a lesser kinesthetic feed-in into the central nervous system is sought, and in the other case the task achieving "meditation" indirectly brings about the relaxation. It is as if a "relaxation" of attitude via meditation brings about skeletal muscle relaxation. The two procedures, though starting from different points, converge on some of the same results. One need not look upon meditation as a mystical procedure in order to have it work.

*Bodily discomfort.* Bodily discomfort is often quite diffuse, so much so that it is difficult or impossible to describe. It often requires other things in connection with it to identify its origin, and to know what to do about it. Fever is often looked for to give discomfort the specific label of illness. Discomfort evokes some anxiety. In fact, one's distress over social situations poorly met, or over behavioral inadequacies of various sorts produces symptoms which are difficult, if even possible, to distinguish from personal discomfort brought about by physical means. It is this indistinguishability that is the crux of the whole question of what to do to relieve the distress. Discovering which of the two origins lies at the bottom of the distress marks real progress.

*Worry.* Relief from worry, while being based on external situations and the ability to resolve the difficulties involved, can in part be obtained by reducing sensory input, namely, the kinesthetic feedback from tense muscles.

*Sleep.* Sleep is dealt with in a separate essay. Here, again, some of the same agents and/or procedures that have already been mentioned may be resorted to.

*Anesthesia.* Both suppression of awareness and relaxation of muscles are involved in anesthesia.

## ISOLATION AND SENSORY DEPRIVATION

In order to most fully understand the role of the sense mechanisms, it is helpful to discover the consequences of limiting sensory impingement on sense organs. To the extent that impingements can be reduced, the individual is approaches a kind of vacuum. Ordinary moment-to-moment existence is an interplay between the organism and the surrounds. The surroundings form a kind of sustaining or balancing agency for it. When not acted upon by outside influences, the neural processes within the individual can run off into curious tangents. This shows that the usual environment exerts a stabilizing control on the individual.

On the other hand, when a person becomes annoyed, it is easy to feel that it is the environment which distorts his activities and purposes. While this may be very real, what happens when stimulation is considerably reduced or withdrawn demonstrates the benign results of the ever-acting environment.

Sensory mechanisms are the means whereby we contact the environment. Some situations—called isolation—fail to contain the stimulus ingredients we need. In experimental situations in which isolation is contrived, the condition is now called *sensory deprivation* and a number of investigations of the behavior of individuals thus deprived have been made. These have been quite enlightening and have clarified the fact that the human organism needs considerable stimulation in order to carry on life as we now know it.

Under natural circumstances, man lives in a context which provides constant stimulation. The energies vary in amount, kind and pattern from instant to instant. To provide an experimental environment totally without stimulation is impossible, but by special means it can be reduced to a minimum.

When the term *sensory deprivation* is used, it refers to the sensory input itself. When *isolation* is used, it often refers to the matter from the standpoint of the experiencing person and is more particularly an organism-centered term. The reason for dealing with isolation and sensory deprivation here is simply to show the other side of the coin from response to stimulation. It takes both aspects to describe more completely human behavior or human existence.

## ISOLATION

Isolation is far from being a new phenomenon. Mystics have practiced forms of it and, in particular, certain Biblical characters have sought it for obtaining what seem highly laudable purposes. It is possible, however, were one to examine only the behavior of mystics, that he would obtain rather distorted notions of what isolation produces. Connected with isolation, particularly among mystics, is the practice of fasting. Fasting can be looked upon as one form of sensory deprivation in itself since the savoring senses are being deprived.

Isolation has four aspects:

1/ Confinement which involves (a) restraint from freedom of movement, and (b) limitation in the use of the exteroceptors, ears and eyes. The environment contains less space; thus while the person is closed in upon, he is also detached. He loses reference which at first is spatial, but later becomes temporal.

2/ Separation from particular places, persons or things (often possessions or facilities). In this category, looked upon broadly, the death of loved ones is an example. In some cases, such as being in sealed cabins of spaceships, the separation is also confinement.

3/ Removal from the general environment. This is the condition generally sought in laboratory experiments in which subjects are kept in the "dark" and in "quiet". Activity is reduced to a minimum by having them lie down. Sometimes their hands are kept in padded gloves so as not to come in contact with edges, hard objects and rough textures. Temperature and humidity are often kept constant so as not to call for bodily adjustments.

4/ Subjection to uniform sensory inputs. From the individual's standpoint this is spoken of as monotony. This may annoy, but the result intended, which is pertinent here, is a form of reduction in response. For example, some uniform inputs come to be hardly sensed.

One of the well-known modern reports on the effect of isolation is the story that Admiral Richard Byrd told about his experiences in the Antarctic. According to plan, he spent six months alone in the Antarctic buried in a small hut under the snow. Innocently enough, he sought this to achieve peace, quiet and confinement and to experience how good they really are. But he soon found the unchanging surroundings in the polar night, with scarcely a sound from the outside, anything but desirable. His tranquility and serenity shifted into a lurid existence. There were hazards such as the danger of carbon monoxide poisoning from his heating stove which proved defective, and bone-chilling cold, plus the possibility of his snow home collapsing, which brought on a kind of fear. However, this changed into a kind of apathy that made him scarcely able to carry on the routines of eating, drinking and even of keeping warm. He lay in bed hallucinating and repeating all sorts of bizarre notions.

His state included the feeling of being almost at one with his surrounds and the universe, a kind of loss of individual identity. Time became timelessness. Whereas all of this may seem strange and startling, it should be expected if one considers that life is made up of the fabric that comes from sensory inputs. With these brought to the very minimum, what is the machinery of the brain and nervous system to do? It is a factory. Without input of raw material it first generates its own input through hallucinations, but it finally shuts down.


## ANOTHER CASE OF VOLUNTARY ISOLATION

A report (Price, 1970) which appeared recently of a man who went into a form of voluntary seclusion provides a few details that might be added to what has already been said regarding sensory deprivation and isolation. Let's call the man DP. DP had been a newspaperman and wondered what he would do when he retired. The main feature motivating his decision to spend a year as a hermit was the desire to do what he wanted to. He did not feel that he could do this living at home in his hometown. So he found a cabin in an isolated part of the mountains near Hot Springs, Arkansas, and settled down to do some "in-depth thinking" and some really attentive introspecting. In his hideaway he had no telephone, no radio, no TV, no "yak-yaking." He devoted himself to reviewing his past. He was contacted by outsiders (his sister and brother-in-law) only about once a week, at which time the conversations were confined to "welfare of the family and close friends, things of the past, small talk and banter."

He started by attempting to achieve and maintain a state of "ecstatic eagerness." He was supposedly doing what he had wanted to do for a long time. (Note that Admiral Byrd in the Antarctic hideaway had the same intent.) He could write as steadily as he chose, and he had time to read and time to think about his life. To begin with, he followed a fixed schedule of writing in the morning, reminiscing in the afternoon, and reading and "reflecting" in the evening. He took long walks in the mountains daily. On these walks he wrote about his visual and other sensory experiences.

The first noticeable result was trouble in sleeping, manifested not only in difficulty getting to sleep, but in sleep coming in short snatches, and in his drifting into states midway between sleeping and waking. He woke up more tired than when he went to bed. He greatly missed the news and seemed to find no similar diversions from the little monotonous activities of the day. He found himself becoming very tired. I would say he was greatly bored. He had to invent a number of trivial, transient, routine things to do. He said he tried to involve one or more of his "five senses" and emotions whenever he could.

You will recall that his main purpose for his seclusion was to review his past. It turned out, however, that a great deal that was sad and depressing emerged. He seemed to remember more of what was sad about his childhood and early life and remember it more clearly than the pleasant things.

He found that his living alone made him more talkative. When his sister and brother-in-law came to see him, he talked volubly. But since news was not to be mentioned, they soon ran out of topics. As a result, they talked a lot about a little.

Days did differ even in this seclusion. Weekends seemed to be the most difficult to pass or endure.

He had many vacant and weird feelings. At night he would wake up with what he called "where-am-I" feelings. At times he became almost panicky.

At other times he feared that he would become stalled on a nonproductive island in his writing and that listlessness and lassitude would completely overtake him. As an antidote, he would work relentlessly to try to avoid depression. According to him, this depression arose not only from lack of news from outside and from not being able to talk with people, but from the sameness of his daily routine.

One of his inventions was a word game that he used to control his wild thoughts after going to bed. He would select a letter and then try to think of words beginning with that letter which pertained to the senses (sight, sound, smell, taste and touch).

As time wore on, he became more and more tired and yet resorted to more and more devices to combat his troubles.

Had he read the experimental material now available on sensory deprivation and isolation and the experiences of others in isolation such as those of Admiral Byrd, he might never have undertaken this year of seclusion. At least he finished it with the belief that it is unadvisable to cut oneself off from everyday life for a prolonged period.

There have been hermits throughout history, but few if any accounts of how these people related to their surroundings and how they saw life. There still are people such as Georgia O'Keeffe, the artist, who spend long periods in dwellings by themselves. Even from them we have no extended accounts of what they do and how they manage to enjoy this "seclusion," or extreme reduction in social contact.

In the account of DP, we have the story of a typical human being wanting to achieve certain ends which he believed he could reach only by having distractions and various intrusions eliminated. But what was the result? What he reports is completely in line with the kind of facts that have been learned in experimental situations, namely, that one cannot get along well in a sensory vacuum. DP noted in particular that it seemed helpful to invent ways to involve the sensory and perceptual systems in activity.


SEA VOYAGES ALONE

Some of the most marked accounts of hallucination in rather impoverished environments have come from those who have set out alone in little boats to cross the Atlantic or Pacific Oceans. They typically become dogged by extra (imaginary) personages of various sorts who soon show up and accompany them in their many-week marathon. In such voyages, the skippers have plenty of work to do. In fact, they could well be on 24-hour watches for safety precautions alone. They likewise encounter storms in which they have two or more persons' work to do. The sea with its wild actions provides tremendous degrees and kinds of stimulation for the basic orienting mechanism and haptic stimulation, but it is a context of social isolation. The roar and other sounds induced are by no means quieting to anyone. Inspite of this, it is a situation of isolation and monotony. Something is lacking with all the stimulation that is present. It is a special example of sensory deprivation and is horrendous for the landlubber even to imagine.

## BRAINWASHING

Two things can be done to a person whereby his behavior can be radically changed and old reality can be, for all intents and purposes, fairly well modified. These two things are sleep deprivation and isolation. This is something that apparently we in the United States had far too little, if any, realization of. One of our awakenings came during the Korean War as a result of some of our airmen, who had become prisoners of war, confessing to having dropped germs on the enemy.

It has been found that sleep deprivation is one of the features of the brainwashing procedure. The victim is deliberately kept awake and interrogated especially at night when the usual diurnal rhythms further lower cortical vigilance. The interrogation involves a repetitive series of questions and arguments. Typically such a threatening situation induces excitement (arousal) and no sleepiness. But, when the threat is overwhelming or is combined with constraint, a kind of sleep state emerges.

The prisoner is often prepared for this ordeal by having been kept in prolonged isolation. Experimental sensory deprivation experiments have shown that it not only results in false perceptions but that the records of brain waves (EEG's) show a slowing down into a pattern resembling drowsiness. When isolation is continued for a matter of a couple of weeks, the brain waves refuse to speed up to normal again for a number of days after the ordeal.

With the evidences we now have we can see how prisoners cannot help but have reality so changed for them that they will "confess" to anything the captors plan for them to say.

## EXPERIMENTAL SENSORY DEPRIVATION

The subjects in some experimental studies usually spent the early part of the experiment sleeping. As time wore on, they slept less, became bored and showed signs of being eager for stimulation. The subjects were generally able to tolerate only two or three days on a voluntary basis. Some left before testing was completed.

During the experimental session unusual emotional instability was noted. For example, doing well on tests given them produced great pleasure, but they became upset when they ran into difficulty.

Visual hallucinations were at first quite simple. At first they would see dot patterns. Later the visual patterns became more complex as, for example, growing into complicated designs such as wallpaper patterns. And, finally, they became curious animals. The visual fields often looked tilted. Such experiences first brought on surprise, and then amusement. Later the experiences interfered with sleep and became an irritating nuisance.

Not all hallucinations were visual, however. Voices of people speaking were sometimes heard. One subject experienced what in part may have been a haptic illusion. He experienced himself as two bodies lying side by side, but overlapping. Feelings of so-called "otherness" were also reported, when it seemed that the head was detached from the body.

As was already implied, the subjects (see Heron, Bexton and Hebb, 1953; Bexton, Heron and Scott, 1954; Doane, Mahatoo, Heron and Scott, 1959; and Scott, Bexton, Heron and Doane, 1959) were given a number of tests during isolation. These included tests of tactual form perception, spatial orientation, color adaptation, figural aftereffect and size constancy.

Upon coming out and removing goggles, gloves and other devices worn to minimize sensory stimulation, the subjects seemed dazed. There were often one or two minutes of visual disturbance, such as difficulty in focusing. While objects seemed fuzzy, their colors seemed more saturated than normal. Along with this, there were feelings of confusion, headaches, mild nausea and fatigue—some of these lasting for 24 hours.

## MILD ISOLATION IN INFANTS

A mild form of isolation in the case of infants is exemplified in the work of Brackbill, Adams, Crowell and Gray (1966). These authors made comparisons between periods of no experimental acoustic input ("quiet") and those in which controlled forms of input were used. The studies illustrate several things, but the one thing of relevance is the difference in excitatory state under the two conditions. Salk (1960) presented an acoustic stimulus of 72 beats per minute at 85 decibels to newborn infants in a nursery for four days. These infants were compared with 112 others in a control group who had no acoustic input. The factors noted were weight gain, amount of crying and food intake. Seventy percent of the experimental group gained weight while only 33 percent of the controls gained. The food intake of the two groups was the same, but in the control group there was 60 percent more crying than for the stimulated group. Here the nonstimulated group was given a form of relative isolation, and the isolation turned out to be less favorable than the acoustic stimulation.

The investigation went on to test 41 children (a mean age of 34 months) during a prenap period with each of four different acoustic conditions: no input, 72-beat input, tick of a metronome, and a lullaby. The variable tested was the time taken for children to fall asleep. The mean number of minutes required with no acoustic input ("no sound") was about 20 minutes; with the lullaby, about 18 minutes. The same time was required for the metronome, while there were only about 14.64 minutes under the 72-beat condition. Statistically, there was a significant mean difference between the sound and no sound conditions, while there was no significant difference between the various sound conditions. In quiet, the children were somewhat less able to fall asleep, which means that their excitation levels were higher.

# WHAT HAPPENS TO SENSORY INPUTS?

The typical concept with reference to stimulation of sense organs
and the resulting sensory response is quite out of line with what
actually happens within the body. The common notion is that
once the sense organ is activated, it sends a volley of impulses up
an unbranched pathway to the brain; and, that this volley is the
main basis for the resulting sensory experience. The present essay
is meant to give a brief description of the components of activity
that go into determining what the sensory outcome will be. It
will show that the matter is fairly complex and that the components, aside from the direct neural volley just mentioned, play a
very important role.

## THE RETICULAR SYSTEM

Direct sensory pathways, projection pathways as they are sometimes called, do not act alone. No one of them functions alone
in any natural situation. Each of them, when activated, operates
in connection with a kind of facilitation system. This is the *reticular system,* and is called the reticular *activating* system. It is
called the reticular system because it is a collection of nerve cells
and their interconnections which is more diffuse than the direct
projection pathways from sense organs.

The reticular activating system takes a hand in developing the response to sense organ stimulation. In fact, some authors think that the propagated impulses up the primary sensory
pathways, such as the optic pathway, would in themselves hardly
provide the basis for perceptual response at all (Livingston, 1959).
According to this view, every sensory input must be organized and
integrated with information from other concurrently active sen-

sory systems. This, of course, is dealt with by association areas and "storage" mechanisms of the brain.

The reticular formation includes nerve cells distributed throughout the brain stem, some of which appear as well-defined groupings (nuclei). The formation receives incoming impulses from the spinal cord, the cerebellum and the hemispheres of the brain. It likewise sends impulses to these areas.

Many cells of the formation which sends impulses to higher centers receive branching connections from direct afferent sensory pathways and likewise send impulses to the cortex by way of a system of diffuse connections through various subcortical centers. Direct experimental stimulation of these cells in animals leads to positive *arousal* reactions. So, it is inferred that these cells make an important contribution to wakefulness, consciousness and attention. The reticular activating system is apparently more strongly affected by general anesthetics than the direct sensory pathways themselves. Thus one of the conclusions sometimes drawn is that depression of this system plays a significant part in producing anesthesia.

The evidence is accumulating that sleep is an active state, that is to say one which is not simply a depression or quieting down of the usual ongoing processes in the brain but rather one which comes about through the agency of sleep-inducing structures in the brain.

The reticular formation maintains a state of excitation relative to the sensory systems so that the net effect is either facilitatory or inhibitory with reference to one or the other of them at any given instant. One of the functions of the reticular system is the determination of attention. The inhibitory effect of the reticular system is minimal whenever new, sudden or intense forces impinge on sense organs. It is greatest when the input duplicates other inputs that have been taken to be "unimportant."

This system, however, is not the only part of the brain that is of significance in helping determine the ultimate consequence of the stimulation of sense organs. Certain other portions of the cortex are quite significantly involved.


THE LIMBIC SYSTEM

The cerebral cortex is roughly divisible into two major portions, the "old" and the "new." The *limbic lobe* is the old cortex and is most directly connected to primitive physiological functions. According to MacLean (1958) it is a "common denominator for a variety of emotional and visceromatic functions in the mammal."

The brain structures that are associated with the limbic cortex are the septum, amygdala, the anterior and midline thalamic nuclei, the habenula, and parts of the basal ganglia. While most readers may not be familiar with these structures, they are mentioned to show that a cluster of brain structures have been identified as being closely integrated with the limbic cortex. All of these structures and the limbic cortex taken together are now called the *limbic system*. It seems that this portion of the brain is primarily concerned with self- and species preservation. One portion, when stimulated, gives rise in the animal to alimentary responses such as licking, chewing, eating and retching. The other portion gives rise to actions representing search for food, such as sniffing, searching, attack, and vocalization.

Psychomotor epilepsy patients show some of this primitive reflex behavior during their seizures. During their auras (periods just preceding seizures), they experience alimentary symptoms and strong emotions. They experience thirst, hunger, nausea, fear, epigastric distress and choking.

What we have said so far is that sensory response is initiated by activation of sense organs but does not occur as a simple result from this. This input is aided and abetted, elaborated, diminished, or left almost to "die on the vine" depending upon an associated neural system that parallels the sensory pathway. Evolutionarily older portions of the brain which handle the influences of basic or vital processes come into play before the sensory response is fully elaborated and ultimately appears. The affective or feeling tone of sensory response may partly arise from this limbic activity.

Hence a sensory response many times is a very complex combination of awareness, feeling tone, and motor activity. This result is not properly understood without realizing some of the things just pointed out. Even though the sensory response is looked upon as largely the product of the central nervous system, it is not produced by a restricted and localized part of it. All of the complicated interactions constitute what I call "utilization." Utilization differs from occasion to occasion, and is the neural substratum of what is most generally described in other kinds of terms such as emotion, attitude, memory.

## ILLUSIONS, PERCEPTUAL CONSTANCY
## AND OBJECTIVITY

For the most part, the discussions of sensory processes and perception that we have included have had to do with descriptions of awareness, the satisfaction of needs (bodily and others), and the emotions that accompany or are evoked by perception. We have been dealing with sensory processes and perception from the standpoint of the individual. There is still another pertinent and interesting problem—that of *veridicality*, which has to do with what is ordinarily called truth-telling. This use of the word truth makes it equivalent to the word, reality. However, we shall later discuss another connotation for the two words which will set them apart from each other.

The present problem has to do with the concept of *illusion*. In vision there has long been a group of geometrical figures which have been known as illusions. Illusions also occur in other senses. So, to round out our examination of the senses and perception we shall discuss the various ways sensory experience is related to the world outside of the individual. This is where the question of whether perceptions "tell the truth" comes in.

We live in a world of things (objects). Objects are what they are to us by reason of the way our sensory response mechanisms are affected by the energies the physicist and chemist describe. The ancients believed in a universe of entities with independent existence and that these entities were made known to us by a kind of ghostlike emanation that left us and went to external objects and brought back to us information about them. This was called the *emanation theory*. Today, this sounds absurd. We believe we know better. Nevertheless, recently a man phoned me to find out why hunters perceive other hunters as deer. He seriously and with some self-satisfaction proposed a reason to see what I thought of it. It was nothing but the old emanation theory, in scarcely a new dress.

Most people today still believe in the independent existence of objects, and that our senses make known these objects to us. For example, if we can't see color in the dark, the color is believed to still be there, but we just can't see it. The sophisticated view is not that at all, but that certain physical conditions may be independent of the perceiver and be existent when the individual is prevented from being affected by them, and thus does not perceive. In case of color, it is generally seen as a property of an object. The physical conditions that constitute the object may exist independently of the presence of a human observer. But, for the observer to see color, an additional "ingredient" or factor must exist, namely, photic radiation ("light") which reflects certain wavelengths more than others. So, the painting of a beautiful scene or the portrait of a friend exists only in the physical properties that make up the material of the canvas and paint. Color comes and goes as variably as the levels and wavelengths of illumination change.

What I have just said has been repeated countless times by a few people, but it doesn't seem real or understandable by most people.

Through the senses a physical world is made known to us, and it is a world describable in terms of what we see, hear, taste, smell, and touch. But this is a different description from what physicists and chemists give us. Physicists and chemists describe the world with man left out. And, when they do this, what is the description like? It is a world of energy manifestations having no trees, no cities, no people, no color, nor objects. It is a universe of "particles" or manifestations of energy. We have no reason to reject this description. It is a universal one which the people in science and technology of all nations accept. It involves no language barrier, no political biases, no nationalism. Man as man (a sensing, experiencing creature) is left out. Though this description has been taught even in some high schools for over a half century, it is not a view that is consistently held by most people even today. The other views make one feel better. Most people cannot readily comprehend a universe that is *not* describable in the sensory (experiential) words they have at their command. They cannot stand to accept a world as empty as physicists and chemists describe it. In fact, chemists don't always avoid sensory description since they are constrained by some of the very conditions that apply to all humans. They describe the chemical elements as materials having the properties we sense, like color and solidity. But this is not the ultimate description to which I've just referred. The ultimate and basic description they use daily in their work is given in structural formulae of molecules, etc., and in terms of certain kinds of "reactions."

But what do we do when we come to the study of man? There are two or three major choices, at least hypothetically. One is the ancient choice of conceiving of man as being apart from Nature, and that to study him one does not resort to what we have learned about Nature to account for anything he does. The other is to consider him a part of Nature. This implies that the same general understandings that apply to all else in Nature are to be applied in the study of man.

Most people straddle the two alternatives and, among other things, provide themselves with an additional problem. This straddling view assumes that man's body can be studied as a part of Nature, but that man is something else than his body. So, we have what is called dualism—a mind-body dichotomy.

The emergence of things or objects is most clearly pictured in the way our visual system performs. For this, let's consider the following example. We look and see a dark gray surface. On it a lighter area emerges which may be seen as simply as a spot. In the present case, we see it as a small *disk*, an independent object. We see it as something that looks solid that we can touch and pick up. Before we attempt to do this, it looks hard and, of course, has edges which can be grasped or traced with one's fingers. When we reach to touch it, we find the edges missing, and we can't pick it up. Whatever it is, it is part of the surface on which it exists. Soon we find that it is only a spot of light which perchance has been focused on the gray surface. Thus, when the photic radiation ("light beam") is intercepted, the disk disappears. It can be made to appear and disappear as many times as we wish simply by intercepting the photic beam. Thus we see that what was a real object visually does not have all the properties that we were led to believe it had by looking at it. It is not something that has independent existence. The texture (if any) that we see by looking at it is simply something visual. So are its hardness and tangible edge.

Now what are we going to say or do? Since it failed to have all of the properties expected of it, many people would be satisfied simply to call it an illusion and forget it, looking elsewhere for *reality*. This is the very way the advanced student of perception doesn't act.

Let us look at the light spot again. In spite of the knowledge we have just obtained, it still looks like the little hard disk that could be picked up. What the sense of vision first supplied, it still supplies.

Since we could not gain tactual corroboration for what we saw, the spot is not quite the full-fledged object it would have been had we obtained it. But, whatever it is, it is only what our senses make out of it. Both the initial object properties given by vision and the negation of any kind of object properties by touch were the products of sensory mechanisms. We have nothing outside of what the senses provide to go on. While this case would be counted by some as an illusion, a "mistaken perception," it is an example of what happens every minute of an individual's waking life as he looks about. Visual perception is making something out of the data provided by photic radiation. When the radiation ceases as we turn off the "light," we see nothing. It eliminates visual existence. What we *see* is thus only what is provided by the photic form of stimulus energy.

What you experienced visually, you called an illusion because when you touched the spot, it did not have the solid properties that a tactual thing would have. But what if it had had them? You would not have questioned your visual perception. You would have "known" you were right.

Let us turn the matter around, and use as an illustration an experience of a touchable (tangible) object, a raised spot on a surface. It is in the dark. The photic radiation (stimulation) for vision is absent. So, since you don't see what you touched, you still wonder about it. You want to see it. You know that since you experience darkness, your eyes are not stimulated and you have learned not to expect to see under such conditions. Knowing this, you "turn on the light" and examine what you touched. But let's say the raised area is so slight that it can't be seen. It still has tactile existence, and since you can't move or separate it from the surface or because it doesn't have a sharp edge, it can't be called a thing with the same meaning as if it were independent from the surface. But, since language is loose, you call it a thing, not an illusion. Since you tactilely experience it, though don't see it, you excuse the visual failure by saying the bump is *too slight* to see. This precludes its being an illusion for you. You have found a way to excuse vision for failing to give testimony.

However, if you were to use some sort of instrumentation (magnifying glass, for example) and couldn't visually perceive a raised place on the surface, you would conclude that you had experienced a tactual (haptic) illusion. However, with the excuse you originally used, you likely didn't feel the need of using a device to supplement naked vision. You just relied on touch.

These two cases show that you relied on visual perception and tactual perception in different ways. It is as if you were saying that touch is more real than vision.

Be this as it may, when touch or full haptic perception is all that one has to rely on when vision is precluded, one cannot fully determine the identity and apprehend the nature of something placed in the hand. One wants to see it so that he can obtain additional information. This is strange, for we have just said that touch is in some respects more real than vision. Here we are asking for a "less real" form of evidence to supplement this "more real" kind of evidence.

We could continue this procedure by examining the results obtained from employing the other forms of perception. Were we to do so, we would find that they are related to each other and participate in the daily moment-to-moment affairs of life in various ways, mostly supporting, but at times contradicting each other.

Illusions have been defined in textbooks as *mistaken perceptions.* This is an assertion that deserves a close look. Where was the mistake? On what basis can it be said that any mistake was made? We have pointed out the contradiction between the properties of a thing looked at and a thing touched. Even so, can we say that the visual experience was false? We have been taught in natural science not to expect something for nothing and not to expect nothing for something. Basically, we expect justifiable quantitative relations. By calling an experience an illusion and defining illusion as a mistake, we believe in a result without a cause.

The "mistake" must lie in the implied *use* one makes of the raw sensory data. The visual experience was real—as real as anything could be. So was the tactual one. If we look upon the perceptual end result as a bona fide result of the conditions producing it, we can say that when one is using visual perception, he is employing one set of conditions; when he is using touch, he is employing another set. If he respects the results each of these sets of conditions produces, he need not imply mistakes in the relations between cause and effect.

Some people attempt to explain the sensory contradictions by saying the mechanisms were all right but they obtained the wrong information. What was the basis of the perceptual information in each case? It was the energies that impinged on the various sense organs. These were the energies that the disciplines of natural science describe. As we said before, they constitute the

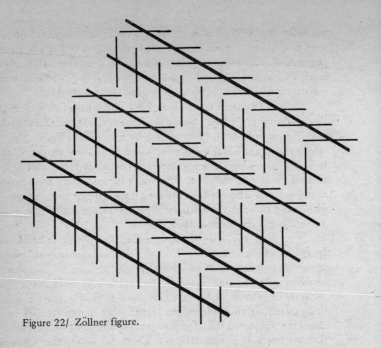

Figure 22/ Zöllner figure.

universe that the physicist and astronomer describe. So, how did any of the senses get "the *wrong* information"? This answer, like the remark about "mistaken perception," is not to be accepted in a detached and comprehensive view of the matter.

There are times when the specific characteristics of given visual "illusions" can be understood if one considers the probable operating principles of the modality in question.

Let us examine several visual "illusions" which from here on we shall more appropriately call *figures*. Many of these figures are named for certain men who pointed them out or studied them.

A good example of a so-called illusion is the Zöllner figure shown in Figure 22. As you see, it consists of several long parallel diagonal lines each of which is crossed by a series of short lines. These run in opposite directions on alternate lines. This is a complex configuration and was not constructed originally to represent any object in Nature. The overall pattern is not seen as strictly two-dimensional. Third-dimensional effects intrude as one views it. One might hazard a guess from the evolutionary standpoint that the human tends to see things in three dimensions, if possible. But we do not need even to make such a guess. All we need to do is to note that if one views the figure in certain ways, portions of it do represent three-dimensional configuration. What is seen, however, is that the pattern as a whole is not so constructed that it represents a *single* three-dimensional object.

The short cross lines of the upper long line appear to lie in a horizontal plane. So do the lines crossing the third diagonal. The other two sets of cross-lines lie in vertical planes. The whole configuration does seem to recede from lower right to upper left. One is viewing the vertical planes obliquely. They recede toward the left of the field. The major inconsistency in the configuration as a whole is that the long lines lying in the vertical planes and those in the horizontal planes do not converge toward a single vanishing point as they should.

On the basis of the fact that the configuration breaks apart—is not one consistent three-dimensional whole, but instead a form of nonsense pattern—one can rightfully ask why he should be expected to be able to regard the long lines as though they were the only lines in the total configuration. Logically, there is nothing to require this. Hence the fact that when one visually extracts the diagonal lines for perceptual consideration he finds they are not seen as parallel is not a basis for saying that what he is seeing is an illusion (a mistaken perception). The real fault lies in what the perceiver is trying to do. He has unwittingly accepted a task which is somewhat nonsensical, if we grant the appropriateness of what I have said initially about the figure being a kind of three-dimensional representation, but not actually a consistent one.

It is true that when given the question of whether the long diagonals look parallel, one looks and finds that they do not. If he measures, he finds that they are geometrically parallel. Since one tends to believe absolutely that the measurement tells the truth, then anything that differs must be a mistake.

The naive person does not recognize that he is operating on the wrong interpretative assumptions when he calls the result a perceptual mistake. Why doesn't he say, since he knows the paper on which the figure is drawn is a plane, that when the figure looks three-dimensional, it is also an example of a mistaken perception—an illusion. No one that I know would ever call a picture of a three-dimensional scene painted on a two-dimensional canvas, an illusion, just because he knows the canvas is two-dimensional. However, he would have to do so if he held the layman's usual beliefs about perception and illusions.

## TRUTH AND REALITY

We often use two words, *truth* and *reality*. Often the contexts in which we find them are somewhat different, but when asking what is meant by truth and what by reality, it seems as though we are asking about the same thing. For instance, how could anything be true if it isn't real, and how could anything be real if it isn't true?

It may be that we judge the real and the true in two different ways. What is true could be something actual, but not something experienced, whereas what is real is often judged by direct experience.

When we judge by direct experience, we often suppose we are judging by an ultimate criterion. Yet we are not always satisfied by the results. We ask about a more basic or ultimate form of existence, and when we do, we are concerned with whether what we experience conforms to this ultimate form.

Part of the time science is looked to for many of the answers to questions that are not answered by direct experience. Other times science is bypassed or disregarded for such answers.

Science in some of its aspects at least brings out the distinction between *truth* and *reality*. Traditional science is conducted to discover essences, laws, generalizations, all of which are abstractions, and they can be said to be true or approach the truth. But, by contrast, the *existence*, the reality of the individual case is left out of the description. Thus, we have it that propositions (laws, etc.) can be true without being real.

The Greeks in their day seriously discussed *universals* versus *specific cases*. This was a form of the same concern that is being expressed today. One does not experience universals as universals; he experiences specific situations as they come and go. These he calls reality.

Science as we view it in terms of laws and principles is a collection of statements of truth, the old Greek type of universals. The student fails to see them in action; hence, he calls for what is real. He wants direct experience or else *examples* of specific situations which convince him they are like his own. He can live vicariously in them.

The concepts and various concerns of today's physical science fail to come close to anything in our experience. Whether or not they do is not considered an issue by the theoretical physicist himself. Newtonian physics was stated in forms that did involve experience. *Force* was a kind of haptic experience. But today's nuclear physics is different. Despite the fact that it does not dwell on matters of direct experience, it succeeds very well in accomplishing a set of "practical" objectives which the man on the street can appreciate. It is the manner in which these objectives are accomplished that is unreal, but represents truth.

Much of textbook psychology deals with truth instead of reality. In this respect it fails to meet all the expectations and needs of those attempting to develop their own understandings.

Might there not be a middle ground, a form of description that is not confined to "single cases," but not given over to the abstractions found in generalizations? Perhaps some kinds of generalizations are needed after all—the kind that are less remote from everyday life than cold statements of law and principle. This has been one of the objectives motivating the present book. Maybe these are part of science, too.

## PAIN AND ANGUISH

Nothing is more important in human experience than pain. It often takes precedence over everything else. Since it is a form of perception, we need to give it some attention.

Like a number of other words in psychology, the term *pain* is used in more than one way. So we will have to indicate what we mean it. First, it is a human experience. This experience differs in certain respects when it is laboratory produced and when it appears in everyday life. This difference, in general, is often recognized by calling the nonlaboratory pain, clinical pain (everyday-life pain).

Laboratory pain has been analyzed mainly in three ways: (1) by thermo-mechanical styli applied to the skin, or *thermal radiation* to the skin's surface, (2) by determining the sensory effects of stimulating cutaneous nerves directly via needles inserted under the skin alongside the nerve in the forearm, and (3) by recording nerve action currents from electrical stimuli applied to sensory nerves and relating this activity to the sensations produced by the same stimuli. In any of these laboratory investigations a reasonable quantitative relation between impingement ("stimulus") and sensory outcome or nerve impulse discharge has been found.

Experiments with animals which, of course, cannot report on experiences, have relied on detection and measurements of body processes and overt reactions rather than reports on sensation. Skeletal muscle responses, such as withdrawal reactions, have been used as detectors. Despite not measuring *experience* (i.e., sensation or feeling) the responses have been called pain or pain responses.

In man, the facts gained from life situations indicate no simple relation between what is felt (and called pain) and the physical intensity of the stimulus. This has long been a kind of puzzle, for it violates the simple expectation of intensity of sensory end result being positively and simply related to the supposed stimulus.

Some of the most marked examples of this puzzling discrepancy have occurred on the battlefield where men badly injured have not felt the degree of pain expected or have denied feeling pain at all. Severe tissue damage often has hardly been felt.

An opposite example of the pain puzzle is the pain produced in terminal cancer and in heart attacks.

A very interesting demonstration of the discrepancy we are talking about has been shown in patients operated upon for relief of clinically manifested "pain" (King, Clausen and Scarff, 1950). In the case of six patients given lobotomies for such relief, all but one were successful. A lobotomy is the cutting across a lobe in the brain to eliminate the action of tissue. Curiously enough, four out of the five relieved patients manifested a *lower* cutaneous threshold on the same side of the body as the lobotomy when tested for pain produced by weak "stimuli" in a test situation. This meant that their sensitivity to mild stimuli was increased. The one patient whose distress was not relieved by his lobotomy showed *bilateral raising* of cutaneous threshold. This meant that this patient, though not helped for his clinical pain, was less sensitive to mild stimuli. It turned out that relief from clinical pain bore no direct relation to the amount of local tissue disturbance needed to produce threshold pain.

Noxious stimuli evoke several classes of reaction in man. These reactions are: *skeletal muscle responses, reactions* mediated by the autonomic nervous system, and *certain kinds of awareness* or experience which may be called suffering. In the early use of the term it was this sensory experience that was called pain. Now the whole complex is included and is called pain. At the same time, any single component is also called pain. So that sometimes one thing and at other times a different thing is called pain.

When the distress outruns the extent of local bodily disturbance, the autonomic nervous system may be contributing to the magnitude and character of the experience.

In cases of extremely unpleasant experience there is often muscle tension. If the experience is an enduring one, there may be a kind of maintained tension. If the exciting cause is sudden and brief, the tension is a kind of withdrawal flexion—an avoidance reaction.

But in all cases the cerebral cortex is involved. The

response is a perceptual one and involves evaluation of the situation. The perception is of threat and harm. It is no wonder then that various kinds of experimental data do not correspond with each other.

Our vocabularly is in need of revamping and sharpening. In fact, what is needed is a better understanding of sensation and perception in general.

The view commonly held at present in regard to sensation is that it is determined in the sense organ. Thus when the sensation is pain, it is supposed to be determined in local tissue, just as visual sensation is supposed to be determined in the eye. This view holds to a simple quantitative relation between the energy of the impingement and the magnitude of the sensation.

It is not fully recognized that the central nervous system is the basis for evaluative behavior (emotion), thinking, and perceiving. Some inputs are received and dealt with as signalling threat; some are received and handled with indifference; and others are dealt with as acceptable, as "good."

Inputs from pain-sense receptors may be reacted to as trivial or may invoke uneasiness. Sometimes the individual is so preoccupied with other stimuli that the input is ignored, as in the case of the men on the battlefield. Any number of different degrees and sorts of preoccupation may exist, or on the other hand, the individual may become fixated on the pain input and treat it all out of proportion to its so-called "objective" significance.

Experimental investigations have enhanced the paradox of the traditional view. For example, a drug used for the relief of local pain should, according to the traditional expectation, raise the *threshold* for feeling pain at that location. But that does not happen. Once the pain reliever is administered, weak local stimuli used to measure pain threshold are just about as effective as before the drug was given. This is certainly a puzzle, for it would have been expected that the alleviation of pain would have taken place by having raised the sensation threshold.

Under some surgical conditions, a subject will report that he is still pained, but that it doesn't hurt. While this may be a fair statement by the victim, it is nonetheless a paradox.

The first step in building a workable vocabulary for the purposes at hand is to choose an overall word that covers the unfavorable side of human experience. *Distress* seems to be a good one. Once adopted, we can ask what kinds of distress may there be. I would say that it might be a good thing to distinguish distress that pertains to or involves some kind of recognizable bodily discomfort ("pain") from the distress which does not. Perhaps all distress sooner or later, or to some small degree, involves bodily discomfort, but nevertheless, a distinction is logical and legitimate here. The distress that does involve bodily discomfort we shall call *anguish*. It is the kind of experience the patient has in terminal cancer, or in a heart attack, or in a lesser way in other cases.

Anguish involves the activation of the pain receptors, but it is the overwhelming personal reaction that ensues when the bodily feeling is bound up with threat and its cognitive consequences. This may seem very strange and sound like empty words, but it takes on more tangible meaning when we remember that some patients who have had brain surgery to alleviate unendurable "pain" report that certainly they still have pain but it doesn't hurt anymore.

The use of the word *anguish*, in addition to *pain*, is one recognition of this distinction. This use represents more realistic thinking than is common.

The next question is how the vocabulary just described handles the experimental laboratory facts and the facts of everyday life.

First of all, our vocabulary eliminates the practice of calling all sorts of discomfort pain. For example, we would not say that some social or economic situation we view, such as poverty, pains us. We would say that it distresses us. We would avoid saying certain things we don't like give us a headache. To say so would be a pure figure of speech. Of course, true headache is a form of pain, and the trouble may turn into anguish if severe enough.

Our outlook clarifies the question of why laboratory experiments often lead to conclusions different from those gained in everyday experiences. First of all, typical laboratory situations are brief and can be escaped from almost at will. They are, therefore, less threatening. They generally involve a lesser degree of stimulation, for often they are *threshold* determinations. Those experiments that encompass the subject and involve stronger and more enduring stimuli provide different results from the more typical experiments. They may produce *anguish*.

Perhaps one fact about pain that has been overlooked is that, as a sensation, it is not set up in a simple manner. The very sensory fibers that are activated in the skin to elicit it do not initially give pain. When weakly stimulated, they result in another sensation. Heinbecker, Bishop and O'Leary (1934) point out that there are four distinct sensations elicitable from electrically stimulating the skin. These are touch, pricking touch, cold, and warmth. Pain is the affective sensation produced by a *more* than threshold impingement (stimulation) of the pricking touch fibers. Thus what is elicitable at threshold is *not* pain. only becoming pain with more intense inputs (Bishop, 1946).

Pain is also a sensation that emerges after summation. Given a brief impingement of a certain intensity, delivering it once may not elicit pain. With a number of repetitions it gradually emerges as pain.

Taking such facts into account, it is less difficult to imagine moving from pain to anguish, without an artificial abruption. Even simple pain as a sensation is a complex rather than a simple one. Hence we do not go from pain, an absolutely simple result, to a complex one that is anguish. In terms of the physiology involved, pain is even complex to start with.

## PHANTOM LIMBS

Experiences of those who have had limbs amputated furnish us with evidence that pain and anguish are experiences that are produced by the action of the central nervous system and do occur in the total absence of the usual sense organs. Amputees often still experience the existence of the limb or limbs that have been removed and about 30 percent of these "phantom limbs" are painful (either periodically or quite chronically).

The pain and/or anguish experienced in phantom limbs is, of course, an example of the cortical basis of awareness.

Pain, of course, is not the only experience in phantom limbs, for they feel realistically present in all respects. The owner of the limb can clench the fist that is not there. He can step out of bed with the leg that is gone. In other words, the experiences have the same characteristics as before amputation and are not simply crude residuals. The central nervous system must be responsible for such a result.

## SLEEP

Regardless of what else sleep can be considered to be, it does represent a state during which the sensory contact and interaction with the environment is different from certain other states, most importantly, the waking state.

The ancients were interested in sleep and developed some very curious notions about it primarily because they interpreted dreams the way they did. If one dreamed he went some place, it was taken as a demonstration that the person (the soul) left the body and actually performed the acts the individual experienced in his dream.

In more recent times, sleep has been studied experimentally. One of the earliest kinds of interest was a study of its depth, and for this, quantitative means were used to determine what it took to waken the individual. Next came the question of what internal conditions cause sleep. This, of course, involved the study of body processes, much of it biochemistry. Here Siamese (conjoined) twins proved useful, for they have a common circulatory system. When it was found that one twin could be asleep while the other was awake, it was concluded that chemical changes in the blood could not be the crucial factor.

One of the other features of sleep that was studied was the bodily movements involved during sleep. Sleepers were watched to determine how often they seemed to rouse and turn over.

The greatest advances have been made with the advent of electrical recording of neural activity. One concern for a long time was the ability to determine when a person is asleep and when awake. Electrical recording of potentials on the scalp (brain waves, EEG's) has helped answer this question. Long before such recording, this question was asked. Long before such recording, it was known that there was a transitional stage between waking and sleep called the *hypnogogic state*.

Another question that persisted was whether or not people can exist without sleeping and, also, how much sleep do people generally need.

Sleep has been found not to be all of one sort as judged by EEG's (electroencephalograms), considered in relation with heart rate and records of throat muscle tension, eye movements, and ease of wakening the sleeper. According to these criteria, sleep is of two kinds. These were originally called *light sleep* and *deep sleep*. The labels have been changed because it has been shown they did not fit the facts in the way used. Now the two are called *normal* and *paradoxical* sleep.

Upon first going into sleep, the sleep is "normal," and only later is paradoxical sleep reached. However, during this later period, the person may alternate back and forth between the two types. Normal sleep is characterized by large slow brain waves, eyes quiescent, heart regular and throat muscles tense. Paradoxical sleep manifests low-voltage rapid waves, rapid eye movements, relaxed throat muscles, and irregular heart rate. Throat-muscle relaxation is the first sign that a period of rapid eye movements is about to begin.

Various limb movements occur during paradoxical sleep, and it is during this sleep that dreams and nightmares occur. Facial twitches occur very often during nightmares. One of the characteristics of nightmares is the experience of being unable to move. The sleeper seems to be pulled toward some very horrible fate while trying to escape but can't. Intermittent twitches and stifled cries are interspersed between periods of rapid eye movements. After about one-half minute, the sleeper is able to wake up.

The attempt to escape from a dream but finding oneself paralyzed is typified in an affliction called *narcolepsy*. Persons with this disorder are abnormally apt to fall asleep under a variety of conditions. In situations that are monotonous, such as when riding on buses and trains or even when walking, sleepiness comes over them. At such times they may tend to bump into people or appear drunk. Sometimes they become sleepy while eating and fall asleep at dessert. This is especially funny to those around, and embarrassing to the person. Recordings have shown that these people pass immediately into paradoxical sleep instead of into normal sleep as others do. After a short period of this type of sleep they may waken and, if they fall asleep again soon, they go into normal sleep. In keeping with the fact that they go right into paradoxical sleep, these persons often have very vivid dreams during their short naps.

This sleep paralysis that narcoleptics report is probably a nightmare for it consists in unpleasant experiences including headless monsters and the like. It also involves feeling paralyzed and thus unable to move.

We have already mentioned the question of the need to sleep. For awhile it was thought that there was actually a need to dream. This idea has given place to the idea of a need for paradoxical sleep. Sleep-deprived persons always fall into normal sleep and narcoleptics always fall into paradoxical sleep unless they have just previously had a period of paradoxical sleep.

All occasions of reduced connection with the environs are not sleep. Of course we know of coma when certain drugs have been administered, and hypnosis which is produced under another set of conditions. Some reactions produced in subhumans in which no vocal instructions, of course, can be given are called animal hypnosis. It seems that animal hypnosis can be induced up and down the animal kingdom from man to cockroach. Other names have also been applied to the state as, for example, sham-death reflex, death feinting, and inhibitory experimental neurosis.

One frequent characteristic of sleep is the fact that a person can sleep and wake up and be unaware that he has been sleeping. This fact comes to attention in two typical situations. One is the allegation of certain persons in the morning, following a night's stay in bed, that they haven't "slept a wink all night long." Many of us have seen a relative lapse into slumber, and even snore, while sitting in a chair. Yet when he wakes up, he denies that he had been sleeping. In fact, I have had my wife tell me a number of times that I had been sleeping while sitting in a reclining chair. In some of those cases, I was able to admit it. It seemed fairly clear that I had, for I had greatly bent my neck and had periodically been aware of trying to straighten up. But, in other cases, I was totally oblivious to having slept. In fact, the naps were short enough that I had no "clock" knowledge with which to check on myself.

Oswald cites a study by Dr. Betty Schwartz in Paris of patients who claimed that they could not sleep at all. In all the cases, EEG electrodes were placed on these patients' scalps, and they went to bed expecting to have another night's full wakefulness. A buzzer was sounded many times during the night, and the signal button which they were to press when they heard the buzz, never got pressed.

Some of these patients did, of course, rouse a bit from time to time and say to the observer, "You see, I'm still awake."

In the morning the patients had no recollection of hearing the buzz or of the times when the observers came in and out of the room.

All sleep is not equally deep. That is, all sleep is not equally a state of relaxation. This was brought out in distinguishing the two kinds of sleep already mentioned. The deeper and longer the sleep, the more marked the transition has to be to get into ambulatory activity. Hence after certain "good nights" of sleep one feels worse than after nights in which there was more dreaming, or the nights in which sleep was definitely intermittent. This is surprising if one does not consider the matter of transition and the amounts of *shift* involved in getting from one state to the other. If one is going to call sleep ineffective just because he does not wake up instantly ready to "rear and tear," he is overlooking the very principle we are talking about.

Let us take an example of the relation of sleep and its transition states and such a common thing as "fatigue." Fatigue is naively looked upon as an energistic phenomenon. One feels tired when he is lacking in energy. This view is staunchly held to in spite of the fact that certain glaring contradictions are fairly commonly recognized. Hence, if one wakes up feeling fatigued or tired, then sleep hasn't done what has been expected of it. Let's say Person X wakes up from a night's sleep. He believes he has to get right up and prepare for the day's work. But, as is fairly characteristic, he becomes introspective. He examines how he feels and quickly concludes he is pretty tired. In a moment or so he remembers that it is Sunday morning and he isn't supposed to go to work. He turns over and prepares to go back to sleep. At this point, further self-examination produces the realization that he is very comfortable. What changed from the instant he was tired to the later instant in which he felt quite comfortable and pleasant? The change certainly was not in some energistic state or in metabolism, as would be expected from eating food. It was a change consequent to realizing that he did not face a task. The very bodily feeling that seemed inappropriate for performing a task now meant something different when no task was required. In the one case it was "fatigue," in the second case it was "relaxation." It was simply that immediately upon waking, a transition period was required before the kind of bodily feelings that make bodily activity thinkable or actually pleasurable would set in. The same bodily feelings were appropriate for sinking back into sleep. One should not, therefore, say that sleep is ineffective when all he is experiencing is the lack of muscle tone existing prior to getting out of bed and making the full transition to active waking conditions.

It is true, however, that the ability to make the transition quickly and well may vary, but failure may not be so appropriately chalked up against sleep, as to something else. In thinking of sleep as restorative, too much is often expected of it.

Apparently, one author regards sleep as a psychonoxious rather than a psychotherapeutic or restorative state. He points out that people may fall ill during sleep. They may go to bed in seemingly good health and serenity, and awaken during the night in states of distress of one sort or another. This may range from anxiety to rage or to depression, or even, in the other direction, to states of euphoria and elation. He thinks that the least frequent experience in awakening is one of refreshment.

The fact that the things this author mentions do actually occur mainly highlights the fact that in sleep the individual is somewhat detached (isolated) from the surrounds, and this leaves him prey to the curious tangents that his internal processes taken when not guided by the environment.

In general, then, the individual is permitted by this very detachment to become reorganized, to recover from the various residual effects of meeting the previous day's confrontments. There are cumulative effects produced, particularly from conflicting forms of response to sensory impingements. Some of these actually accumulate in the form of tensions in both skeletal and visceral musculature. Other processes, too, need to occur to restore certain biochemical conditions to *status quo ante*. This can be considered a feature of homeostasis, even though one hears little about it in such a context.

In two places (Bartley and Chute, 1947; Bartley, 1965), considerable examination has been made of the matter of reorganization in connection with fatigue.

## CROWDS AS POTENT
## PERCEPTUAL ENVIRONMENTS

Having discussed the effects of sensory deprivation, we can see that the human individual thrives on a sizeable amount of sensory input, as clearly demonstrated both by the laboratory findings and the cases of isolation in life situations. The individual, strictly speaking, cannot live in a sensory vacuum. Actually, no physical environment can be a complete vacuum since it always provides *some* sensory stimulation. But where stimulation is reduced to a bare minimum, the individual develops curious experiences and his tested behavior deteriorates. It appears sensory stimulation is a guiding, sustaining and directing influence.

We now wish to discuss a form of a very potent stimulation for the human individual and thereby to go a long way in the direction opposite to deprivation. It would appear that the presence of many people as a context fulfills this requirement. In general, we can call these groups, *crowds*. Crowds, however, are of several sorts and although they have some effects in common they differ greatly, depending upon what the people in them are doing.

Some crowds are *incidental* One of the best examples of this is a sidewalk on a busy street downtown in a big city. There are many people in the immediate area, but you and they are there for independent purposes. The people you see are going in various directions. No one thing connects you all except the geometry of the scene and traffic regulations which govern all. As far as you are concerned, the people are somewhat incidental and, being in that category, they affect you less than under other conditions. Nevertheless, there is a vast perceptual and consequent mood difference evoked between such a scene and an empty street.

This same scene (incidental crowd) may be turned into something else just as soon as a single event of the right sort takes place. Let there be a traffic accident, or sudden rain. The motives of the individuals in the crowd become more alike. The people begin to have a single goal. In the first case it is to see what has happened. In the second case, it is to dash for cover. So, here we have an active, rather than an incidental crowd.

*Active crowds* are of several sorts. (Let it be understood, of course, that in our classification we are not following any recognized sociological scheme.) It may be said that active crowds are polarized in possibly one, two, three, or possibly even more directions. However, as poles multiply, the crowds would take on the characteristics described for incidental crowds.

A singly polarized crowd is one in which all members are involved in a single purpose. A bipolar crowd is one in which there are two subgroups interacting in opposition such as with demonstrators and police. Most often such crowds are actually tripolar, since there are many people besides the two most active groups; they may be thought of as spectators, but constitute a third group. They may seem passive, but they are more involved than they think.

What we wish to talk about with reference to active crowds are the powerful influences they exert on the individuals within them. It is a very different thing to be involved in an action alone than with many, many other people. The very sight of them is an extremely stimulating influence.

With the sight of other people around him bent on the same purpose, the individual ceases to act alone. He is carried away with what he sees going on. He may develop a heroic feeling. Any purpose involved at the moment seems lofty and right regardless of what it is. In such situations, perception leads directly to mood and drive, and this is the reason that descriptions of social activities so quickly lose sight of the fact that behavior rests on sensory input. We insist on not making that mistake. The crowd situation is primarily an example of perception at work, mediating between the environment and the moods it induces. At every instant the sensory mechanisms are at work discriminating and feeding in data to the higher centers of the brain where they are utilized both for action (response) and for orientation (mood).

It would be impossible to describe aptly at this point all the usual things that take place within the individuals involved. We know of no study of crowds, mobs and riots that has been so conducted as to disclose all that happens to the individual in such situations, but what happens in a true riot is undeniably overwhelming.

In this country for the most part, few people had any firsthand experience with *active* crowds except at football, basketball, hockey, and other games where most of the activity is channeled into more harmless modes of expression. This absence of violent crowds has not been the case throughout history, even in the Western world.

England in the eighteenth century twice saw Parliament pass Riot Acts defining the inciting situation and what was to be done about people congregating under certain conditions. It was recognized that the congregating of people together (even when only a few) sometimes posed a threat to peace, property and life. The appropriate officer was to "read the Riot Act" and thereby make it illegal for the individuals to continue their assemblage. Looting was one of the known associates of rioting and dire penalties were prescribed for it.

The essence of all this was that an essentially different set of behavioral influences was recognized to be at work under these conditions and that, therefore, different measures had to be used to treat behavior. But this is not recognized in this country even by most intelligent people today. Those who have been participants in riots or even those who have been more than passive members of the third pole can well testify to the unusual moods and driving forces that operate in such situations. By comparing how one feels and what one will do in these cases with how one usually feels, reasons, and behaves, one hardly recognizes the behavior as his own. It is that different.

While what we have just been describing is mood, passion, and overt behavior, the basis for the whole thing is the sensory and perceptual machinery. One *sees, hears*, and through additional senses comes into contact with this active people-filled situation, and things *look different, sound different*, and *feel different*.

In books such situations are generally described as *social* situations. But most times the word, *social*, is used as a neutral way of saying that things are different when they involve people than otherwise. The describer stops with the label of social. It is true that in many fundamental ways the principles of sensory stimulation are the same whether or not they involve people as stimuli. It is also true that when one perceives his immediate environs as containing other persons, added potency and other differences do come into play.

When many people are actively involved and when this action is thwarted, overwhelming forces are let loose within the individual. The vehicle for this is to be sought and found in the perceptual and sensory processes.

Despite our civilization's being quite old, it has not tried to understand this well enough to know or put into practice the appropriate actions to take. It is incumbent upon the students of sensory processes and perception to study the matter more fully and let their results be known. In fact, there is enough known now to necessitate something being taught children about crowds and riots.

# EXTENSIONS OF OUR SENSORY MECHANISMS

It is entirely in keeping with the tenor of our discussions on sensation and perception to include a few remarks about what we shall term the extensions of human sensory capacities. They are all around us and we are familiar with most of them, but it is not common to regard them as extensions of sensory capacity. It would be helpful to do so.

Most of these extensions pertain to the senses of sight and hearing, and can be classed as devices which sharpen these senses and those which extend their range over great distances in space. Some of the specific devices that we will mention do both.

The most familiar device is our eyeglasses. They provide for our seeing clearly at greater distances and for increased visual acuity in examining small items. The usual binoculars or field glasses enable us to see distant objects better. They enlarge the images of these objects on the retina and curiously enough this makes the objects look closer rather than larger. Some distortions are introduced but these are generally overlooked by most users of field glasses. Range-finders in gunnery are still another form of sensory extension. A much greater extension of our visual range is brought about by telescopes which enable objects at astronomical distances to be examined. Along with *direct extension* of vision go two forms of collateral extension. One is long-range photography and the other is television, which give us pictures. Radar and sonar, the one for air and the other for underwater detection of objects, extend the sensory appreciation of the environment in a different way.

Certain other devices are used to enhance or even usefully distort the optical inputs to the eye from certain targets. Stereoscopes belong to this class. By the use of two different views of a scene, the third-dimensional features are exaggerated. Rangefinders operate on much the same principle and, in turn, enable more accurate gunnery.

Still another device which enables further sensory appreciation is the common slide projector which uses small pictures to produce huge ones, life-size or greater, and thus enables the visual detection of features not possible with small pictures.

A further optical device that enables people to see and appreciate environmental objects is the periscope, used on underwater vessels to see objects above the surface in various directions. Periscopes enable us to see around corners, too.

Close to the periscope is the bronchoscope which is used to see the interior of respiratory passages such as the trachea and bronchi.

As well as extending vision to cover great distances we are now able to go in the opposite direction—to enabling vision for tiny things. The microscope has been with us for about four centuries and it has been improved from its crude beginnings to the electron microscopes of today which provides detection of small items by magnifying them by a factor as large as 300,000 times. The ordinary microscope generally has a range of 25 to let's say 900 diameters. Put into different terms, some people allege that electron microscopes can make linear dimensions of about 24 trillionths of an inch visible.

We turn now to the extensions of hearing. The most widespread among them is possibly the telephone whereby we can talk to other people anywhere in the industrially developed world. Public address systems are used routinely for enhancing the voices of speakers and for other sound sources. Next in this category is radio, which can reach astronomical distances.

One of the commonly used extensions of the ability to hear is the physician's stethoscope for listening to the heart and respiratory passages. Such devices as the stethoscope are now surpassed by monitoring devices which can be attached to persons and function during vigorous bodily activity at a distance from the recording station. This overall device, of course, also makes heart activity visible and could have been mentioned along with the other extension of seeing, for what is obtained is a wave picture on a strip of recording paper.

A last category of sensory extensions we shall mention is the group including probes, forceps and tweezers. These are haptic, of course, and allow the person to deal with objects too tiny to grasp with the naked fingers, too inaccessible for fingers to reach, or with problems in which the muscles are too weak to cope.

There are still other devices, but the ones just mentioned are sufficient to emphasize the existence of sensory extensions and suggest the importance they have in our lives. They also demonstrate that a great deal of modern technology has to do with complementing human senses.

We live in a world which provides us with all these things from childhood up and so take them for granted, seldom wondering what a world without them would be like.

# glossary

analgesic

A *mild* sedative such as aspirin.

analysis

A mode of abstracting something from a system in which it is a part. The item extracted is not fully like the item as it is a part of the system. Hence there is some degree of artificiality to all analysis. Chemistry provides some of the best examples. We say water is $H_2O$ but the properties of H and O, taken separately, have little resemblance to those elements as components of water. The proper understanding of what analysis is and what use can be made of it is one of the very most basic features of science.

anguish

The state in which stimulation of pain receptors is utilized to indicate danger. Thus a form of distress emerges that is often quite intolerable. Instead of simply calling this experience *pain*, it is preferably called *anguish*. It seems to follow a different set of relations to sensory input, and also to the drugs given for its alleviation, than does simple pain.

anosmic

The inability to smell odors.

approach,
environment-
centered

The practice of beginning with impingement characteristics in the attempt to predict behavioral outcome. This is the traditional approach and has kept experimental and the more humanistic forms of psychology apart.

approach,

The practice of using the organism rather

| | |
|---|---|
| organism-centered | than the impingement as the point to start from in viewing various matters about behavior. In this approach the principle of utilization is employed. |
| auditory | Having to do with hearing. Since the word is an adjective, it labels the hearing system. |
| axillary | Pertaining to the armpit. |
| biological science | The disciplines that deal with organisms in terms of physics and chemistry. |
| blind, adventitious | Becoming blind sometime after birth. |
| blind, congenital | Born blind. |
| causal system | A system in which there is cause and effect. In natural science it is an energistic system with units of weight, power, distance, force, velocity, time, etc. Other (would-be) causal systems are supernatural or preternatural (outside of nature). It is common for people to go outside of nature to explain natural phenomena. Science is not built that way. |
| centrifuge, human | A huge, heavy turntable on which human subjects can be tested for effects produced by various velocities, changes in velocity, etc. |
| cutaneous | Pertaining to the skin. |
| decibel | A unit of energy. Its most common use is in designating an acoustic stimulus. |
| display | Any action that communicates with another animal. |
| dorsal | Pertaining to the back. |
| dualism | The belief that man is made up of two components—a body and a nonmaterial entity which can exist independently from it. Actually, many dualists contradict themselves when they make mind and body independent, since they contend at the same time that there are no disembodied spirits, minds or whatever. |

| | |
|---|---|
| edema | Swelling of tissue. |
| energistic | Having to do with energy and force, e.g., watts, footpounds, and other such units. |
| energy | A basic feature of nature. |
| erotic | The quality of something that arouses sexual desire. It is thus said that certain literature is erotic, while on the other hand certain haptic stimuli are said to be erotic. |
| eroticism | The practice of arousing sexual desire by what is said, what is shown, or by the use of touch. |
| estrous | The sexual cycle in females. |
| explanation | An account of the conditions under which something happens, in such a way as to relate it to a causal system. It turns out that personalistically any such description that satisfies the questioner is an explanation. It is an account which relates a specific event to the general class of phenomena to which it belongs. Thus an explanation uses known principles to account for the single event which is up to that moment a kind of unknown. |
| haptic | A form of perception in which sensitivity and response to mechanical influences on the organism are involved. "Haptic" is derived from a Greek word signifying "able to lay hold of." Haptic perception involves not only touch, temperature and pain, but also the receptors of the muscles, tendons and joints. |
| heat load | The amount of heat contained in the body above or below a certain reference level. Thus there are both positive and negative heat loads. |
| homeostasis | The combination of all the processes which operate toward maintaining balance in the body. The cells of the body are |

viewed as living in a chemical and thermal environment. This internal environment is made up of the fluids of the body. Part of homeostasis is describable in terms of time processes. This is to say that cells are involved in maintaining homeostasis. Some of these cells are sense cells (receptors). Hence sensory systems or modalities are involved.

impingement
Energy which reaches sense organs.

individual
A term used when the human is referred to in a more general way. In some cases it contrasts single humans from groups.

integument
The covering of the body, especially the skin.

item
A term used when the perceiver is not involved. Traditionally, *object* is used both for perceptual units and for units that are not people's experiences. *Item* is the preferable term for the latter.

kinesthesis
The sensory system of receptors in muscles, joints, and tendons.

labyrinth
The part of the inner ear having to do with relations of the person to gravity.

material
Any kind of data or other content that constitutes the substance being dealt with.

materialistic
A quality attributed to various views and theories that omit something non-physical as being part of the universe. The word materialistic has meaning only in a dualistic framework or premise. Monisms are neither materialistic nor non-materialistic. The word *materialistic* is used by some as an intended denouncement of a given theory or idea.

mechanical
Anything that involves contacts, pushes, pulls, compressions and twists. Some other concepts involved are movement and velocity. Man senses mechanically

expressed energy mainly through the haptic sense.

**mentalism**  A viewpoint or system in which only conscious behavior is considered psychological. Older psychologies were defined as studies of consciousness or mind, or of "mental life." Take, for example, the word *assume*. It would mean consciously taking something for granted, not acting as if the behavior were based on lack of awareness.

**monism**  The belief that there is only one kind of system or entity that makes up the human, instead of there being two (mind and body). The phenomena that the dualistic calls *mind*, stem from body process.

**natural science**  Basically, it is chemistry and physics, but when biological phenomena can be dealt with energistically, they become a part of natural science.

**nystagmus**  Involuntary horizontal eye movements ordinarily characterized by a slow drift in one direction and a quick reverse movement. These alternate and continue for some time.

**object**  A term applied to what a person perceives. People live (perceive) in a "world of objects."

**observer**  The term used for a subject when, in a perception experiment, he is called upon to make observations, report on sensation, etc.

**olfaction**  The sense of smell.

**organism**  The biological word for an animal, including the human.

**otolith**  The prefix oto = ear, lith = stone. A part of the inner ear sensitive to head posture and often called the otolith organ.

**pain**  A kind of unpleasant sensation or experience that stems from the activation of certain receptors. Under restricted laboratory conditions this experience is never as overwhelming as in clinical situations. Pain as meant here is a form of sensation. In clinical situations the peculiar state of the individual is such that small sensory inputs to the central nervous system are utilized to produce threat and thus pain becomes *anguish*.

**parathyroid gland**   A gland having to do with calcium metabolism.

**perception**   The immediate discriminatory result of energy reaching sense organs. This discrimination is expressed at the personalistic level and is not based solely upon action at a single set of sense organs. It is the utilization of the input to all sense organs being activated at the time.

**person**   The organism acting as a unit in relation to environmental conditions impinging on it.

**personalistic**   Anything that is expressed by the organism acting as a unit (as a person). The more traditional term used here is *psychological*. But since this word involves so many naive conceptions about the organism, it is a far less appropriate word to use in a systematic and sophisticated language about the organism.

**physical**   Commonly that which can be touched or otherwise sensed as existing. The body is said to be physical. In the more restricted definition, physical is that which pertains to physics, a scientific discipline. There the data are basically quantities of energy with no qualitative characteristics whatsoever. Newtonian physics did deal with phenomena that were experienced, but the attempt has been to leave man out of the measurements, etc.

| progestational | Promoting gestation. Pertaining to those substances and processes active in the menstrual cycle or during pregnancy. |
|---|---|
| proprioceptor | A special class of sense organ sensitive to overall body position or one of the limbs. The organs are in muscle, tendons and joints and in the labyrinth. |
| psychophysical | The data obtained by the method of psychophysics are said to be psychophysical. This is a category coordinate with the physical and the informal responses that arise in any informal situation. Thus in psychology there are the *physical* (stimuli), *psychophysical,* and the purely behavioral or experimental *psychological.* |
| psychophysics | A laboratory investigation procedure, wherein certain formal manipulation of impingement (stimulus) conditions are used. The procedure involves certain designated ways in which the data are treated when obtained. |
| savor | To detect, discriminate, enjoy or dislike, through nasal and oral stimulation. The term *savory* is often used to indicate pleasant odors and/or tastes. |
| sedative | A substance which allays discomfort by lessening or obliterating pain or anguish. |
| sensation | The experience resulting from activation of sense organs. |
| sensitivity training | Training used by certain groups in psychology whereby individuals are enabled to react to the social environment better. |
| stimulus | Energy which reaches sense organs and induces a response of the organism. |
| subject | The human or other animal as used in an experiment, or in any scientific study. |
| subpersonalistic | A term applicable to processes within the organism, when abstracted by analy- |

sis. Actually, the organism is always acting as a unit, but by abstraction we can artificially isolate various processes and study their essential characteristics as if affected by no other processes. For example, there is the process of digestion. It can be described, but how digestion actually occurs in any given case depends upon the other processes going on in the organism at the same time. This is to say, how the person is performing.

surrogate | That which substitutes for another.

taste | One of the sense modalities involving the results produced by activating taste buds in the mouth. Since the results obtained do not stem from this form of stimulation alone, two terms are needed. Olfaction (the sense of smell) and other senses are often involved also in producing what is ordinarily called taste. *Taste* then can better be the name for the sensory experience produced by putting something in the mouth. In such a case, *gustation* can be the name for the results of stimulating taste buds, one of the components of the overall situation.

thermal | The form of energy that is involved in activating temperature receptors. When we say something is cold, we are using a word to indicate how it feels, not giving a quantitative account on a thermal scale.

thigmotaxis | The movement of an organism with reference to a solid object.

tonic | Pertaining to muscular tension.

transcendental meditation | A form of concentrated continued thought or contemplation, instigated and guided by a form of doctrine holding that reality is essentially mental or spiritual in nature. *Oriental* would be a fair synonym in this case for *transcendental*.

| | |
|---|---|
| tropism | Response in simple animals to some feature of the environment. |
| utilization | The use which the organism as a person makes of energy that impinges on sense organs. This energy is simply raw material, so to speak. Some patterns of energy can be utilized in many ways; the use that can be made of other patterns is much more limited, hence there is a more predictable relation between impingement and personal response. |
| ventral | Pertaining to the front of the body. |
| vestibule | See *Labyrinth*. |

# references

Adler, J. Chemoreceptors in bacteria. *Science,* 1969, *166,* 1588-1592.

Anonymous. Please do touch the daisies. *Time,* July 25, 1969.

Anonymous. The unlikeliest product. *Time,* December 26, 1960.

Anonymous. Wanted: Girl who will live in a cold tent. *The State Journal,* Lansing, Michigan, February 8, 1970.

Atcheson, R. Rubbing the right way. *Holiday,* 1970-71, Dec.-Jan., 22-26.

Baldwin, A. L. *Behavior and development in childhood.* New York: Dryden Press, 1955.

Bartley, S. H. *Fatigue: Mechanism and management.* Springfield, Ill.: Charles C. Thomas, 1965.

Bartley, S. H. *The human organism as a person.* Philadelphia: Chilton Books, 1967.

Bartley, S. H. *Principles of perception, second edition.* New York Harper & Row, 1969.

Bartley, S. H., and Chute, E. *Fatigue and impairment in man.* New York: McGraw-Hill, 1947.

Beach, F. A. Analysis of the stimuli adequate to elicit mating behavior in the sexually inexperienced male rat. *J. Comp. Psychol.,* 1942, *33,* 163-207.

Beach, F. A., and Gilmore, R. W. Response of male dogs to urine from females in heat. *J. Mammal.,* 1949, *30,* 391-392.

Beach, F. A., and Levinson, G. Effects of androgen on the glans penis and mating behavior of castrated male rats. *J. Exp. Zool.,* 1950, *114,* 159-168.

Bedichek, R. *The sense of smell.* New York: Doubleday, 1960.

Beecher, H. K. *Measurement of subjective responses.* New York: Oxford Univ. Press, 1959.

Beidler, L. M. The chemical senses. *Ann. Rev. Psychol.,* 1961, *12,* 363-388.

Bermant, G., and Westbrook, W. H. Peripheral factors in the regulation of sexual contact by female rats. *J. Comp. Physiol. Psychol.,* 1966, *61,* 244-250.

Bexton, W. H., Heron, W., and Scott, T. H. Effects of decreased variation in the sensory environment. *Canad. J. Psychol.,* 1954, *8,* 70-76.

Bienfang, R. *The subtle senses.* Norman, Okla.: Univ. Oklahoma Press, 1946.

Bierrien, F. K. The effects of noise. *Psychol. Bull.,* 1946, *43,* 141-161.

Bishop, G. H. Neural mechanisms of cutaneous sense. *Physiol. Revs.,* 1946, *26,* 77-102.

Bowlby, J. *Attachment and loss; Vol. I, Attachment.* New York: Basic Books, 1969.

Brackbill, Y., Adams, G., Crowell, D. H., and Gray, M. L. Arousal level in neonates and preschool children under continous auditory stimulation. *J. Exp. Child Psychol.*, 1966, *4*, 178-188.

Brackbill, Y., and Fitzgerald, H. E. Development of sensory analyzers during infancy. In L. P. Lipsitt and H. Reese (Eds.), *Recent advances in child development and behavior, Vol. 4.* New York: Academic Press, 1969.

Brannon, J. B., Jr. Linguistic word classes in the spoken language of normal, hard of hearing, and deaf children. *J. Speech and Hear. Res.*, 1968, *11*, 279-287.

Bronson, F. H., Eleftheriou, B. E., and Garick, E. I. Effects of intra- and inter-specific social stimulation on implantation in deermice. *J. Reproduction and Fertility*, 1964, *8*, 23-27.

Bruce, H. M. An exteroceptive block to pregnancy in the mouse. *Nature*, 1959, *184*, 105.

Bruddenbrock, W. von. *The senses.* Ann Arbor, Mich.: Univ. of Mich Press, 1958.

Burton, M. *Phoenix re-born.* London: Hutchison, 1959.

Burton, M. *Animal partnerships.* London: Warne and Co., 1969.

Carmichael, L. Behavior during fetal life. In *Encyclopedia of psychology*. New York: Citadel Press, 1951.

Carr, W. J., and Caul, W. F. The effect of castration in rat upon the discrimination of sex odours. *Anim. Behav.*, 1962, *10*, 20-27.

Carr, W. J., Loeb, L. S., and Dissinger, M. E. Responses of rats to sex odors. *J. Comp. Physiol. Psychol.*, 1965, *59*, 370-377.

Carthy, J. O. *An introduction to the behavior of invertebrates.* New York: Macmillan, 1958.

Chipman, R. K., Holt, J. A., and Fox, K. A. Pregnancy failure in laboratory mice after multiple short term exposure to strange males. *Nature*, 1966, *210*, 652.

Collias, N. E. The analysis of socialization in sheep and goats. *Ecology*, 1956, *37*, 228-239.

Collins, L. G. Pain sensitivity and ratings of childhood experience. *Percept. Mot. Skills*, 1965, *21*, 349-350.

Cutsforth, T. D. *The blind in school and society.* New York: Amer. Foundation for the Blind, 1951.

Davenport, W. Sexual patterns and their regulation in a society of the Southwest Pacific. In F. A. Beach (Ed.), *Sex and behavior.* New York: Wiley, 1965.

Dember, W. N. *Psychology of perception.* New York: Holt, Rinehart and Winston, 1965.

DeReuck, A. V. S., and Knight, J. (Eds.). *Hearing mechanisms in vertebrates.* Boston, Mass.: Little, Brown & Co., 1968.

Dixon, N. F., and Dixon, P. M. "Sloping water" and related framework illusions: Some informal observations. *Quart. J. Exp. Psychol.*, 1966, *18*, 369-370.

Doane, B. K., Mahatoo, W., Heron, W., and Scott, T. H. Changes in perceptual function after isolation. *Canad. J. Psychol.*, 1959, *13*, 210-219.

Dominic, C. J. Observations on the reproductive pheromones of mice. I. Source. *J. Reproduction and Fertility*, 1966, *11*, 407-414.

Doty, R. L. Homospecific and heterospecific odor preferences in sexually-naive *Peromyscus maniculatus bairdi* and *Peromyscus lencopus*. Unpublished doctoral dissertation, Department of Psychology, Michigan State University, East Lansing, Michigan, 1972.

Doty, R. L., Carter-Porges, C. S., and Clemens, L. Olfactory control of sexual behavior in the male and early-androgenized female hamster. *Hormones and Behavior,* 1971, *2,* in press.

Doty, R. L., and Levine, R. L. Odor preferences of female *Peromyscus maniculatus bairdi* for male mouse odors of *P. m. bairdi* and *P. lencopus* as a function of estrous state. *Amer. Zool.,* 1970, *10,* 479.

Douglas, R. J. Cues for spontaneous alternation. *J. Comp. physiol. Psychol.,* 1966, *62*, 171-183.

Drillien, M. Studies in prematurity. Part 4: Development and progress of the prematurely born child in the preschool period. *Arch. Dis. Childhood,* 1948, *23,* 69-83.

Dröscher, V. B. *The magic of the senses.* New York: Dutton, 1969.

Eakin, R. M. The third eye. *Amer. Scientist,* 1970, *58,* 73-79.

Eakin, R. M., Stebbins, R. C., and Wilhoft, D. C. Effects of parietalectomy and sustained temperature on thyroid of lizard, *Sceloporous occidentalis. Proc. Soc. Exp. Biol. and Med.,* 1959, *101,* 162-164.

Eibl-Eibesfeldt, I. *Ethology: The biology of behavior.* New York: Holt, Rinehart and Winston, 1970.

Falk, J. L. The grooming behavior of the chimpanzee as a reinforcer. *J. Exp. Anim. Behav.,* 1958, *1,* 83-85.

Feldman, S. Visual projections to the hypothalamus and preoptic area. *Ann. N. Y. Acad. Sci.,* 1964, *117,* 53-58.

Fieandt, K. von. *The world of perception.* Homewood, Ill.: Dorsey, 1966.

Fish, M. P. Animal sounds in the sea. *Scientif. Amer.,* 1956, *194,* 93-102.

Frank, L. K. Tactile communication. *Etc.,* 1958, *16,* 31-79.

Freud, S. Notes upon a case of obsessional neurosis. In *The standard edition of the complete psychological works of Sigmund Freud, Vol. 10.* London: Hogarth Press, 1959.

Frisch, K. von. *Bees: Their vision, chemical senses, and language.* Ithaca, N. Y.: Cornell Univ. Press, 1964.

Furth, H. G. *Thinking without language.* New York: The Free Press, 1966.

Gagge, A. P., Herrington, L. P., and Winslow, C.-E. A. Thermal interchanges between the human body and its atmospheric environment. *Amer. J. Hygiene,* 1937, *26,* 84-102.

Gartlan, J. S., and Brain, C. K. Ecology and social variability in *Cercopithicus aethiops* and *C. mitus.* In P. Jay (Ed.), *Primates: Studies in adaptation and variability.* New York: Holt, Rinehart and Winston, 1968.

Gault, R. H. An unusual case of olfactory and tactile sensitivity. *J. Abnorm. Psychol.,* 1923, *17,* 395-401.

Gesell, A., Ilg, F. L., and Bullis, G. E. *Vision, its development in infant and child.* New York: Hoeber, 1949.

Gibson, J. J. Observations on active touch. *Psychol. Rev.,* 1962, *69,* 477-491.

Gibson, J. J. *The senses considered as perceptual systems.* Boston: Houghton Mifflin, 1966.

Goda, S. Spoken syntax of normal, deaf and retarded adolescents. *J. Verb. Learn. Verb. Behav.,* 1964, *3,* 401-405.

Griffin, D. R. Echolocation by blind men, bats, and radar. *Science,* 1944, *100,* 589-590.

Griffin, D. R., and Galambos, R. The sensory basis of obstacle avoidance by flying bats. *J. Exp. Zool.*, 1941, *86*, 481-506.

Griffith, C. R. An experimental study of dizziness. *J. Exp. Psychol.*, 1920, *3*, 89-125.

Hafez, E. S. E., and Schein, M. W. The behavior of cattle. In E. S. E. Hafez (Ed.), *The behavior of domestic animals*. Baltimore, Md.: Williams & Wilkins, 1962.

Hamilton, J. Direct experience and alcoholism. In *Symposium: Perception and alcoholism*. Edmonton, Alberta: Department of Psychology, University of Alberta and Division of Alcoholism, Alberta Department of Health, 1968.

Hammett, F. S. Studies of the thyroid apparatus. *Endocrinol.*, 1922, *4*, 221-229.

Harlow, H. F. The nature of love. *Amer. Psycholog.*, 1958, *13*, 673-685.

Harlow, H. F., and Suomi, S. J. Nature of love—simplified. *Amer. Psycholog.*, 1970, *25*, 161-168.

Harper, R. S., and Stevens, S. S. A psychological scale of weight and a formula for its derivation. *Amer. J. Psychol.*, 1948, *61*, 343-351.

Harrison, R. J., and Montagna, W. *Man*. New York: Appleton-Century-Crofts, 1969.

Hazzard, F. W. A descriptive account of odors. *J. Exp. Psychol.*, 1930, *13*, 297-331.

Hediger, H. *The psychology and behaviour of animals in zoos and circuses*. New York: Dover, 1968.

Heider, K. G. The Dagum Dani: A Papuan culture in the highlands of West New Guinea. *Viking Fund Pub. in Anthropol.*, 1970, Vol. 49.

Heimer, L., and Larsson, K. Mating behavior of male rats after olfactory bulb lesion. *Physiol. and Behav.*, 1967, *2*, 207-209.

Heinbecker, P., Bishop, G. H., and O'Leary, J. Analysis of sensation in terms of the nerve impulse. *Arch. Neurol. and Psychiat.*, 1934, *31*, 34-53.

Heron, W., Bexton, W. H., and Hebb, D. O. Cognitive effects of decreased variation to sensory environment. *Amer. J. Psychol.*, 1953, *8*, 366.

Hersher, L., Richmond, J. B., and Moore, A. V. Maternal behavior in sheep and goats. In H. L. Rheingold (Ed.), *Maternal behavior in mammals*. New York: Wiley and Sons, 1963.

Hess, E. Attitude and pupil size. *Scientif. Amer.*, 1965, April, 46-54.

Hess, E. H., and Polt, J. M. Pupil size in relation to mental activity during simple problem solving. *Science*, 1964, *143*, 1190-1192.

Hicks, C. B. Your mysterious nose. *Today's Health*, 1965, *53*, 35+.

Hoebel, A. E. *Anthropology: The study of man, Third edition*. New York: McGraw-Hill, 1966.

Hollingworth, H. L., and Poffenberger, A. T. *The sense of taste*. New York: Moffat Yard, 1917.

Hollwich, F. The influence of light via the eyes on animals and man. *Ann. N. Y. Acad. Sci.*, 1964, *117*, 105-131.

Hooker, D. *The prenatal origin of behavior*. Lawrence, Kansas: Univ. Kansas Press, 1952.

Howard, W. E., Marsh, R. E., and Cole, R. E. Food detection by deer mice using olfactory rather than visual cues. *Anim. Behav.*, 1968, *16*, 13-17.

Huxley, A. *After many a summer dies the swan*. New York: Harper, 1939.

Jacobson, E. *You must relax*. New York: McGraw-Hill, 1957.

James, W. *The principles of psychology*. New York: Holt, 1890.

Jay, P. Primate field studies and human evolution. In P. Jay (Ed.), *Primates: Studies in adaptation and variability*. New York: Holt, Rinehart and Winston, 1968.

Jöchle, W. Trends in photophysiologic concepts. *Ann. N. Y. Acad. Sci.*, 1964, *117*, 88-104.

Jones, D. E. H. The stability of the bicycle. *Physics Today*, 1970, *4*, 34-40.

Jöres, E. *Dent. Arch. Klin. Med.*, 1933, *175*, 244 (cited by Hollwich).

Kahneman, D., and Beatty, J. Pupil diameter and load use memory. *Science*, 1966, *154*, 1583-1585.

Kalmus, H. The discrimination by the nose of the dog of the individual human odours and in particular the odour of twins. *Brit. J. Anim. Behav.*, 1955, *5*, 25-31.

Kalmus, H. The chemical senses. *Scientif. Amer.*, 1958, *198*, 97-106.

Kalogerakis, M. G. The role of olfaction in sexual development. *Psychosom. Med.*, 1963, *25*, 420-429.

Keller, H. *Story of my life*. New York: Doubleday, 1954.

Kellogg, W. N. *Porpoises and sonar*. Chicago: Univ. Chicago Press, 1961.

King, H. E., Clausen, J., and Scarff, J. E. Cutaneous thresholds for pain before and after unilateral prefrontal lobotomy. A preliminary report. *J. Nerv. Ment. Dis.*, 1950, *112*, 93-96.

King, J. E., Becker, R. F., and Markee, J. E. Studies on olfactory discrimination in dogs: (3) Ability to detect human odour trace. *Anim. Behav.*, 1964, *12*, 311-315.

Kinney, J. A. S., Luria, S. M., Weitzman, D. O., and Markowitz, H. Effects of diving experience on visual perception under water. *U. S. Naval Submarine Med. Center*, Groton, Conn., 1970, Rep. #612.

Kitzler, G. Die Paarungsbiologie einiger Eidechgen. *Z. Tierpsychologie*, 1942, *4*, 353-402.

Kuno, Y. *Human perspiration*. Springfield, Ill.: Charles C. Thomas, 1956.

Lancaster, J. B., and Lee, R. B. The annual reproductive cycle in monkeys and apes. In I. DeVore (Ed.), *Primate behavior*. New York: Holt, Rinehart and Winston, 1965.

Landau, A. Ueber ein tonischen Lagereflex beim alteren Säuglung. *Klin. Wschr.*, 1923, *2*, 1253-1255.

Landis, C., and Hunt, W. A. *The startle pattern*. New York: Johnson Reprint Corp., 1968.

Lardner, R. Your perfume...Su! *Pagent*, 1959, *15*, 122-126.

Lawick-Goodall, J. Van. The behavior of free-living chimpanzees in the Gombe Stream Reserve. *Anim. Behav. Monogr.*, 1968, *1*, 161-311.

Lawick-Goodall, J. Van. A preliminary report on expressive movements and communication in the Gombe Stream chimpanzees. In P. Jay (Ed.), *Primates: Studies in adaptation and variability*. New York: Holt, Rinehart and Winston, 1968.

Le Magnen, J. Les phenomenes olfacto-sexuels chez le rat blanc. *Arch. Sci. Physiol.*, 1952, *6*, 292-332.

Livingston, R. B. Central control of receptors and sensory transmission system. In J. Field, H. W. Magoun, and V. E. Hall (Eds.), *Handbook of physiology; Section I: Neurophysiology*. Baltimore, Md.: Williams and Wilkins, 1959.

Lounsberry, M. Sensitivity training goes to church. *The State Journal,*

Family Weekly Suppl., Lansing, Michigan, August 9, 1970.

MacFarland, R. *Human factors in air transportation.* New York: McGraw-Hill, 1953.

MacKintosh, J. H., and Grant, E. C. The effect of olfactory stimuli on the agonistic behavior of laboratory mice. *Z. F. Tierpsychologie,* 1966, *23,* 584-587.

MacLean, P. D. The limbic system with respect to self-preservation and the preservation of the species. *J. Nerv. Ment. Dis.,* 1958, *127,* 1-11.

Magnus, R. *Körperstellung.* Berlin: Springer, 1924.

Maier, R. A. The role of the dominance-submission ritual in social recognition in hens. *Anim. Behav.,* 1964, *12,* 59.

Marg, E. The accessory optic system. *Ann. N.Y. Acad. Sci.,* 1964, *117,* 35-52.

Mariscal, R. N. A field and laboratory study of the symbiotic behavior of fishes and sea anemones from the tropical Indo-Pacific. *Univ. Calif. Pub. Zool.,* 1970, *91,* 1-43.

Marler, P. Aggregation and dispersal: Two functions in primate communication. In P. Jay (Ed.), *Primates: Studies in adaptation and variability.* New York: Holt, Rinehart and Winston, 1968.

Mason, W. A. Use of space by *Callicebus* groups. In P. Jay (Ed.), *Primates: Studies in adaptation and variability.* New York: Holt, Rinehart and Winston, 1968.

Mathews, L. H., and Knight, M. *The senses of animals.* New York: Philosophical Lib., Inc., 1963.

McGraw, M. B. *The neuromuscular maturation of the human infant.* New York: Columbia Univ. Press, 1943.

McHose, J. H., and Ludvigson, H. W. Differential conditioning with nondifferential reinforcement. *Psychonom. Sci.,* 1966, *6,* 485-486.

McNally, W. J., and Stuart, E. A. Physiology of the labyrinth reviewed in relation to seasickness and other forms of motion sickness. *War Med.,* 1942, *2,* 683-771.

Mead, M. The swaddling hypothesis: Its reception. *Amer. Anthropolog.,* 1954, *56,* 395-409.

Melzack, R. Phantom limbs. *Psychol. Today,* 1970, October, 63-68.

Michotte, A. *La perception de la causalité.* Louvain: Institute Supérieur de Philosophie, 1946.

Miller, J. W., and Goodson, J. E. Motion sickness in a heliocopter simulator. *Aerospace Med.,* 1960, *31,* 204-212.

Milne, L., and Milne, M. *The senses of animals and men.* New York: Atheneum, 1962.

Milne, L., and Milne, M. *The mating instinct.* New York: Signet, 1968.

Moncrieff, R. W. *The chemical senses.* Cleveland: Chemical Rubber Co., 1965.

Moncrieff, R. W. *Odour preferences.* London: Leonard Hill, 1966.

Money, J. Psychosexual differentiation. In J. Money (Ed.), *Sex research: New developments.* New York: Holt, Rinehart and Winston, 1965.

Montague, A. M. F. The sensory influences of the skin. *Tex. Reps. on Biol. and Med.,* 1953, *11,* 291-301.

Moore, R. E. Olfactory discrimination as an isolating mechanism between *Peromyscus maniculatus* and *Peromyscus polionotus. Amer. Midland Naturalist,* 1964, *73,* 85-100.

Morris, D. The feather postures of birds and the problem of the origin of social signals. *Behaviour,* 1955, *9,* 76-111.

Morrison, R. R., and Ludvigson, H. W. Discrimination by rats of conspecific odors of reward and nonreward. *Science*, 1970, *167*, 904-905.

Munz, L., and Löwenfeld, V. *Plastiche Arbeiten Blinder*. Brünn: Rohrer, 1934.

Murphy, M. R., and Schneider, G. E. Olfactory bulb removal eliminates mating behavior in the male golden hamster. *Science*, 1970, *167*, 302-304.

Nelson, T. M. Hue memory deficit among alcoholics. In *Symposium: Perception and alcoholism*. Edmonton, Alberta: Department of Psychology, University of Alberta, and Division of Alcoholism, Alberta Department of Public Health, 1968.

Novick, A. Acoustic orientation in the cave swiftlet. *Biol. Bull.*, 1959, *117*, 497-503.

Ortavant, R., Mauleon, P., and Thibault, C. Photoperiodic control of gonadal and hypophyseal activity in domestic mammals. *Ann. N.Y. Acad. Sci.*, 1964, *117*, 157-193.

Oswald, I. *Sleep*. Baltimore, Md.: Penguin Books, 1966.

Parkes, A. S., and Bruce, H. M. Olfactory stimuli in mammalian reproduction. *Science*, 1961, *134*, 1049-1054.

Payne, R. B. Giant cowbird solicits preening from man. *The Auk*, 1969, *86*, 751-752.

Petter, J. J. The lemurs of Madagascar. In I. DeVore (Ed.), *Primate Behavior: Field studies of monkeys and apes*. New York: Holt, Rinehart and Winston, 1965.

Piaget, J. *The construction of reality in the child*. New York: Basic Books: 1954.

Pickett, J. M. Tactual communication of speech sounds to the deaf: Comparison with lipreading. *J. Speech and Hear. Dis.*, 1963, *28*, 315-330.

Price, D. My year alone. *Modern Maturity*, 1970, June-July, 9-11.

Raab, W. *Ges. Exp. Med.*, 1939, *106*, 154 (cited by Hollwich).

Ralls, K. Auditory sensitivity in mice: *Peromyscus* and *Musmusculus*. *Anim. Behav.*, 1967, *15*, 123-128.

Ratner, S. C. Comparative aspects of hypnosis. In J. Gordon (Ed.), *Handbook of clinical and experimental hypnosis*. New York: Macmillan, 1967.

Révész, G. *Psychology and art of the blind*. New York: Longmans Green, 1950.

Reyniers, J. A. Germ-free life studies. *Lobund Reps.*, 1946, No. 1; 1949, No. 2.

Riley, D. A., and Rosenzweig, M. Echolocation in rats. *J. Comp. Physiol. Psychol.*, 1957, *50*, 323-328.

Rock, I., and Harris, C. S. Vision and touch. *Scientif. Amer.*, 1967, *216*, 96-104.

Rock, I., and Victor, J. Vision and touch: An experimentally created conflict between the two senses. *Science*, 1964, *143*, 594-596.

Rogers, W. L., Melzack, R., and Segal, J. R. "Tail flip response" in goldfish. *J. Comp. Physiol. Psychol.*, 1963, *56*, 917-923.

Rowan, M. K. A study of the Colies of Southern Africa. *The Ostrich*, 1967, *38*, 63-115.

Russell, W. M. S. On comfort and comfort activities in animals. *UFAW Courier*, 1959, *16*, 14-26.

Salk, L. The effects of the normal heart beat sound on the behavior of the newborn infant: Implications for mental health. *World Ment. Hlth.*, 1960, *12*, 168-176.

Schein, M. W., and Hale, E. B. Stimuli eliciting sexual behavior. In F. Beach (Ed.), *Sex and behavior.* New York: Wiley and Sons, 1965.

Schludermann, E., and Zubeck, J. P. Effect of age on pain sensitivity. *Percept. Mot. Skills,* 1962, *14*, 295-301.

Schneider, C. W., and Bartley, S. H. A study of the effects of mechanically induced tension in the neck muscles on the perception of the vertical. *J. Psychol.,* 1962, *54*, 245-248.

Schneirla, T. C. Theoretical consideration of cyclic processes in Doryline ants. *Proc. Amer. Phil. Soc.,* 1957, *101*, 106-133.

Schon, M. Psychological effects of hypophysectomy in women with metastatic breast cancer. *Cancer,* 1958, *11*, 95-98.

Schutz, W. C. *Joy: Expanding human awareness.* New York: Grove Press, 1967.

Scott, T. H., Bexton, W. H., Heron, W., and Doane, B. K. Cognitive effects of perceptual isolation. *Canad. J. Psychol.,* 1959, *13*, 200-209.

Shirley, M. A behavior syndrome characterizing prematurely-born children. *Child Develop.,* 1939, *10*, 115-128.

Simmons, K. E. L. Feather maintenance. In A. L. Thompson (Ed.), *A New dictionary of birds.* New York: McGraw-Hill, 1964.

Simmons, K. E. L. Anting and the problem of self-stimulation. *J. Zool., London,* 1966, *149*, 145-162.

Skinner, B. F. *Verbal behavior.* New York: Appleton-Century-Crofts, 1957.

Slessers, M. Bathing behavior of land birds. *The Auk,* 1970, *87*, 91-99.

Smith, F., and Miller, G. A. *The genesis of language.* Cambridge, Mass.: M.I.T. Press, 1966.

Smith, F. V., Van-Toller, C., and Boyes, T. The critical period in the attachment of lambs and ewes. *Anim. Behav.,* 1966, *14*, 120-125.

Smith, K., and Sines, J. O. Demonstration of a peculiar odor in the sweat of schizophrenic patients. *A.M.A. Arch. Gen. Psychiat.,* 1960, *2*, 184-188.

Smith, K., Thompson, G. F., and Koster, H. D. Sweat in schizophrenic patients: Identification of the odorous substance. *Science,* 1969, *166*, 398-399.

Solove'ev, I. M. The significance of the training of unvoiced hearing for the development of perceptual activity in deaf-mute children. (Russian Translations on Speech and Hearing) *Amer. Speech and Hear. Assoc.,* 1969,#4, 121-136.

Sparks, J. H. On the role of allopreening invitation behaviour in reducing aggression among Red Avadavats, with comments on its evolution in the Spermestidae. *Proc. Zool. Soc. Lond.,* 1965, *145*, 387-403.

Sparks, J. H. Allogrooming in primates: A review. In D. Morris (Ed.), *Primate ethology.* New York: Doubleday, 1969.

Stebbins, R. C., and Eakin, R. M. The role of the "third eye" in reptilian behavior. *Amer. Museum Novitates,* 1958, No. 1870, 1-40.

Stein, M., Ottenberg, P., and Roulet, N. A. A study of the development of olfactory preferences. *A.M.A. Arch. Neurol. Psychiat.,* 1958, *80*, 264-266.

Strand, R. Studio emphasizes pleasures of sound. *The State Journal,* Lansing, Michigan, November 8, 1970.

Stratton, G. M. Vision without inversion of the retinal image. *Psychol.*

Rev., 1897, 4, 341-360, 463-481.

Sweeney, D. R., and Fine, B. J. Pain reactivity and field dependence. *Percept. Mot. Skills*, 1965, *21*, 757-758.

Szebenyi, A. L. Cleaning behaviour in *Drosophila melanogàster*. *Anim. Behav.*, 1969, *17*, 641-651.

Tervoort, Rev. Fr. B. T. Esoteric symbolism in the communication behavior of young deaf children. *Amer. Ann. Deaf*, 1961, *166*, 436-480.

Vinacke, W. Z. Illusion experienced by aircraft pilots while flying. *J. Aviat. Med.*, 1947, *18*, 308-325.

Wallace, R. K. Physiological effects of transcendental meditation. *Science*, 1970, *167*, 1751-1754.

Wallis, D. I. Behaviour patterns of the ant, *Formica fusca. Anim. Behav.*, 1962, *10*, 105-111.

Warren, R. M., and Warren, R. P. Auditory illusions and confusions. *Scientif. Amer.*, 1970, *223*, 30-36.

Wasserman, E. A., and Jensen, D. D. Olfactory stimuli and the "pseudo-extinction" effect. *Science*, 1969, *166*, 1307-1309.

Wendt, G. R. Vestibular functions. In S. S. Stevens (Ed.), *Handbook of experimental psychology*. New York: Wiley, 1951.

Wheeler, W. M. *Ants: Their structure, development, and behavior*. New York: Columbia Univ. Press, 1910.

Whitten, W. K. Modification of the estrous cycle in the mouse by external stimuli associated with the male. *J. Endocrinol.*, 1956, *13*, 399-404.

Windle, W. F. *Physiology of the fetus*. Philadelphia: Saunders, 1940.

Winslow, C.-E. A. Man's heat exchange with his thermal environment. In *Temperature, its measurement and control in science and industry*. New York: Reinhold, 1941.

Winslow, C.-E. A., Herrington, L. P., and Gagge, A. P. Relations between atmospheric conditions, physiological reactions, and sensations of pleasantness. *Amer. J. Hygiene*, 1937, *26*, 103-115.

Witkin, H. A. The perception of the upright. *Scientif. Amer.*, 1959, *200*, 50-56.

Wrightstone, J. W., Aranow, M. S., and Muskowitz, S. Developing reading test norms for the deaf child. *Amer. Ann. Deaf*, 1963, *108*, 311-316.

Zemlin, W. R. *Speech and hearing science: Anatomy and physiology*. Englewood Cliffs, N. J.: Prentice Hall, Inc., 1968.

# index

228 93

75 76  9 8 7 6 5 4 3